PENGUIN
RAJ OF TH

Tapti Roy has taught history in Kolkata, and in Dubai where she currently resides. She is the author of *The Politics of Popular Uprising—Bundelkhand in 1857* and the article 'Disciplining the Printed Text: Colonial and Nationalist Surveillance of Bengali Literature', in *Texts of Power—Emerging Disciplines in Colonial Bengal*. She used to write a weekly column titled 'Cause, Culture and History' for the *Asian Age*.

Raj of the Rani

TAPTI ROY

PENGUIN BOOKS

PENGUIN BOOKS
Published by the Penguin Group
Penguin Books India Pvt. Ltd, 11 Community Centre, Panchsheel Park,
New Delhi 110 017, India
Penguin Group (USA) Inc., 375 Hudson Street, New York, New York 10014, USA
Penguin Group (Canada), 90 Eglinton Avenue East, Suite 700, Toronto,
Ontario, M4P 2Y3, Canada (a division of Pearson Penguin Canada Inc.)
Penguin Books Ltd, 80 Strand, London WC2R 0RL, England
Penguin Ireland, 25 St Stephen's Green, Dublin 2, Ireland
(a division of Penguin Books Ltd)
Penguin Group (Australia), 250 Camberwell Road, Camberwell,
Victoria 3124, Australia (a division of Pearson Australia Group Pty Ltd)
Penguin Group (NZ), cnr Airborne and Rosedale Roads, Albany,
Auckland 1310, New Zealand (a division of Pearson New Zealand Ltd)
Penguin Group (South Africa) (Pty) Ltd, 24 Sturdee Avenue, Rosebank,
Johannesburg 2196, South Africa

Penguin Books Ltd, Registered Offices: 80 Strand, London WC2R 0RL, England

First published by Penguin Books India 2006

Copyright © Tapti Roy 2006

10 9 8 7 6 5 4 3 2 1

ISBN-13: 9780143062219   ISBN-10: 0143062212

Typeset in *Sabon Roman* by SÜRYA, New Delhi
Printed at Baba Barkhanath Printers, New Delhi

To Ma and Daddy
and
as always for Anwita and Animesh

Contents

Acknowledgements

It has been quite a challenge writing this book since I was away from home in circumstances not entirely conducive to research. Those who helped me get back my bearings were old friends, new acquaintances and, as always, my family.

For the initial encouragement to write this book, I owe deep gratitude to Kamini Mahadevan. I am equally indebted to Gautam Bhadra for endorsing the proposal and remaining my sternest critic and the most supportive mentor.

With a sense of déjà vu I returned to the alcoves of National Library, Kolkata, to do the research. I am thankful to Swati Majumdar and Ashim Mukhopadhaya for making me feel as if I had never been away and for pandering to my demands for old, frayed and sometimes inaccessible resources in the National Library during my rushed stay in the city.

I availed of the generosity and hospitality of many in the course of my research and travels. My friend Sumita Sen put us up in Delhi without complaint. K.N. Agarwal made all the arrangements for our stay and comfort in Jhansi and also introduced me to Dr Mahendra Lal Verma to whom I am obliged for crucial insights. Despite his frail health, Dr Verma spent long hours taking me around the town and filling me in on details of the life and times of Lakshmi Bai. During my many visits to the Jhansi fort, Manoj Kumar Verma, the deputy director of the Archeological Survey of India, was always patient and supportive. He took me to Om Shankar Khare 'Asar' who, in turn, let me use his published papers and generously shared with me his impressive research on Jhansi, its surroundings and the Rani. The scholars of Jhansi warmly received an unknown researcher into their learned inner circle, for which I am grateful.

I wish to thank Prabhat Munshi of IIT Kanpur for the comfortable stay and pleasant evenings on campus and Mrs Mahendrajit Singh for the warm welcome to her beautiful home.

Formal acknowledgements are seldom adequate to convey how much one owes friends and family. P.J.O. Taylor made a trip to the India Office Library just so that he could copy some important correspondence for me. I know just saying thank you to him is not enough. I am grateful to all my friends, Joyshree Roy, Tapati Guha-Thakurta, Kaushik Mitter, Sweta Ghosh, Subhadra De, Hari Vasudevan, Anjan Ghosh and Shubhramoni De for being there for me always. I wish to thank Sudhir Kartha, president and CEO of Emirates College for Management and Information Technology for allowing me some relief from my responsibilities and granting me leave. I wish my friend Shomita Ghose was here to see the book done.

Once more, like many times before, my family stood by me firm in their faith and support. In their own ways all of them—Anwita, Animesh Basu, Sushil and Leena Roy, Aniles and Hashi Basu, Urmi, Arijit, Sriparna Ray, Sudeep, Malabika, Sagnik, Ruchika and Sattick Roy and Amitesh, Sutapa and Diptangshu Basu—helped me believe that I could complete the book, whatever the circumstances may be. My uncle Ashis Guha would have been very proud of me and I like to believe that his blessings still remain with me even if he is not.

Finally, I am grateful to Nandini Mehta for her critical comments on the first draft of the book and to Manjula Lal and Prita Maitra for helping me improve on that substantially. Needless to say, I remain responsible for any flaws that may still remain in the book.

Preface

They say in Jhansi that the best thing that ever happened to their town was Lakshmi Bai. This town, a major railway junction in the province of Uttar Pradesh that is close to 400 years old, and links western India with the east through a network of railway lines, still feels that it owes its fame to a young Rani who ruled for four-and-a-half years. Spread out in the shadow of the fort, Jhansi palpably keeps alive the memory of the Rani with her image on horseback imprinted all over. She is at crossroads, on hoardings splashed across the sky, in parks, at the base of the fort, her ubiquity confirming what people believe.

Association with her has also brought fame. Outside the railway station is the bust of Vrindavan Lal Verma, winner of the Padma Bhushan for his literary works in Hindi, who is best known for his novel based on the life of the queen. People quote him as the authority on the life and times of Lakshmi Bai. Verma, whose great-grandfather was killed in the war of 1858, was brought up on stories that his great-grandmother and grandmother told of the uprising and of Rani Lakshmi Bai. The novel, published in 1968, was his tribute to Anand Rao, his great-grandfather, and the queen Rao died fighting for.

Verma referred to Dattaraya Balwant Parasnis's account of Lakshmi Bai as the only single authoritative biography; its Hindi translation appeared in 1938.

It may seem surprising that despite an incredible career, it took eighty years for Indians to write a comprehensive description of her life. It was not because she was forgotten, but that people who lived during her time did not leave any writing behind. And, quite a few of those who knew her were too afraid of reprisals to profess links with her. Thus, in the first fifty years after her death, Lakshmi Bai's memory remained veiled in silence. Silence offered a perfect setting for apocryphal stories about the mysterious Rani who died on the battlefield in the cause of her land. People could not talk about her but nothing stopped them from remembering Lakshmi Bai in the image that they created—the self-sacrificing heroine and martyr.

In the subsequent decades of India's freedom struggle, nationalist scholars acclaimed the uprising of 1857 as a fight of the people for their religion and their land. It became known as the 'First War of Indian Independence', which in some ways was true if we regard the endeavour to rid the country of white rule as the first sign of aspiring for freedom. The portrayal of Lakshmi Bai and what she stood for served the essential purpose of stirring nationalist fervour. While it was being recounted, however, the story of the Rani and her personality stood taller than the larger narrative of the uprising of 1857. In many ways, she was alone in her magnificence, the singular figure in a gallery of heroes.

Rani Lakshmi Bai also became the protagonist in a different kind of story—fiction by British writers to dramatize the horrific experience of the mutiny in which an Oriental queen, full of passion, added a thrilling dimension. Invariably, she was both vengeful and lustful and in at least two out of three fictional writings, she is depicted as being in love with an Englishman. Lakshmi

Bai became legendary on a different account, quite in the fashion of a heroine.[1]

The first critical assessment of the uprising and therefore its chief champions, appeared a hundred years later to commemorate the centenary of 1857. Western-educated, middle-class urban Indians, who now wrote histories, found the form of protest by the rebels of 1857 outmoded compared to the modern party politics that they felt eventually won the nation its Independence. The rebellion of 1857 was regarded as regressive, one which, if successful, would have turned the clock back. It sought to empower feudal forces of the zamindars and the rajas who acted in their own interests, which rarely extended beyond the boundaries of their own dominion. These modern studies rarely focussed attention on a single figure. Rani Lakshmi Bai became one of the many feudal overlords who resisted British intrusion into her land and fought them because they invaded her kingdom. Parasnis was thus the first to write a full account of the Rani, using as much as he could of contemporary official and non-official sources. He uncovered the limitations of her resistance and the fact that she was helplessly pushed into war.

If British official correspondence is taken into account, it is impossible to overlook Lakshmi Bai's constraints. Vrindavan Lal Verma took objection to Parasnis's account and felt that such appraisals downplayed the Rani's unique individuality and role. In order to correct such a depiction, he chose to write a novel where he would be unfettered by the need to cite sources. He indulged in literary licence whenever he felt it necessary to portray the Rani as the undaunted leader of her people determined to defy the British. If there were inconsistencies and contradictions, he chose to overlook them. Within the ambit of the novel, it made no difference.

In the 1960s, there were a number of other biographies written in English and Indian languages. After more than a hundred years, Rani Lakshmi Bai's image found concrete shape as historians and scholars explored her life and the circumstances that made her what she was. The human face of the Rani emerged through these writings. However, the biographers had to walk the tightrope between adulation and objective study of her circumstances, and her achievements and limitations. Often, the first overtook the second concern.

In 1957, Amrit Lal Nagar translated a Marathi travelogue by Vishnubhatt Godse called *Majha Pravas*. Godse was the only writer who had met the Rani and was present during her most critical hours. Subsequently, Nagar's translation became very popular and was widely used by scholars. Meanwhile, following Verma, the tradition of writing novels on the Rani continued. Even today in Jhansi, scholars like Mahendra Lal Verma and Om Shankar Asar, with extensive knowledge about Lakshmi Bai and her times, claim to be novelists with a penchant for history of the region and its Rani.

The legend of the Rani has been perpetuated in modern politics too. The stories that grew around her continue to offer a kind of moral and emotional sustenance to Bundelkhand, otherwise marginalized since its split and absorption into the larger provinces of Uttar Pradesh and Madhya Pradesh. Neither has she escaped caste politics. One of the characters in Verma's novel was a young woman called Jhalkari. She was supposed to have been born low and was married to a soldier in the Rani's army. She had a strange resemblance to Lakshmi Bai and was supposed to have fought while the Rani escaped. For quite some time, the British thought she was Lakshmi Bai herself and therefore did not pursue the real queen.

There is a historical problem with this subplot in the larger story. But today, scholars in Jhansi are divided over the authenticity of Jhalkari. It makes no difference to the broader theme but does contribute to the politics of caste and divisions between the higher and lower groups. The Rani was a Brahmin who was saved because a low-caste woman gave up her life.

What made Lakshmi Bai so singular? How did a young Marathi woman come to wield so much influence in a strongly Rajput-dominated region? It is not only Jhansi but the whole of Bundelkhand that seeks fame through her. How has she overshadowed the proud Bundelas? Or for that matter, how did she rise above her limitations to remain such a central figure both in her land and in her times? There are no clear answers and in trying to look for them, one would be guilty of reducing history to predictable factors that are drawn from a different context.

In the present study, I have tried to locate Lakshmi Bai within the wider context of her time and space. It is not my intention to debunk any opinion. For what people feel about her has contributed to the figure of Lakshmi Bai and it is impossible to separate the Rani from her image. It is not required either, for the image is as relevant as the historical person. I have therefore tried, where it seems relevant, to integrate authenticated incidents with imagined ones in the same narrative. There is very little information in the book that is not already known, as most of my sources are printed works by scholars. I have used archival sources, which are essentially British official correspondence, to underscore the wider circumstances in which she evolved and operated. The limitations of this biography are obvious for there is practically no first-hand account of her times except Godse's. Even local scholars of Jhansi refer to Verma and Godse as the final word on the Rani.

There are twelve chapters to the book and the first describes the places of her early life in Banaras, Bithur and Bundelkhand. In most of the accounts of Lakshmi Bai, descriptions are often too narrowly focussed on her. I feel if we pan the spotlight wider, the brilliance of the principal protagonist emerges brighter. It is worth studying, for example, how a small kingdom that was in a welter of crisis and hopelessly dependent on British support, emerges as the focus of national attention. This was not because of the soldiers who mutinied in 1857 but because of a young widowed Rani who refused to let matters lie in British hands.

The narrative continues up to the time when Lakshmi Bai's world changes with the tragedy of the deaths of her son and husband. It not only transforms her world but also metamorphoses her from a widow to a warrior, determined and bold, who takes on the British without faltering or fear.

Three years shape the individual that fascinated both the Indians and the British. The heroine is born. She is, however, unprepared for what is coming, the mutiny of soldiers in Jhansi, but when it occurs, she rises to the occasion. Much of the book is about 1857, the year Lakshmi Bai had not only to take effective charge of her town of Jhansi, but also protect her larger kingdom.

Next is the year 1858, when the British march with their counter-insurgency forces upon Bundelkhand in what amounts to an invasion. Lakshmi Bai's dilemma is whether she should support rebellion over the order that she has come to personify. Her hesitation is not because she is afraid but because she is uncertain.

In the interlocking of British and Indian narratives,

Lakshmi Bai helplessly watches her town being torn asunder. Finally, there is a series of battles in Kunch, Kalpi and Gwalior that ends in the death of this indefatigable fighter.

Controversies chased Lakshmi Bai when she was alive; they continued even when she died. How much was she involved in the uprising? How much did she know? Was she responsible for the killing of the whites in Jhansi? How did she herself die? The British had no tangible proof of her complicity in the rebellion but were not sure if she should be allowed to go free. She was far too fiery to be completely innocent, they reasoned.

Lakshmi Bai died because her personality was too large for the contemporary British officials to contend with and trust. She became the victim of the very indomitable spirit that made her immortal.

Mine is a small effort to pay respect to this extraordinary woman in Indian history.

1

New Beginnings

During the eighteenth century, Marathi-speaking conquerors from the western part of the Indian subcontinent spread all across north India, taking political advantage of the vacuum created by the declining power and authority of the Mughals. In the process, they formed an alternative power base to local rajas and feudal lords. The Marathis were great military organizers and strategists. They were also deeply committed to their faith, and invested their military success with spiritual sanction. Bithur was a popular destination in the Marathi pilgrim itinerary, whence they went to attend fairs.

Bithur's fame can be traced back to Hindu mythology. Brahma, the first of the gods in the Hindu trinity, was believed to have performed his horse sacrifice here—even today, this event is commemorated with an annual fair. According to popular myth, the nail of the horseshoe is embedded in the soil beneath the river and can be seen when the tide ebbs. Valmiki, the composer of the *Ramayana*, lived in a forest hut close to Bithur, where Sita took shelter after being abandoned by Ram. Her sons Lav and Kush were born in Valmiki's ashram and Ram was reunited with them here. Temples built in the memory of both Valmiki and Sita are still places of worship.

Within more recent historical memory, Bithur became both famous and lively after the Marathi Peshwa, Baji Rao II, surrendered to the British in 1818 and, on being asked to leave Pune, the capital of the Marathi kingdom, chose to live in Bithur.

Baji Rao's choice of the place may have had a lot to do with its mythological associations.

The Peshwa was granted an annual pension of eight lakh rupees, a generous amount in those times. He was allowed to maintain three guns and 500 armed men, for the maintenance of which he was assigned part of Bithur and the village of Ramel in revenue-free tenure.[1] It was certainly a handsome grant, though no match for the thirty-four lakh rupees he lost by being forced out of Pune. No limit was put on the number of civilian retainers he could keep, an estimate putting the figure at 16,000— to begin with. The district gazetteer gives the number of Marathis living in Bithur in 1847 at 13,647.[2] It was only natural that with the decline of Pune, followers and dependents of the royal house would scatter and follow their master.

The Peshwa built his palace in the middle of a sprawling compound, adjoining which grew a busy, thickly-populated Marathi settlement. His two brothers chose to reside in different places: Chimnajee Appa moved to Banaras, and Umrae Rao, his adopted brother, went south to Chitrakoot, both famous as centres of pilgrimage and oft-visited by Marathis from the west.

When Chimnajee Appa took up residence in Banaras, the holy city already had a substantial population of Marathis, thanks to a leader called Amrit Rao, who had settled there in 1803 with 4,000 retainers. In Chimnajee Appa's retinue was a family with the surname Tambe.

Today, the fourteen-kilometre stretch from Kanpur to Bithur looks like any other landscape of semi-urban north India. Narrow, ill-maintained roads run through fields growing pulses, sugar cane, corn and wheat, with scattered hamlets and stray buildings breaking the monotony of an endless expanse of half-grown crops. Nearer the town of Bithur, houses are clustered closer together till, over the last two kilometres to the river, the road becomes a narrow lane that meanders through a maze of closely constructed buildings jostling for space. The road ends at the riverbank, a paved, rectangular space with a row of small temples along the right, and rundown constructions grown over with weeds and plants on the left. The path that runs along the riverbank is lost in thick undergrowth.

Nothing reminds you today of the thriving pilgrim town that Bithur used to be, except the temple priests who speak of old times and ancient glory. There were, once upon a time, fifty-two separate paved ghats reserved for the kings who visited this town when it celebrated as many as twelve religious melas every year. The rich and pious also built rest-houses along the bank to provide for their annual visit. Melas meant large gatherings of people and a lot of business that kept Bithur busy practically throughout the year.

Banaras, too, was a particularly popular town, with a significant number of Marathis living there.[3] By the end of the century, there were close to 30,000 Marathi immigrants in Banaras, including Brahmins, traders and followers of the rich and the noble who chose to live in the holy city. They built temples, including the most famous Vishvanath and Annapurna, bathing ghats, rest-houses and, of course, mansions for themselves.[4] Festivals such as the Ganesh Chaturthi were introduced and became popular because of the Marathis. They also contributed to the tradition of popular folk theatre in Uttar Pradesh and thereby remained culturally important in places like Banaras even after their control was weakened by British rule.

The Tambes were a Karhad Brahmin family from Vai in Sattara. Krishna Rao Tambe had been a soldier in Peshwa Baji Rao I's army who rose to the rank of commander during the third battle of Panipat at the time of Baji Rao II. He was among the few who returned from the disastrous campaign. His son Balwant Rao followed in his father's footsteps and served the Peshwa's army for as long as he could. By the time Balwant's sons were born in the early nineteenth century, the Marathis were a defeated power and a career in the army held little promise. Balwant Rao was particularly close to Chimnajee Appa, and decided to relocate to Banaras rather than Bithur.[5] He built a house close to his patron's house at Assi ghat, where most of the Marathis lived.[6]

Balwant Rao Tambe had two sons, Moropant and Sadashiv. Moropant started working for Chimnajee on a monthly salary of fifty rupees.[7] By then he was married to Bhagirathi Bai from the Sapre family in Karar.[8] She was beautiful and, like all Marathi Brahmin girls, well versed in Hindu mythology. Bhagirathi Bai gave birth to a daughter whom she named Manikarnika after the river Ganges. In their rather peripatetic life, this was a moment of sheer joy for Moropant and Bhagirathi. The beautiful child was called Manu at home. The world, however, remembers her as Lakshmi Bai.

There are differences among scholars about the date and year of her birth. Vrindavan Lal Verma writes that she was born on 11 November 1836. According to Mahasweta Devi, she was born on 21 November 1835 in the Assi ghat house.[9] Parasnis puts the date at 14 Samvat or 16 November 1835.[10]

Two events that have been historically authenticated occurred after her birth. Chimnajee Appa died in June 1832[11] and—bereft of his patron—Moropant Tambe had to look for an alternative source of income. Baji Rao, who went for his brother's funeral, invited some of his close confidants to Bithur, and Moropant was one of them. It is uncertain if they actually accompanied him back or followed him, but this was shortly after Chimnajee died.

When Moropant moved home yet again, his daughter Manu was a child of three. If Manu had been born in 1835 or 1836, as claimed, then that would mean that Moropant continued to stay on in Banaras for eight years after his patron's death. This he did not. He took his wife and young daughter to Bithur almost immediately after and this event puts the date of his daughter's birth somewhere close to 1828.[12] This would make her a twenty-nine-year-old woman during the time of the uprising in 1857. Robert Hamilton, the British official who met her in 1854 and 1855, corroborated this when he wrote his impressions to historian John Kaye of the young Rani being around twenty-eight or twenty-nine years old.[13]

While in Banaras, little Manu regularly visited the temple of Vishvanath with her parents. Her devotion and piety were largely due to her upbringing in a staunch Marathi home. In Bithur, Moropant found work at the Peshwa's court for the same salary of fifty rupees. But shortly after they moved, Bhagirathi Bai died. Manu was all of four. The grief-stricken Moropant resolved not to marry again, but raise his daughter with the help of his aged mother.

In a country that swears by astrology, a hero's birth can never be an ordinary one, without significant signs that prophesy the extraordinary turn events will take. The astrologers seem to have read Manu's horoscope right.

She was born to be queen and bring everlasting fame to her family. True enough. But for her, Jhansi would have faded from historical memory, dredged up only to show how unfair Lord Dalhousie had been. Without 1857, even Dalhousie would have been forgiven.

Moropant Tambe took the astrologers' forecast seriously, and set out to groom his daughter for the role she was destined to play. Most Marathi women of her time were taught to read, write and recite the scriptures, and Manu was put through the rigours of a proper Sanskrit curriculum. Her special training was in riding horses, using swords and firing guns, unlike the ordinary women of her times.[14] Her mother and grandmother constantly told her stories from the epics and infused in her a deep sense of awe for men and women of ancient India who stood for truth and freedom.

The qualities of a warrior queen that she exemplified in her life were not apocryphal. She was trained in the skills of riding and fencing, unconventional for any woman of that period. She could not have learnt them later when she grew up and was married into a protected, conservative royal family. At the same time, she remained a devout person, extremely diligent about performing all religious rites.

Baji Rao II had two daughters but no son to inherit his property. Some believed that there was a curse on the family of the Peshwas, that they were denied sons because of their past sins against Brahmins, committed for furthering political ambitions. Perhaps to atone for those sins, Baji Rao chose to be in a holy place and spend his exile in spirituality. He came to Bithur accompanied by his two wives and quite a substantial amount of personal treasure, which the British neither examined nor seized.[15] What followed was something of an exodus as a large number of families from Maharashtra trailed their traditional patron, unable to find alternate means of livelihood under the new regime. Baji Rao proved to be a very considerate and generous benefactor. The pension granted to him by the British government had actually taken into account that he would need to support 'a large retinue of faithful adherents'.[16] He provided for his kinsmen well without indulging in waste. Out of his pension, he saved and invested in public securities that by 1851 were worth nearly 80,000 rupees.

Among the followers were Madhavrao and his wife Ganga Devi, pious Brahmins from a village named Venu who came to Bithur in 1827 with their three-year-old son, Sririshi. Baji Rao took a fancy to little Sririshi and decided to adopt him as a son who would perform his funeral rites and inherit his property. On 7 June 1827, Sririshi was initiated into his new status as the son of Peshwa Baji Rao II with a new name, Nana Dhondu Pant, who grew up to be better known as Nana Sahib. Subsequently, Baji Rao adopted two more sons, Raghunath Rao and Gangadhar Rao, also called Bala Sahib.

Baji Rao served the British well. During the war with Afghanistan, he lent the East India Company five lakh rupees. In the Punjab war, he offered to raise a thousand horses and an equal number of foot soldiers at his own cost.[17] Whatever his motives, his loyalty to the British rulers now was tested and proven without a doubt.

In 1839, he drew up a will stating that he had adopted three sons. His second son Raghunath Rao had died, leaving behind a son, Pandurang Rao. Now Baji Rao had two sons and a grandson to bequeath his property to. Nana Dhondu Pant, as the eldest, was to inherit both the title and the pension of the Peshwa. Given that he had done so much to help them, Baji Rao was certain that the British were going to approve the adoption. He was, however, mistaken. His plea was turned down, though the matter was left open for further consideration, perhaps after his death.[18]

Shortly after the adopted son Nana Dhondu Pant came to live in the palace, a new playmate made an appearance—a little girl named Manu. Her father Moropant Tambe, as an employee of the Peshwa's office, had been given quarters in the sprawling palace where several other retainers lived. Later, he built his own house close to the palace and little Manu's proximity and association with the palace was never severed.

Manu was intelligent, lively, energetic and vivacious. The ageing Peshwa grew very fond of her, calling her 'Chhabili'.[19] She must have been indulged in every way. Manu was allowed to take lessons with the boys in the palace and quickly acquired a working knowledge of Sanskrit, Hindi and Persian in addition to her mother tongue, Marathi.[20] She also displayed a remarkable penchant for outdoor activities that she trained for with the boys. 'Manu flew kites, ran races, watched wrestling matches with keen interest, and learned to ride, shoot, and fence.'[21]

A fairly objective and critical biography written in 1966 by John Smyth attributes the talent and character of the future Rani to her being 'a tomboy of great force'. Her widowed father may have allowed her to spend time with the boys, unable to control 'her high spirits and physical energies'. She was thus free to attend lessons that the boys took, such as shooting and riding. But 'these details of her childhood must be conjectural', for nothing was recorded for decades after her death in 1858.

Trying to match her early upbringing with her later actions, Smyth sums up, 'It would seem... that she had unique gifts which were rapidly developed through the role she was called upon to play. It is a well-known phenomenon that a personality often grows to the size required by circumstances... But of course her particular natural attributes were tailor-made for the job.'[22] Clearly there were bits of all—her natural talent, her unusual upbringing and the extraordinary times in which her singular fate was to unfold. Finally, oral history immortalized her, contributing to the creation of a larger-than-life persona.

One late afternoon, Moropant Tambe was waiting at the gate of the Peshwa's palace for his daughter Manu. She went riding every afternoon with her friends Nana Sahib and his brother Bala Sahib, but that day they were late. The elderly Peshwa joined Moropant, and both began to wonder what was keeping the children, when from a distance they saw Nana's horse returning without the rider, foaming at the mouth with fear and exertion. The two men panicked and were about to send other horsemen in pursuit when they observed another horse in the distance. As it came closer, they saw Nana covered in blood, with Manu riding the horse. Neither Nana nor his brother was able to speak. The girl in their company explained the fall with complete composure.

She said they were riding home when Nana suddenly speeded up and threw a challenge at Manu: 'Let's see who rides faster.' Manu spurred her horse and had forged ahead when she suddenly heard Nana's cry. As she looked back, she found him lying on the ground, his head bleeding. She stopped and turned her horse. Nana had fallen, hitting his head on a hard surface. It hurt, but the injury was not deep. Manu patiently helped him stand up and get on her horse, and then mounted behind him. Her composure notwithstanding, the entire palace was in a commotion tending to the young prince.

Moropant could not hide his pride at the manner in which his daughter had taken charge of the situation. It augured well, he thought. Later that night, however, he was quite unexpectedly cross-questioned by Manu. The little girl was surprised that there was so much of uproar over such a trifling. Nana was not a baby, and his injury was so little. What was the fuss about? She had been brought up on stories from the *Mahabharata* where young heroes like Abhimanyu died fighting without a shadow of fear. Moropant had no answer except to blame the fuss on circumstances. Manu promised she would never be cowed down like Nana and that all her life she would demonstrate unwavering courage.

Moropant sighed and asked her to go to sleep. It had been a long day, after all.

A couple of days later, Manu went to see Nana. He looked pale and somewhat weak. Manu lost her patience. She was certain that he was malingering so that he would continue to be pampered. With some annoyance, she asked him why he always bragged about wanting to emulate the Marathi heroes when a slight injury kept him in bed for days. She insisted that they go riding that afternoon. Nana was shocked at her suggestion. What if a jolt opened up his barely healed wound? What if he fell down again? Nana was also a bit irritated by Manu's scorn and embarrassed by his own weakness. The Peshwa entered the room while the two were arguing, and Moropant followed him. Baji Rao, usually very indulgent of Manu, was somewhat peeved at her for raising her voice at Nana. He mildly chided her for talking so much. To ease the tension, Moropant suggested that Nana be taken for a joyride on the elephant that had been specially fitted with soft cushions. He hoped that the threesome could go for their daily saunter and the tension between the teenagers would ease.

Manu was very excited at the thought of riding an elephant, for she had never ridden one. Elephants were kept for special occasions when the Peshwa rode; as a mere friend of his adopted son, she never had the privilege. This evening she was going to fulfil her long-cherished dream, for she had often fantasized that she would ride her own elephant. She ran ahead of the others to where the elephant was waiting with the mahout, a beautifully decorated howdah on its back. Nana was brought and helped up to the seat. His younger brother Bala Sahib followed him. Manu impatiently waited for her turn. She requested Baji Rao to ask his men help her sit on the howdah too. Before Baji Rao could say anything, Nana told the mahout to start. The mahout swung his whip and the elephant stood up. Baji Rao said a little loudly, first to his older son and then the younger, that they should take Manu with them. Nana was in no mood to comply, and ordered the mahout to start.

The two rode past Manu, standing there shocked and incredulous. She felt tears pricking at the corners of her eyes, but she was too proud to shed them. The Peshwa went back to his palace. Manu turned to her father and said that she must ride and he should ask the mahout to stop. Moropant was also upset at Nana's behaviour and more than a little surprised. He reasoned with his daughter that she could ride another day. She stood angry and unconvinced. As she continued to pester him, Moropant lost his cool and snapped back at her: she was not destined to ride an elephant, and that was that. Manu was stunned by her father's rebuff, for seldom had he spoken to her in this manner. She stood silent for a while and then replied, 'I am destined to have not one but ten elephants.'

There is not a single biography of Rani Lakshmi Bai

that does not mention this incident, especially the last bit—Manu being turned down by Nana and her confident claim. Vrindavan Lal Verma describes the incident at length. If this story is apocryphal, no one knows who invented it; if it is true, it is not known who recorded it.

In yet another story, Manu is said to have stopped a raging elephant by jumping on its trunk and pacifying it. According to Joyce Lebra-Chapman, 'Since the elephant symbolises kingship in India, these episodes with elephants were significant portents of her later role as well as early demonstrations of her bravery and spirit.'[23]

2

Coming of Age

Meanwhile, Moropant Tambe was beginning to worry about his daughter. It was customary to get daughters married before they reached puberty, and Manu was well past the age. Almost as an answer to his prayers, Tantia Dikshit arrived in Bithur from Jhansi, where he lived. A learned Brahmin, a well-known astrologer and highly regarded by the entire community, Dikshit was on a tour of Marathi settlements. According to Verma, he was supposed to have visited Banaras, Nagpur and Pune, and now on his way back, he came to pay his respects to the Peshwa in Bithur. He was greeted with all formalities due to a senior Brahmin.

Tantia Dikshit is said to have proposed first to her father, Manu's marriage to Gangadhar Rao, the Raja of Jhansi, who was a widower without children. There are different unauthenticated versions of the story. One is that Moropant Tambe had shared his concerns regarding Manu with Dikshit, who asked to see her horoscope. He was very impressed with the excellent configuration of stars and confirmed that she was born to be queen. Baji Rao concurred that she was a girl of exceptional talent and intelligence. Dikshit returned to Jhansi and sought the

Raja's consent. Gangadhar Rao agreed only on condition that the girl's father had no objections to the difference in their ages. According to the popular version, the Raja was past forty when he married for the second time. In reality, he was in his late twenties. A formal proposal was sent and Moropant Tambe readily agreed.

In another account, Tantia Dikshit made the offer of marriage as soon as he saw Manu and heard of her good qualities. Moropant was thrilled with the proposal. Given their difference in status, the Raja could not come to the bride's house as was customary—Manu and her father had to travel to Jhansi instead. The match was finalized by the Raja sending a large convoy laden with presents for the young bride. Moropant agreed to go to Jhansi with his daughter. One of Nana's closest friends, Tantia Tope, accompanied them.

Young Manu left a carefree childhood behind and walked into the one destined to make her a legend.

The marriage of Manu to the Raja of Jhansi made the dreams of Moropant Tambe a reality. What the fond father was oblivious of was the beleaguered legacy that his future son-in-law had inherited.

From whichever direction one enters the town, the fort of Jhansi, perched atop a small hill, is the first visible landmark. It stands sombre in its grandeur, witness to the ravages of history. By medieval Indian standards, the fort of Jhansi is neither large nor impressive. The outer ramparts enclose approximately forty-nine acres of land, but if one excludes the outer moat, most of the inner complex is within the wall surrounding fifteen acres. The more prominent buildings in the fort are the temples, the palace and several scattered low buildings. These were built by the men who controlled Jhansi fort in turn—the Bundelas, the Marathis and finally the British.

The fort overlooks the land they call Bundelkhand, home to the feisty, stubborn Bundelas. The region has now been truncated into two halves that fall in the provinces of Uttar Pradesh and Madhya Pradesh. But originally, the five districts of Banda, Hamirpur, Jalaun, Jhansi and Lalitpur that comprised Bundelkhand squatted squarely on the route that joined the Western Ghats with eastern India.

Bundelkhand was a difficult terrain and still is hard, stony land interspersed with craggy hills and deep ravines, which makes any regular, extended stretch of cultivation impossible. On the journey from Gwalior to Jhansi across Bundelkhand, patches of agriculture can be seen, interrupted by undulating land and low hills covered in shrub. Depleted, unproductive soil supports a sparse population, making widely dispersed settlements and huge areas of wasteland hallmarks of this region. For a good part of the nineteenth century, the 'cry... was not for broad acres to till but strong arms to guide the plough'.[1] Except for congested towns like Jhansi, the ravines and gorges still remain the unmistakable mark of Bundelkhand, where the number of houses to a mile in 1853 was less than half of what was found in the Doab. The ratio does not appear to be very different 150 years later.[2]

Survival in these difficult conditions was a struggle, and those who managed to do so became naturally tough. Different groups of people intermittently settled here—Rajputs, Brahmins, agricultural castes such as the Lodhis, Gujars, Kurmis Ahirs, and low-caste Khangars and Chamars—over centuries till the Bundelas rose to occupy and consolidate political rule here in the sixteenth and seventeenth centuries. Thereafter began a more or less regular succession of kings, local landlords and privileged tenure holders. In their characteristic manner, British officials branded the Bundelas as 'men prone to turbulence, and habitually and continually engaged in hostile contests—men impatient of control, who acknowledged no law but that of force'.[3]

One of the Bundela chiefs, Rudr Pratap, founded the town and kingdom of Orchha after defeating the other chiefs in 1507. Ten kilometres north-west of Orchha, on a low hill called Bangra, one of his successors, Bir Singh Deo, built a fort in 1613, perhaps for strategic reasons, though he called it Mauj Mahal (recreation palace). A popular story goes that Bir Singh Deo was showing, from the top of one of his palaces, the new fort he had built on Bangra hill to his friend the Raja of Jaitpur. The Jaitpur Raja, on being asked if he could see it well, remarked he could, but in a haze, *'jhainsi'*. Bir Singh Deo decided to call the place Jhainsi and this eventually became the colloquial Jhansi.

Subsequently, other Bundela chiefs built bases in places like Datia in the north and Mahoba in the east. While one of them occupied a larger domain, his brothers and close kin received land for their support on special terms. They formed the aristocracy, next in line to the chiefs and—being members of the same family—formed a closely-knit clan. As people, they were passionately attached to their land and pride. To reinforce this, they evolved certain practices and conventions of landholdings that became distinctive of this region.[4]

Looking for the Thugs in his famous expedition, W.H. Sleeman found, 'There is hardly a single chief of the Hindoo military class in the Bundelkhand or Gwalior territories, who does not keep a gang of robbers of some kind or other, and consider it as a very valuable and legitimate source of revenue.'[5] In search of bandits, Thugs and the cult of Kali a century and half later, Kevin Rushby came looking for all of them to the region of

Bundelkhand, 'one renowned for lawlessness'.[6] He was told on his visit to Jhansi that this was a land famous for countless small rajas, some of whom sponsored robbers. The barren, stony terrain, capricious rainfall and uncertain agriculture did not sustain any regular agrarian life. Resorting to banditry was often the only alternative amidst those craggy hills and piles of boulders.

Bundelkhand must have been a troubled kingdom for the Marathis. The most successful regional power in western India to emerge in the shadow of Mughal decline was drawn into the political struggle of Bundelkhand by Chatrasal Bundela, who in the early eighteenth century conquered and consolidated almost the whole of Bundelkhand, extending control over the east, the south and the west. As Mughal control waned and local Rajputs weakened in disunity, intermediary groups like the Bundelas rose. But because of its positioning, Bundelkhand knew no lasting peace or stable rule. There were several pretenders to power and Muhammad Khan Bangash, the Nawab of Farruckabad, was one who wanted control over the entire region. Farrukshiyar, the Mughal Emperor, granted this Rohilla chief the large jagir of Allahabad with jurisdictions overlapping Chatrasal's kingdom. In trying to claim his rights over the area, Bangash clashed with the Bundela. It was a long drawn-out battle in which the Rajput fared badly in the initial phases.[7] Chatrasal surrendered and, together with his family, was confined in the fort of Jaitpur in 1728. Between December 1728 and February 1729, Chatrasal Bundela got in touch with the Marathis, who formed a powerful regional force under the leadership of the Peshwas, the prime ministers of the kingdom. The Peshwa at this time was Baji Rao I, perhaps the most talented and ambitious in a long line.

During Holi on 4 March 1728, Chatrasal sought

special permission from his new master to celebrate the festival with a lavish function at his home. Convinced that the Bundela, now over eighty years old, was incapable of posing any resistance to his men, Bangash allowed him to leave the fort with his men. Eight days later, the Peshwa marched into Bundelkhand leading a strong Marathi army. By August, the Rohilla chief was defeated and driven out of the Bundela land.[8]

Grateful for the Peshwa's help, Chatrasal divided his kingdom among his two sons and Baji Rao. The Marathis got the region in the west, including Jhansi, his eldest son Hardi Sah got portions in the south-east, and his second son, Jagat Sah, territories in the north. The aged Bundela died in 1731, but it was more than a decade before the Marathis came to live in and rule Jhansi. For some time, they chose not to govern this region directly, and instead decided to impose *chauth*, a tribute that guaranteed Marathi protection, on the smaller principalities that technically fell within their domain. The Raja of Orchha, Bir Singh Deo, refused to pay the levy, opposed the Marathi force sent to realize the amount and killed their general Jyotibai Scindia. In retaliation, the Marathis sent another force under the charge of Naru Shankar. Bir Singh Deo was defeated and captured in the fort of Jhansi. He was later released and restored to his kingdom on condition that he give up the fort of Jhansi and pay a huge indemnity including money and land to the Marathis.

Naru Shankar was appointed the first Marathi subedar, or Governor of Jhansi, in 1742. But it was a charge fraught with constant threat. He was recalled in 1757 but reinstated four years later. Naru Shankar was succeeded by his nephew, Vishwas Rao Lakshman, who governed Jhansi for three years from 1766 to 1769. The man who followed was Raghunath Rao Newalkar. With him began the hereditary rule of Jhansi by a single family, the Newalkars. This was the family Lakshmi Bai married into.

Raghunath Rao proved to be the most effective of the chiefs of Jhansi after Naru Shankar.[9] At the same time, smaller Marathi principalities emerged in Jalaun and Gurserai. By the end of the eighteenth century, in an interlock of political claims, the Bundelas came to share power with the Marathis. In a strange turn of fate, however, the Rajputs lost out and had to settle for the smaller jagirdaris or landholdings, while the relatively more prominent political centres, such as Jhansi and Jalaun, went to the Marathis. The kingdom of Banda comprising territories in the east, next to Allahabad, was seized by Ali Bahadur, the illegitimate son of Baji Rao I. But the Rajputs remained in effective control as proprietors of land of varying sizes and privileges. What made their domination almost inviolable were the horizontal clan linkages that tied through relations of blood and marriage everyone from the Bundela retainer to the landlord, and higher still, to the regional prince. The Bundelas were particularly strong in Jhansi and further south. There were other Rajput clans like the Puars and the Kuchwahas, the Sengars and the Bais, organized more or less on similar patterns.

It thus could not have been easy for the Marathis to rule. Naru Shankar concentrated on settling and building up the town of Jhansi by inviting Marathi Brahmins from the Deccan and encouraging artisans to come and stay. Markets were set up and *bastis* or neighbourhoods of various craftsmen and merchants grew. The court of Jhansi became specially known for patronizing learned Brahmins. They also built temples to their presiding deities, Ganesh and Lakshmi, that attracted annual pilgrims apart from supporting families of Brahmins in the town. The temple of Lakshmi, one-and-a-half kilometres away from the heart of the town, overlooked a large and beautiful tank and was among the most striking structures and examples of Marathi architecture. It was also the most frequently visited temple and the one Lakshmi Bai never failed to make her weekly trips to. Between themselves, Naru Shankar and Raghunath Rao gave Jhansi a new look and a new life. It was the most beautifully decorated town in the region and certainly the busiest and most travelled to. All this was before Lakshmi Bai's time.

Inside the fort, Naru Shankar built two temples—a small shrine of Ganesh close to the entrance and another dedicated to Shiv—at Jhansi fort. The impressive five-storey Panch Mahal, which was the royal palace, was originally built by the Bundelas and later improved upon by the Marathis. Behind that was a two-storey structure for the court and its officials. The Shiv temple was built on a slope on the north-eastern side that was reached by a flight of steep stairs. All colonial bungalows set in the middle are reminders of further invasion and occupation of the fort. But it was most lived in, busy and best maintained under the Marathis.

It is said that 4,000 people could live in the fort in the best of times. Separate quarters for soldiers ran along the thick wall that had several and separate gates for pedestrians, horses and the Raja's elephants. Inside were beautifully laid-out gardens and open spaces with fruit trees, flower beds and well-manicured green grass.

Outside the fort, the town of Jhansi grew into a busy marketplace. Unlike its present chaos and disorderly expansion, Jhansi used to be a prettily laid-out town that stretched along the eastern side of the fort. Three hundred metres from the fort, Raghunath Rao built a palace on a busy market street. This was where Lakshmi Bai spent her last years, which is why it is now known as Rani Mahal. In one of its meandering lanes, amidst the clamour and noise, stands the temple to Ganesh, the god who overlooks all earthly matters and ensures that everything is set right. The most prominent feature of Jhansi, however, was its bazaars that sold a whole range of luxury goods, like silks, brass utensils and paintings, and specialized cloth.[10] The Marathis were quite struck by the beauty of Jhansi, its gardens and undulating landscape.[11] Unlike the rest of Bundelkhand, the town received a lot of rainfall. Thus, it was in every sense an oasis in the midst of a desert.

Naru Shankar's success had been largely independent of assistance from Pune. It is doubtful if he regularly sent tribute to the capital. Certainly, by the time of Raghunath Rao, Jhansi had for all practical purposes become free of control from the Peshwa's court. But now they had to contend with the rising British power. Raghunath Rao chose not to antagonize or get in the way of the colonial government. He refused to give shelter to Chait Singh of Banaras, regarded as a renegade by British officials.[12] In 1796, Raghunath Rao abdicated the throne in favour of his brother Sheo Rao Hari and retired to Banaras to devote the rest of his days to spirituality. In all likelihood, he was afflicted with leprosy and wished to spend his last days in the holy city, for here, in the waters of the Ganga, he drowned himself.

Outside Jhansi was the countryside and the Rajputs to reckon with. There were close to 700 villages in the kingdom spread over Puchore, Kurehra, Mhow, Bijairaghogarh and Pundwaha, each of which was later converted into a unit of administration under the British. The Marathis remained largely confined to Jhansi and other towns like Gurserai. As rulers, they did not want to disturb the customary land tenures or proprietary rights of Bundelkhand and let land be owned by powerful Rajput landlords. The Bundelas, the Kuchwahas, the Chauhans, the Puars and the Sengars by intermarriage created a strong, resilient community of landholding brotherhood, very jealous of their rights. The Marathis were aware of this and the Rajput tradition of resistance by banding together and going on a rampage. They let them alone and instead chose a headman for each brotherhood who was designated 'mehtey' and granted an allowance either in land or money for collecting the dues of the government from other members. These men were usually 'lineal descendants of the eldest branch' of the chief landholding clan. In villages held by more than one caste or clans, separate mehteys had to be appointed for each and the allowance distributed according to land held by the brotherhood.[13] The Marathi government imposed a demand on the total out-turn of crops. If the season was good the entire revenue was raised; if not, as was often the case, the officials collected all they could, hoping the balance would be made up in future.

There used to be a practice called *dekha parkhi*, or review by sight. The revenue was fixed on paper but collected on the basis of what was raised on land. And the amount was decided after a physical inspection of the fields.[14] Agricultural loans, called *tuccavi*, were also granted to landholders.[15] It is doubtful if, despite such concessions, the Bundelas took to Marathi rule very well, but in the absence of any information on the period from the end of the eighteenth century till the beginning of the next, we can say little. The more important Bundela chiefs, however, treated the Marathis with deference.

And then the British arrived. Marathi power collapsed in the wake of a series of battles which the British army won. With every victory and treaty that followed, they occupied larger and larger portions of territory. In an agreement supplementary to the Treaty of Bassein, the Peshwa gave up claims to all his substantial territories, which included the province of Bundelkhand, yielding a revenue of thirty-six lakh rupees.[16] This meant that as a subsidiary of the Peshwa, the kingdom of Jhansi was now bequeathed to the British. The British chose not to administer it directly. In February 1804, the East India Company signed a treaty with Sheo Rao Hari, allowing him to continue his rule and even promising him protection of the Peshwa. This was to be the crucial point of contention later—as a tributary state, Jhansi could be independent only under certain conditions. The subedar had to pay his annual tribute, promise to assist the British if they were at war with neighbouring states, and pledge never to help anyone who was not on friendly terms with the colonial government.[17]

There were only three states in the region with which the East India Company signed separate and formal treaties as independent principalities. They were the Bundela kingdoms of Orchha, Datia and Sampthar. The rest, a total of twenty-six chiefs of states in Bundelkhand who were holding their estates under *sanads*, were bound by deeds of allegiance and thus dependent on the British. In reality, everyone had to acknowledge the supremacy of the British government and was thus obliged to offer military service. On their part, the British reserved for themselves the prerogative to interfere in local politics whenever it suited them.

*

Ramchandra Rao was declared heir to the throne of Jhansi in 1811, when his father died. The decision was taken by his grandfather Sheo Rao Hari, who made the announcement at the sacred thread ceremony of Ramchandra Rao when the boy was eight. Gopal Rao Bhao, a trusted lieutenant, was appointed guardian of the minor heir. As the paramount power in the region, the British were informed of the Raja's decision. Sheo Rao retired to Banaras and subsequently died there.[18] The young Ramchandra became the subedar at the age of fourteen in 1814.

Ramchandra Rao had a fairly long and rather eventful career. Within the family, he had had to face persistent resistance from his mother Sakhubai who resented his growing independence in state matters. The people of Jhansi talk of an incident in which she conspired to murder him. Ramchandra was a keen swimmer, and every morning would go to swim in the taal, or tank, next to the Lakshmi temple. Sakhubai, it is said, got iron spikes planted in the water to kill him when he entered it. A soldier named Lalu Kodalkar found out about the conspiracy and alerted the subedar. Sakhubai had the soldier murdered, but her own complicity became evident, and she was made a prisoner in one of the forts under the jurisdiction of Jhansi.

Of primary concern to Ramchandra Rao was sorting out his relationship with the British government. In 1817, Peshwa Baji Rao II surrendered completely to the East India Company and by the Treaty of Pune, gave up all claims to Bundelkhand, including the state of Jhansi. The seventeen-year-old Ramchandra Rao, on the advice of his mentors, chose to demonstrate his unequivocal allegiance to the colonial government. The chiefs of Jhansi from the time of Raghunath Bhao had been among the most faithful and devoted subjects of British rule, and equally dependent on it. Ramchandra Rao continued the trend. In the wake of the changed political fortunes, the British government signed defensive treaties with all the local chiefs of Bundelkhand in 1817. The one with the subedar of Jhansi signed in November 1817 recognized him and his successors as the hereditary rulers of the state. Thirty-six years later, Lakshmi Bai reminded the British Governor General of this commitment.[19]

Ramchandra Rao proved a very loyal subject of the British. During the Anglo-Burmese war of 1824, he contributed generously to the commissariat department of the British army and a year later advanced 70,000 rupees as annual tribute. He also agreed to maintain a body of troops that was later turned into the Bundelkhand Legion. In return, he asked the British government for a favour. The chief of Jhansi was a simple subedar. Surely, he submitted, his recent acts of support to the British government proved him to be a faithful ally and one who held a high status among other chiefs of the region. He would thus like to be conferred the title of 'Maharaja'.[20]

In 1832, William Bentinck, the Governor General of India, on a tour of north and central India, visited Jhansi. It was indeed a rare event, and the large audience hall at the top of the palace was magnificently decorated. Amidst all the glitter, Ramchandra Rao was awarded the title of Maharaja and described as the 'devoted servant of the glorious King of England'.[21] As a biographer describes, 'The simple-minded Ramchandra, overwhelmed by this honour, begged to be allowed to adopt the Union Jack as the flag of Jhansi. The request was granted, and the flag was hoisted over the highest tower of Jhansi fort.'[22] According to this account, it was Ramchandra Rao's obsequious behaviour towards the British that caused 'a rebellion on the part of some chiefs whose self-respect was outraged'.[23] This opinion seems hard to defend since the

Rajput chiefs of Datia and Orchha had on previous occasions been as open in offering assistance to the British as the Marathi ruler now. Towards the Raja of Jhansi, they may have had ill-will for quite different reasons.

While the Governor General was expressing his government's appreciation of a loyal subject, his able and much commended lieutenant was having a harried time nearby. There was a sudden increase in crime in Bundelkhand, and as the man in charge of the Thugee and Dacoity department, William H. Sleeman had not a moment of respite. Petty crimes were fairly rampant in this part of the world, and the chiefs often had to be warned against them. In 1830-31, there was an increase in incidents of what Sleeman called 'Thugee'. His concern seemed to be that these miscreants could not be easily detected or apprehended because of the protection and shelter they received from the local chiefs. The ones most guilty were the states of Orchha and Datia. The Raja of Jhansi, Sleeman felt, was not at fault except that he needed to exert himself a little more to capture these men.[24]

So wrapped up was Ramchandra Rao in his newfound glory and in his life in Jhansi, that he had been overlooking conditions in the countryside till the situation grew serious. If the Rajputs in the villages were resentful, they had every reason to be. The years 1830-31 in Jhansi saw successive bad harvests that proved disastrous. People already living on the edge were reduced to begging and hopeless poverty, a condition that could not have made the proud Rajputs happy. In 1833-34, the local Collector sent his report with the observation that pestilence and famine 'was such as have rarely afflicted so intensely any other portion of the globe'.[25] Early in 1834, the Governor General's agent based in Jabalpur, too, reported a famine in the whole of central India for the past year. But while the rest of the region was able to slowly recover, Bundelkhand reeled under the crisis. A huge number of people migrated, making the situation worse. The casualty rate every day was phenomenally high. At least fifteen people died of starvation daily in those two years.[26] It is not surprising that the same letters from local officials carried reports of a spate of crime in Bundelkhand.

What came to the surface in the crisis was the unconcealed antagonism between the Marathi ruler and his Rajput subjects. The friction was exacerbated by the fact that the rulers of Datia and Orchha belonged to the same Rajput clan as some of the powerful and disaffected people of Jhansi.

When the Raja of Jhansi was unable to ignore the crisis any more, he wrote to the Governor General in Ootacamund in the summer of 1834 describing instances of crimes and violence in his kingdom, adding that he was certain the Rajput chiefs of Datia and Orchha were supporting the men involved. One group of people under constant threat were the mahajans, or moneylenders. Several of them were captured and carried away into the Orchha and Datia territories. People from these neighbouring states plundered granaries in Jhansi and escaped before they could be caught. In some cases, mahajans were put under threat and forced to carry their movable properties to Orchha and Datia, only to have them taken away by the chiefs. A landlord named Parichat, active in the Gwalior region, seized Ramchandra Rao's courier, who had been sent to fetch water from the sacred river Ganges at Bithur, and several others from the state. He also captured merchants carrying grain from the Ganges-Yamuna belt, and took them to a village in Orchha. Amidst widespread scarcity and starvation, the fact that the Marathis were importing grain from outside for their townsmen could not have endeared them to the starving Rajputs.

West of Jhansi, the thakurs of Udgaon, Jigni, Noner and Bilhari laid waste large portions of land by plundering and destroying villages, and not letting farmers cultivate the land. The Raja was forced to send troops to put them down. But Ramchandra Rao felt he could not do this alone as it was proving to be impossibly expensive. He asked the British government for help, convinced that his former loyalty would prevent the governors from turning him down. Both the monsoon and the winter crops had been destroyed and without assistance, he would not be able to restore normal agriculture.[27]

Already, the military operations were a huge drain on the exchequer and the revenue of the kingdom was reduced to twelve lakh rupees a year. The Raja was forced to borrow money from the British and sahukars, or moneylenders, in Gwalior, but despite that could not avoid a large arrear of payment to his soldiers.[28] This created a situation that his successor was hard put to resolve.

Ramchandra Rao died at the age of twenty-nine in 1835, neither a happy ruler nor a successful one. Since he had no son, he adopted his sister's son, Krishna Rao, shortly before he died. There were two other claimants to the throne, his uncles Raghunath Rao and Gangadhar Rao. While his mother Sakhubai, since released from prison, championed the cause of her infant grandson in the hope of becoming the guardian of the infant, the two brothers staked their claims as the sons of Sheo Rao Bhao. The arbiters, of course, were none other than the British. Not willing to have another minor as the ruler of the sensitive state, they ruled against Krishna Rao.

Raghunath Rao became the new Maharaja of Jhansi despite the fact that he was in an advanced stage of leprosy. Thus began the new phase in the history of Jhansi, one of continuous crisis and increasing dependence on the British. Jhansi had a very high price to pay.

3

Marital Bliss, Shortlived

No sooner had the news arrived in Jhansi than the town began celebrating. For the proposed marriage of Gangadhar Rao to Manu, daughter of Moropant Tambe, was to be a festive occasion after a long time. The last five years had been terribly grim.

Raghunath Rao died in 1838, three years after he inherited the throne from his nephew, leaving behind a trail of scandal and a legacy besieged with crisis.

Despite their claim to the highest social rank as Brahmins, the Marathi governors seemed to have a penchant for Muslim mistresses. Baji Rao I's affair with Mastani has passed down in history with various romantic embellishments. Raghunath Rao had no heir from his legally wedded wife Janki Bai, but his mistress Lacho had two sons—Ali Bahadur and Nasrat Jung. Ali Bahadur was the more ambitious of the two and managed to get from his father, during the latter's brief rule, the right to collect revenue from eighty-five villages.[1]

It was thus hardly surprising that he should stake a claim to the throne of Jhansi when it fell vacant in 1838. He was not alone. There were his stepmother, Janki Bai, the legitimate wife of Raghunath Rao, Krishna Rao, the adopted son of Ramchandra Rao whom the irrepressible Sakhubai backed very strongly and finally, Sheo Rao Bhao's youngest son, Gangadhar Rao.

Raghunath Rao's reign had been an unqualified disaster. His extravagance and debauchery proved expensive—even disastrous—for the state and its economy. Revenues had fallen to a paltry three lakh rupees, villages were mortgaged to moneylenders in Gwalior and Orchha, and arrears of payments to soldiers had mounted hugely. To make matters worse, the Rajput landlords in the countryside were still sullen and unreconciled.

Differences among pretenders to the throne did not make matters any better. As the paramount power, the British intervened hastily, appointed a commission that upheld Gangadhar Rao's claim over others as the surviving descendant of Sheo Rao Bhao, the original signatory of the treaty with them. Gangadhar Rao, however, did not immediately get to enjoy his newfound authority. The agricultural season of 1837-38 was as bad as the one in 1833-34 and beginning April 1838, plundering began once more. Merchants were waylaid, villages looted, and goods carted away. Gangadhar Rao was unable to restore order and sought British intervention.

S. Fraser, the British agent at Banda, received a letter from the Raja's lawyer stating that things were quickly getting out of hand. There was a certain moneylender called Lalu Bakshi who, the letter alleged, was responsible for all the recent troubles. Bakshi moved to Gwalior and gathered armed retainers to perpetrate raids and outrages on Jhansi. Lalu Bakshi must have had a huge outstanding loan that he did not know how best to recover.[2] Matters rapidly worsened. On 1 October, one of the Raja's officials was killed while he was on his way home at nine at night, causing a great deal of consternation and excitement in the town. This time there was someone else to blame: Sakhubai, the mother of Ramchandra Rao, who resented the throne being taken away from her grandson. She mobilized the disgruntled soldiers and guards of the fort who had not been paid for months, and had little hope in their new Raja. By November 1838, the districts fell into complete disarray. Before the situation got any worse, British officials decided that Jhansi should be administered on behalf of the Raja, for they feared that Jhansi's troubles would spill over to their districts, where clansmen of the disaffected would be only too eager to sympathize and join in the fray.[3]

The British had to go to some length to overcome the resistance of soldiers whose salaries were long overdue in Jhansi, and occupy the fort on 5 January 1839.[4]

For four years, Gangadhar Rao was a king without a kingdom. He was granted a monthly allowance for his upkeep. According to Om Shankar Asar, he was not even allowed to live in Jhansi but assigned quarters in a small fort in Burwa Sagar.[5]

Nothing much is known about these years of his life. His wife Ramabai died young and for a long time he had not contemplated remarrying.

He spent his time pursuing what he loved most, the creative arts. He patronized painters and musicians, though his heart lay in theatre. Gangadhar Rao built a huge theatre hall adjoining the city palace. In all likelihood, he built it after inheriting the kingdom. When Manu came to Jhansi as a newly-wed bride, Gangadhar Rao was deep into theatre, both acting in and directing plays. He was particularly fond of Sanskrit plays. In his time, women did not perform on stage (the only exception was a woman called Motibai who performed regularly on stage for the

Raja of Jhansi. After his death, she became a loyal follower of Rani Lakshmi Bai), and it is said he loved dressing up and acting in women's roles. Gangadhar Rao was not a tall man, somewhat thickset and serious-looking. His make-up artist had to work hard on him to turn him into an alluring heroine.

Opposite the palace, he built a library with a huge collection of handwritten manuscripts, classics, poetry, drama, ancient spiritual texts like the *Puranas*, books on Ayurveda, Tantra and astrology. Scholars from far travelled to Jhansi to consult the library.[6]

During these four years, the British found governing Jhansi not easy at all. Captain Ross, appointed as the superintendent of Jhansi, was able to double revenue by systematizing and regularizing collection. What he found much more difficult was dealing with the Rajput landlords, who had been up in arms for the past few years. In the political uncertainty, a few landlords of Noner, Jigni, Bilhari and Udgaon took to imposing an illegal tax called 'taki' on villages, as a kind of security money that would save the people from being plundered. Among themselves, they carved out territories from which each of them would raise money.

Only with the intervention of Captain Beadon, commanding the Bundelkhand Legion in Jhansi, were they forced to concede in March 1840. Their small forts, called 'garhis', were captured and disarmed. It was apparent that these thakurs, since the beginning of Marathi rule in Bundelkhand, had been 'uniform in their opposition to the chiefs of Jhansi, and a source of constant intimidation and oppression to the villages in their vicinity'. The Marathis, in contrast, were always compliant and on the side of law, and never gave the British any reason to find fault.[7] It would be very different some years later.

None of this disturbed Gangadhar Rao's involvement with the theatre except that there was a matter of his personal life to be sorted. He needed a queen and an heir to the throne. It is not known why he waited so long to get a wife. Biographers give different reasons for his 'late' marriage, although he was no more than twenty-nine when he married for the second time. According to Mahasweta Devi, the Newalkars were Brahmins of the Karhera clan and it was not easy to find a suitable consort for them.[8]

Vishnubhatt Godse, traveller and ardent admirer of Lakshmi Bai, has not been very charitable to Gangadhar Rao. According to him, the ostensible reason was that the Raja's horoscope discouraged early remarriage. The real reason was that Gangadhar Rao was known for his bad temper and intolerant nature, and not many were willing to give their young daughters to him. The Raja's obsession with the stage did not bode well for his reputation either. People did suspect that he may have been impotent or gay, according to D.V. Tahmankar. 'On occasions he played female parts, as was the custom in India, where there were no actresses until the twentieth century. But the enjoyment he found in these performances and his liking for women's dress became common knowledge in Jhansi.'[9]

This side of his nature was incompatible with the general impression, later reported by British officials, that he was stern by nature. He was certainly somewhat taciturn and withdrawn.

In 1841, Tantia Dikshit, the court astrologer, came home with news of a girl who was in every way suitable to be the Rani of Jhansi. She was from the right Brahmin clan; she was educated, well-spoken and pretty. And, of course, she had the best recommendations from none other than Peshwa Baji Rao II. Even though in reduced circumstances, the Peshwa was still the seniormost Marathi leader, and his counsel could not be ignored. Gangadhar Rao agreed to the proposal and sent a large convoy laden with presents as a token of his consent and formal engagement to Manu.

Since Moropant Tambe was lower in the hierarchy to the Raja of Jhansi, he could not expect the bridegroom to come to his house to ask for his daughter's hand. Tambe made the journey instead. The marriage was fixed for May 1842.

Manu and her father, accompanied by a small group, arrived in Jhansi and were put up in a house not far from the palace, opposite the Ganesh temple where the marriage was to take place.

In Vrindavan Lal Verma's novel, Manu had the first glimpse of her husband from the window on the first floor of the house. She was watching the horses and their riders more keenly than her future husband-to-be when a young girl of about her age came forward to pay her respects. There were two others who followed. These three girls were the famous companions of Lakshmi Bai—Sundar, Mandar and Kashi—and were said to have remained by her side till their death.[10]

The Ganesh temple, set in one of the narrow lanes of the town, was a typical Marathi construction built on two floors around a rectangular hall, at the end of which was the sanctum for the idol. Surrounding the hall on the first floor ran a corridor with a hanging balcony for the women to watch the ceremony. Before the altar in the hall downstairs, arrangements for the marriage were lavishly laid out that day in May 1842. Members of the royal family and those close to it crowded around the hall, women and children on the first floor, eagerly waiting for the nuptials to begin. Outside, there was a huge crowd. People lined the streets from the crack of dawn, to see their Rani and Raja proceed to the palace in the fort after the wedding. Manu was dressed in the family diamonds of the Newalkars and taken in a palanquin to the temple across the lane. She took her place next to Gangadhar Rao with both trepidation and excitement. This was the moment that she had been waiting for all her life. Before the bride and the groom were to walk around the fire seven times, the priest bent down to tie the end of her sari to the groom's wrapper. Manu spoke out clear and loud, 'Tie the knot firmly so that it is not easily undone.'[11] After the wedding, as the royal couple made their way to the palace on palanquins, a huge cheer rose from the crowd, blessing their new Rani. Manu was given a new name. She became Lakshmi Bai, Rani of Jhansi.

The celebrations were extravagant, as becoming of the wedding of the Raja of Jhansi. Sweets and coins were distributed generously among the residents of Jhansi and guests from outside. There were hundreds of Brahmins who had come to Jhansi for the occasion. They were presented with money and expensive gifts as they showered the newly-wed couple with their blessings. Guns were fired in salute and in the evening, the town was resplendent with dazzling fireworks. Nothing in the splendid celebrations reminded the people of the town that the kingdom had not been returned to the Raja and that he was still a pensioner. This did not bother the bride's father nor did the disturbances raging not far from the town of Jhansi seem to lessen the gaiety. The wedding had the usual spectacle of a Hindu marriage and the expenses may have been borne by the Raja from his private funds. Or perhaps hagiographical literature on the Rani of Jhansi, unable to describe her marriage in any lesser terms, let imagination run riot. After all, this was the moment of her transformation from a simple Brahmin girl to a queen.

The year boded well for Gangadhar Rao. The British returned Jhansi to its ruler. His Rani, people preferred to believe, brought the kingdom back truly in the manner of the goddess of wealth—Lakshmi—as, before the year ran out, the British concluded a treaty with Gangadhar Rao, restoring his estates back to him. Since this region was still somewhat explosive, they decided to maintain a military force for its protection. There already was a small contingent called the Jalaun Legion. It was now to be called Bundelkhand Legion with its station in Jhansi on a piece of land that the Raja conceded not far from the town. In course of time, this area grew into the cantonment that was to play such an important role in the subsequent drama. To bear half the cost of maintaining the force, Gangadhar Rao had to forsake two parganas, or provincial subdivisions, yielding an annual revenue of a little over two lakh twenty-seven thousand rupees. This did not seem to trouble the Raja too much, for it brought him the much-desired sense of security amidst the turbulent Rajputs.

Captain Ross, the deputy collector for Jhansi, had made short-term revenue settlements with landholders, which still had two years to run. The Raja was asked to honour the British commitment.

Gangadhar Rao, however, needed no counsel. He proved to be an able and competent ruler, and increasingly quite popular too. His revenue management was particularly successful. Once the British settlements expired, the Raja entered into fresh five-year agreements. He pitched the rate high, but backed it up with an efficient system of collection that blended severity with lenient concessions as and when required. The Raja took personal interest in the organization and running of the revenue machinery. He made sure that his state honoured all rights and privileges that traditional landholders had been enjoying. Little wonder that—after Sheo Ram Bhao—he was the first Newalkar to bring reconciliation and peace between the Rajputs and Marathi rule in Jhansi. Since there was not much need of the Bundelkhand Legion, it was disbanded in 1848, but a small force of British soldiers remained in the town.[12]

There was a remarkable decline in crime rates both in the town of Jhansi and in the surrounding regions. People could leave their doors open at night and sleep without a care. Gangadhar Rao appointed responsible men in charge of security and demarcated separate domains for each of them. If there were any incidents of theft, the man in charge had to replace the goods lost. Several times, the loss was compensated from the Raja's own treasury. This is a traditional form of crime management.[13] But he was known to be a very stern ruler whom the subjects both admired and feared. He improved roads and sanitation which, together with peace and security, improved trade and commerce. When Vishnubhatt Godse visited Jhansi in 1856 or when Atkinson did a statistical survey of the region, people spoke of Gangadhar Rao's rule with fondness and blessed his soul.

The Raja built around him a team of exceptionally talented assistants, among whom prime minister Raghav Ramchandra Sant, chief lawyer in the royal court Narasimha Rao and Nana Bhopatkar, in charge of the judicial administration of the entire kingdom, were the leading officials. They identified sensitive areas where the thakurs had been active, and by sending troops in some cases and extending gestures of friendship in others, all were brought round to the support of the Jhansi raj.[14] At the same time, Gangadhar Rao built his own strong army of 5,000 soldiers, 2,000 policemen, 500 cavalry, 100 specially trained guards and four guns.[15] He was said to have had quite a collection of horses and elephants.

His personal favourite was an elephant named Sidhbaksh. The howdah was made entirely of gold. All his horses and elephants were gorgeously decorated, and special craftsmen from Banaras were engaged for making the howdahs and the saddles for them. These added grandeur and glory for the first time to the kingdom of Jhansi.

Flattering biographies of Lakshmi Bai attributed the splendour of the Jhansi court to the coming of the Rani, like a blessing from the goddess of wealth. The years were happy and the kingdom prospered. Not only did admiring writers pen eulogies of Jhansi, visitors like John Lang, the impartial British journalist and lawyer and the stern British agent for central India, Robert Hamilton, could not resist admiring the court and the magnificence of Jhansi, its collection of horses and elephants. Even the most complimentary account of the Rani could not have credited this to her. They were proof of Gangadhar Rao Newalkar's accomplishments.

With the British, the Raja of Jhansi kept a deliberate distance, making sure that his personal dignity was never compromised. Once, Dussehra fell on a Sunday, when the Raja led a traditional ceremonial procession. The officer commanding the British force sent word that his men would not be present since they did not carry arms on the day of Sabbath. The Raja replied that he had been bearing part of the cost of maintaining the contingent in Jhansi and if they did not comply with his command, he would withdraw support. The men promptly reported for duty.

Gangadhar Rao was a man of diverse talents, at once strong and sensitive. British accounts sometimes confuse his reign with the ineffective ones of his immediate predecessors. His reputation is also eclipsed by his Rani's dazzling career. But Gangadhar Rao would hold out as an exceptional ruler on his own.

Young Lakshmi Bai must have been overawed as she stepped into the Panch Mahal, a massive five-storey building with a few floors below the ground. After the fashion of all local architecture, there was a long and fairly wide hall in the middle with small rooms along three sides on each floor. On the fourth side ran a narrow staircase, all the way up. The walls and the ceiling were richly covered with frescoes painted in earthy colours of brown, green and red. The Rani's rooms on the ground floor were equally ostentatiously adorned.

For Manu, it was not easy to adjust to the life of a Rani, cloistered in the palace and confined to the fort, her every step determined by protocol. But it was a life that she had grown up believing was fated for her. As a part of the marriage arrangement, her father Moropant Tambe was offered the position of a sardar in Jhansi with an annual salary of Rs 3,600 and living quarters. Now that Manu was settled, he decided to remarry. The Khanwalkars lived in Gurserai, and Basudev Shrirao had a young daughter, Chima Bai, about the same age as Manu. Moropant married her and began a new family in Jhansi. They had a son and a daughter.

Lakshmi Bai grew up from a restless child into a dignified woman who was very striking to look at. She was of middle height, with handsome features and very large eyes. As queen, she was richly adorned with jewels, especially pearls. She had a fetish for cleanliness and disliked anyone who was not neatly turned out. It is once again difficult to be certain about Lakshmi Bai's relationship with Gangadhar Rao. Myths abound.

According to Godse, Lakshmi Bai was not happy. 'Her husband was a man of very stern nature and his regime was very severe too. She was not given any sort of freedom. Moving out of the palace was out of the question; she wasn't even allowed to move within the palace freely.'[16]

This seems something of an exaggeration, especially as Mahasweta Devi talks of a growing rapport between the couple. She relates how Gangadhar Rao surprised the Rani one day with a palanquin crafted in silver by special artisans from Banaras. The cushions inside, embroidered in gold threads and edged with tassels, were equally spectacular. Lakshmi Bai was charmed, and used it for her trip to the Mahalakshmi temple. It was a breathtaking sight as the procession moved to the sound of shehnais played by musicians who sat on the second-floor porch of the temple so that their music wafted all the way to the town and people knew that the Rani was on her way to Lakshmi mandir. People gathered for alms and blessings that were never offered without a glimpse of the pretty Rani.[17]

It is unlikely that Lakshmi Bai was completely housebound or strictly prohibited to go out. According to Om Shankar Asar, even though for the first few years her movements were restricted, Gangadhar Rao came to regard his wife's wisdom and sagacity highly and often sought her advice on matters of importance.[18] It is doubtful if she was allowed to ride openly or practise any outdoor activity such as sword fighting or shooting. It is equally unlikely that she trained her companions and maids at riding and the use of arms while Gangadhar Rao was alive.[19]

Between the couple, there grew a warm understanding. Contrary to popular versions, Gangadhar Rao was not very much older than Lakshmi Bai. He was twenty-nine when they married, she fifteen. Probably as a mark of his affection and attachment, the Raja decided to undertake a pilgrimage with his wife. This could not have been a customary practice, and clearly Gangadhar Rao was breaking conventions to please his Rani. For nothing would give Lakshmi Bai greater pleasure than to visit her childhood haunts in Banaras. Religious and God-fearing as she was, the opportunity of praying in the temples where her father and mother had taken her must have been the high point of her life as the Rani of Jhansi. There was also a shadow hanging over their lives because, despite being married for nine years, they did not have a child. The couple decided to seek the blessings of the gods.

The Raja wrote to the Governor General about his proposed journey and requested him to make appropriate arrangements. They set out in the beginning of 1851 for Banaras, which was to be their first halt. The British made sure that the royal party was received well wherever it halted, offered the best of hospitality and security befitting a king. In cases where it was not up to the mark, Gangadhar Rao did not hesitate to complain, and his grievance was promptly addressed.

It was a large party, for a huge entourage of servants and assistants accompanied them. At Banaras, they spent some time offering prayers at all the temples, making donations to the poor and pious, and organizing feasts for the Brahmins. Lakshmi Bai visited the temples and the endless lanes lined with shops and wares. From Banaras, they went to Gaya, where Hindus offer prayers to the souls of departed ancestors. On the way back, they stopped to bathe in the holy confluence at Prayag. Gangadhar Rao wanted to go further east to the Jagannath temple at Puri, but urgent matters forced him to change plans.

Lakshmi Bai was in the family way. The couple, away from the stringent rules of protocol, must have spent happy hours together and, freed of tension, the young Rani conceived her first child. Nothing could have brought Gangadhar Rao more joy than the news that he was to have an heir to his throne after all. The party returned in the summer of 1851 to one of the most festive welcomes in Jhansi. The whole town gathered on the streets of Jhansi to watch the Raja and Rani return, escorted by twenty-one elephants and cavalry.

For Lakshmi Bai, those months must have been by far the best of her married life. As the wife and Rani, she was fulfilling what was then regarded as the most important duty of a wife—that of bearing a child and possibly the future heir to the throne of her husband. The expectant mother was given all the care she required while the priests in the temple offered special prayers for the well-being of the family.

It was on the eleventh day of the moon in late November that Lakshmi Bai gave birth to a son. Joy and excitement broke all bounds. Gangadhar Rao was beside himself with delight. In the evening, the fort and the entire town were illuminated as fireworks announced the birth of the scion. The next morning, a ceremonial parade of troops, elephants and horses was organized in commemoration of the occasion. The Raja had elephants sent to different parts of the kingdom to distribute sugar among the people, a traditional Marathi custom of sending 'sweet news'. In Jhansi, public feasts were planned and food and clothes distributed among the poor. No expense was spared to share the Raja's ecstasy with the people.

It was a cheer that did not last long. The child was born weak and despite all attention, did not gain weight. It is not known what astrologers had predicted, but they certainly did not prepare the royal couple for what was to come. Three months later, just as the town had woken to a jubilant day greeting the new prince, it was plunged into the abyss of gloom when the baby died. The infant had been critically ill for a couple of days and priests were chanting mantras day and night, hoping for a miracle. When it did not happen and the child died, the Raja was inconsolable. In the coming months, he grew increasingly moody and irritable. He stopped attending the theatre and gradually began to lose interest in most of the things around him. This gradually told on his health. He lost sleep and his appetite. There was a visible deterioration in the Raja's condition from the beginning of 1853. As the year wore on, his health showed further signs of decline.

The Raja, however, refused to let his indifferent health come in the way of any public ceremony, especially if it was religious. During the autumn festival traditionally called Navratri, it was customary for the royals to walk to the Mahalakshmi temple after a whole day's fast. Gangadhar Rao insisted on walking the distance despite his weakness. Lakshmi Bai tried to reason with him and so did Moropant Tambe. Gangadhar Rao remained adamant. The exertion proved too much and, soon after this in September, Gangadhar Rao was bedridden. Initially, the exact cause of his ill-health remained undiagnosed and untreated. Gangadhar Rao, as a staunch Hindu Brahmin, refused to be treated by anyone but local Ayurvedic doctors.

These must have been the worst years of Lakshmi Bai's life. Young Manu could never have imagined in her darkest thoughts that within two years, everything that she cherished in life would gradually elude her. There is no record of her personal suffering after her son died. When her husband fell ill, she refused to leave his bedside except for her daily prayers and rituals. She must have silently been preparing for what was to come.

4

Years of Loss

Major D.D. Malcolm, the political agent for Gwalior, Bundelkhand and Rewah, based in Gwalior, 145 kilometres north-west of Jhansi, was a busy and somewhat worried man from about October 1853. He was told that the Raja of Jhansi, Gangadhar Rao, had been taken critically ill, and was not likely to recover. Malcolm's apprehensions were of two kinds: that any political uncertainty may trigger trouble among local Rajput landholders. Therefore, there had to be a peaceful transfer of power. And herein lay his second worry.

Would the Raja adopt a son, now that he was not getting better? Adoption was a delicate affair. Within eight months of taking over in 1848, the new Governor General, the Marquis of Dalhousie, issued a decree that the British government would in future 'legally' and 'justly' appropriate all territories that lapsed to its control and, in the absence of natural heirs, adoption would not be permitted. There were going to be exceptions, but strictly for political reasons that served British interests. He also said that he was personally against any further extension of British frontiers. At the same time, he could not as a

practical Governor ignore the advantage of consolidating
territories 'by taking possession of States that may lapse in
the midst of them'. They may not add to the government
fortunes but would certainly contribute to greater peace
of mind for its officials. Resorting to the inimitable
colonial metaphor, he added, these 'petty, intervening
principalities' were sources of annoyance and did not
contribute much to the treasury either'.[1] Would any
exception be made in the case of Jhansi?

Malcolm turned to the person regarded an expert of
this region because of his extensive travel—W.H. Sleeman.
Sleeman wrote back confirming the agent's worst fears.
The local pundits would most certainly try to convince the
Raja and Rani that they should adopt in order to secure
their own incomes. Sleeman, who had met Gangadhar
Rao, felt that the Raja was not very keen. 'I think the
Raja himself told me one day that all he cared about was,
in case of his death, that his widow should be made happy
and comfortable. The conversation took place on a visit
he paid me when no one was present. He had no relative
that he cares a straw about.'[2]

Malcolm knew he had to exercise his own judgement
and act accordingly. He explained in his report to the
Secretary in Calcutta that he wanted to secure for the
British government the rights of a paramount power over
Jhansi and to pre-empt disturbance and turmoil. The
principality stood between British territories in the north
and south and its absorption would strengthen British
control over central India.

At the same time, he started what was to be a long
correspondence with Major R.W.W. Ellis, who had recently
taken charge as the political assistant for Bundelkhand
stationed in Jhansi. On 29 October, Malcolm wrote
detailed instructions to Ellis. There were two possibilities,

he wrote. The Raja may express a wish to adopt or actually adopt while still alive, or the Rani may adopt a child after his death. Whether the first adoption will be sanctioned was subject to ratification by the Government of India. But it was important that locally they should provide for all contingencies such as may arise following the death of the Raja. Ellis must take charge of Jhansi and its treasure, which was in danger of being plundered. If the Rani adopted, the son would have the right to inherit only the personal property or wealth that belonged to the family. Malcolm also wanted Ellis to suggest the amount of pension they should be proposing to the Government of India for the widowed Rani. He, however, insisted that someone senior should be present in Jhansi at the time of the Raja's death.

Malcolm and Ellis were not on the best of terms. Right then Malcolm seemed somewhat peeved that Ellis was planning a short holiday with his wife without informing his senior. He learnt about it from another junior officer. He added that he would have no objections to Ellis's intended pleasure trip so long as it was within a short distance of Jhansi.

Ellis ignored the jibe and in his reply to Malcolm's demi-official letter on 1 November 1853, stated that since he was expected to take charge, he would require military support. He asked Malcolm to instruct officers commanding the Kanpur division and Scindia's forces that they should be ready to come to Jhansi should the need arise.[3] This seemed a fair demand. But Malcolm felt that Ellis would not face any resistance if he handled the situation with 'judgement and firmness'.[4]

Ellis did as he was told, and frequently checked upon the Raja's health. He was suffering from chronic dysentery, which was certainly not past cure in the nineteenth century. But the Indian doctors in Jhansi did not appear very competent. Ellis met a few senior members of the Raja's court like Lahori Mull, Narasimha Rao, Appa Rai and Fatehchand on 16 November and apprised them of the necessity of taking adequate measures to prevent disturbances in the event of the Raja's death. They were not to release prisoners, for example.[5]

On the morning of 20 November, Ellis received a letter from Gangadhar Rao saying that he had adopted a boy of five, named Damodar Gangadhar Rao or Anand Rao, a descendant from his grandfather, to ensure that his family continued in the event of his death. He hoped he would recover and since he was not too old, could still have children of his own. If that did not happen and he succumbed to his illness, his widow should be allowed to manage the kingdom so long as the boy was a minor.

On receiving this letter, Ellis and Captain A.P. Martin, officer commanding the Bundelkhand Legion, rushed to the palace to meet the Raja and found that his condition had deteriorated greatly. The letter was read out, and this process had scarcely finished when Gangadhar Rao was seized with a convulsive fit. The two officers hurried out.[6] Ellis went back to look up the Raja the same evening and took along with him Dr Allen, the medical officer in Jhansi. The Raja had been brought down from an upper room to one on the ground floor, adjoining the women's quarters. Dr Allen prescribed medicines that the Raja consented to take only if mixed with Ganga water and purified by his own Brahmin servants. An Indian doctor was sent to stay with the patient at night, administering medicines as required. Once the British left, the Raja changed his mind and refused to take any medicine. The Indian doctor was asked to go home.

The following afternoon on 21 November at 1 pm,

Raja Gangadhar Rao of Jhansi died. Malcolm received a 'kharita', or letter, addressed to him by the Raja, written on the same day that he had adopted his son and had earlier written to Ellis. It was very similar to the one to Ellis, except that it quoted the treaty that the British government had signed with Ramchandra Rao in 1817, acknowledging his claim and that of his heirs and successors to the hereditary rule of Jhansi. Gangadhar Rao hoped that the British government would take into account the fidelity and 'attachment' that the Rajas of Jhansi had always shown to the British government and consider his adoption with favour. Dalhousie's directive had shaken local confidence, and no one was any longer certain.

British officials had little time to lose. Ellis, on hearing the news, rushed to the fort to offer condolences to Rani Lakshmi Bai. What was far more pressing was the need to guard the treasury and the prison. There was more than two-and-a-half lakh rupees in cash and an equal amount of valuables in gold and silver and other currencies. The people inside the fort watched with disgust as they saw Ellis put seals on the locks of the rooms where the treasure was kept, in their hour of deep distress, even before their Raja had been cremated.[7] Ellis had no time and even less patience for such emotions. A hundred soldiers and thirteen non-commissioned officers were sent to the fort to help the troops maintain peace. But the number was inadequate to keep watch over 250 prisoners and a fairly spread-out fort. There was also the rest of the town and the immediate surroundings to protect.

Captain Martin wrote to Ellis expressing misgivings, and Ellis once more asked Malcolm if the Gwalior Contingent could be raised to the strength of a full regiment and separate detachments sent to the forts of Kurehra and Mau-Ranipur to pre-empt Bundela uprisings.

Malcolm agreed and in his report to J.P. Grant, the officiating Secretary to the Government of India, wrote that he had asked Brigadier Parsons, commanding the Scindia's contingent, to send additional companies to Jhansi.[8]

Governor General Dalhousie was away from the capital. Urgent missives were sent from the office of the president of the Council of India to Malcolm and Ellis. On 16 December, Under-Secretary to the Government of India J.W. Dalrymple's mail to Malcolm summed up the government's stand: 'You will take due measures to preserve public tranquillity. No change should be made in any of the native modes of administration; and you will be careful not to commit the Government regarding the adoption, either by confirming or rejecting it.'[9]

The only reference to Lakshmi Bai was in the long report that Malcolm wrote to the Secretary on 25 November, shortly after the Raja died. 'The widow of Gungadhur Rao, in whose hands he has expressed a wish that the government should be placed during her lifetime, is a woman highly respected and esteemed, and I believe fully capable of doing justice to such a charge.'[10] He advised that she be told that she would be allowed to keep all her husband's personal property, the palace in the town and a generous allowance to maintain her family and retainers. He also suggested that she should be paid a pension of 5,000 rupees every month. The estate of Jhansi should be incorporated with the other districts of Bundelkhand, now under the charge of the commissioner of Jabalpur.[11]

Lakshmi Bai stayed by the Raja all through his illness. On the 19th morning, the Raja summoned his senior officials Narasimha Rao, Lahori Mull and Lala Fatehchand and the Rani, and said that he wished to adopt a son. He asked all present to consult the holy scriptures and find a time that would be most appropriate. They also had to look for a child belonging to the same lineage who seemed suitable to 'succeed him as ruler of Jhansi'.[12] Everyone agreed, as did the Rani, but not without some foreboding regarding the future and the Raja's frail health. Adoption was clearly the last resort of a dying ruler to ensure that his property did not fall apart.[13] Her worries did not prevent her from overseeing all arrangements for the ceremony on 20 November. She prayed a little longer than most days that morning.

Anand Rao, the five-year-old son of Vasudev Rao Newalkar, was selected for adoption. The family priest Banaik Rao conducted the ceremony called Sangkalpa. The boy sat on Lakshmi Bai's lap as his natural father gave up claims on him and his adopted father blessed him with all rights of an offspring.[14] It was a very touching moment for both Gangadhar Rao and Lakshmi Bai. Their close advisers Narasimha Rao, Moropant Tambe and Lala Tatti Chand were present at the ceremony. When Ellis and Martin visited the palace, Lakshmi Bai retired behind the curtain, as was customary for an Indian queen.[15]

Gangadhar Rao's condition worsened palpably in the course of the day and evening of the 20th. The Raja was brought down to the ground floor next to the Rani's quarters. Lakshmi Bai ordered special prayers be offered in all the leading temples of the city and a more elaborate one in the Mahalakshmi temple. In the evening, the palace was specially lit up while inside, the queen sat in misery, praying hard that the tragedy she feared would not come to pass. No miracle took place and, by the next afternoon, Lakshmi Bai became a widow. She was inconsolable. As the news spread, Jhansi grieved for the Raja it had lost and for the Rani. An elaborate funeral procession carried the body of Gangadhar Rao to the bank of the lake opposite the Mahalakshmi temple for cremation.

Lakshmi Bai, however, did not have the luxury of mourning her husband's death for long. Malcolm forwarded, together with his covering note dated 15 December, what was the first of a series of letters from her to the British written within three weeks of the death of her husband. She sent it to Ellis for being forwarded to Malcolm. Addressing the Governor General, the Marquis of Dalhousie, the Rani began her appeal with a reminder of the past relations the Rajas of Jhansi had with the British. The first treaty was with Sheo Rao Bhao, and then with his grandson Ramchandra Rao in 1817 that confirmed not only his rights but also those of his heirs and successors. The treaty subsequently signed between Sleeman and Gangadhar Rao guaranteed all benefits of the earlier treaty including claims of heredity. This became the standard line of argument in favour of the right of succession of the adopted son. According to Hindu scriptures, whoever undertakes the funeral rites of a man and offers libations to his soul, enjoys all the rights of a natural-born son. In this case, Anand Rao, a child from the same clan as Gangadhar Rao was selected and adopted by the Raja strictly according to Hindu laws. Later named Damodar Rao Gangadhar, he performed all the rites that a son has to after the death of his father. The local British officials, Ellis and Martin, were privy to all that the Raja had done. The Raja had also 'made the boy over to the protection and favour of the British Government'. The final argument was that adoptions were approved in the case of at least three neighbouring kingdoms of Orchha, Datia and Jalaun. There was no reason why Jhansi should be different.[16]

Ellis added a note saying that she was right about Orchha and Jalaun but not about Datia. He also sent a genealogical tree of the Newalkar family that he had prepared from information from the court, confirming Anand Rao's place in the order of descent. He was the only British officer who made a daily visit to the Rani's palace and these meetings did not fail to leave their mark on him. On 24 December, he wrote to Malcolm, 'I beg leave to observe that we have a treaty of alliance and friendship with the Jhansi as well as the Urcha (Orchha) States, and that I cannot discover any difference in the terms of the two which would justify our withholding the privilege of adoption from one state and allowing it to the other.' He went on to argue that the right of the 'native states' to adopt was clearly acknowledged by the court of directors in 1839. '. . . it appears to me that it would be opposed to the spirit of enlightened liberality which dictated those orders, if the privilege was to be now refused to families created by ourselves as a reward for the services rendered to the British Government, on the grounds that they were not of so ancient an origin as others.'[17] To this note, Malcolm refused to make any comment, but sent it to the Secretary in Calcutta.[18]

Within weeks of the demise of the Raja of Jhansi, two men staked claims to the throne and sent appeals to Ellis's office. The first was Krishna Rao, son of Ramchandra Rao, former Raja and nephew of Gangadhar Rao. Ellis dismissed his claim outright, even as he reported the matter to Malcolm. The second aspirant was slightly more serious. Sadashiv Narain, a young man of twenty-five, was the son of Narain Rao, a second cousin of Gangadhar Rao living in Parola. Ellis was inclined to dismiss him as well, but as Malcolm observed, if any claim was to be admitted from the family, 'this individual is actually the nearest relative left to claim the *gaddi* on these grounds'.[19]

The Rani and her coterie of counsellors, including her father and Narasimha Rao, were bracing for the worst. Lakshmi Bai's journey from being the wife of the Raja of Jhansi to a Rani quite on her own was beginning now. On 16 February, Lakshmi Bai sent a second letter to the Governor General. It referred to two provisions in the treaties that the Rajas of Jhansi had signed with the British over time. The treaty with Sheo Rao Bhao signed in 1804 guaranteed his rights provided he and his successors offered the British complete allegiance and support. The loyalty of the Rajas of Jhansi had never faltered—the Rani's letter cited instances of loyalty that the Jhansi raj had displayed and the manner in which the British government had reciprocated with compliments and honours. The second referred to the treaty that her husband Gangadhar Rao had signed with the British much later in 1843, after it had been returned to him.

Here the argument got sharper. In the second article of the treaty, the principality was confirmed to both the '*warisan*' and the '*janisinan*' of Gangadhar Rao. *Warisan* meant direct heirs while *janisinan* referred to successors. 'Treaties are studied with utmost care before ratification; and it is not to be supposed that the term *janisinan* used in contradistinction to *warisan* was introduced in an important document of this kind, of the authority almost of a revelation from Heaven, without a precise understanding of its meaning, the advantages of which are further explained by the clause declaring the gift then made to have been one in perpetuity to the family.'[20] The argument had some moral force, suggesting that if the British withdrew their support now, it would be tantamount to a betrayal. The Raja adopted Anand Rao only because of these terms of the treaty and had officially in the presence of Major Ellis and Captain Martin put his ward under the 'care and protection' of the British government.

The appendices included four precedents where the British had confirmed adoptions by the rulers of the neighbouring states of Datia, Orchha, Jalaun and Algi and letters of appreciation by earlier Governor Generals to the Raja of Jhansi.

As is well known, because practically all textbooks include these affairs in their description of the causes of the uprising of 1857, Jhansi was not the first and certainly not the last state to be faced with such a crisis. Dalhousie took his first stand within four months of his arrival in India in 1848. The Raja of Satara, a Marathi territory of some significance, died without a natural heir. For the first time, the question arose: would the Raja's adopted son be allowed to continue independent rule or be included in British dominions? While local British officials were sympathetic, the Governor General was unequivocal in his decision that in the absence of a natural heir, the family would have to forfeit its rights. As if by a strange quirk of fate, a number of rulers died without natural heirs. In January 1851, Peshwa Baji Rao II died, leaving a will stating that all his property should be passed on to his adopted son Dhondu Pant or Nana Sahib. Since the annual stipend of eight lakh rupees was a personal grant to the Peshwa, the government replied, there was no reason why it should be continued to his adopted son. When Nana Sahib learnt of this, he appealed to the court of directors and subsequently to the authorities in England. According to the novelist Vrindavan Lal Verma, Tantia Tope visited Jhansi shortly after Lakshmi Bai's son was born and told her about the situation in Bithur.[21] Gangadhar Rao and Lakshmi Bai must have learnt of the death of the Peshwa and what followed. In the winter of

1853, Nagpur, another important Marathi province, lost its ruler. The last of the Bhonsles did not have a son, nor did he adopt one. Thus, the entire property was sequestered, including the palace, much to the mortification of the mother and wife of the late Raja. The women wanted only their royal palace to be restored and appealed first to the Governor General and then to London.[22]

Lakshmi Bai and her advisers thus could not have been unaware of the practice of sending appeals to the British government and the precise course of arguments that was conventionally followed. In the case of Jhansi, however, it was as much the correspondence and appeal as the singular personality of the Rani that stood out in the next few years. She did not belie Malcolm's assessment of Gangadhar Rao's widow being a capable woman. As one of her biographers Michael White wrote, there were two sides to her personality. The first was her looks, at once beautiful, majestic and captivating, 'far removed from the generally accepted type of her countrywoman. But there was a strength of character emphasized in every line of her distinctly Aryan features, a force of will, a mystical power in every flash of her lustrous eyes, in every movement, in every word, however gently spoken, warning' the officials that she was 'no shrinking, simple zenana maiden'.[23] We will find how the officials were able to see the Rani who should have been behind purdah.

Despite being surrounded by her husband's advisers, Lakshmi Bai appears central to all the activities that were taking place. She had legal experts counselling her on the appeals to be made to the British but she drafted large portions of them in Urdu herself. At the same time, Lakshmi Bai consciously nurtured a public image. True to convention, she took to wearing white saris but, contrary to custom, she did not shave her head nor did she stop wearing jewellery. She continued wearing her favourite pearls and braided her hair carefully and differently for various occasions. She also made sure that apart from the daily court that she attended, the people of Jhansi saw their Rani when she went on her daily visit to the temple. When dealing with British officials, however, Lakshmi Bai was always behind purdah.

While Lakshmi Bai was drafting her second petition, British officials were busy sending their reports to the capital for the Governor General to take his final decision on Jhansi. Major Ellis's opinion was completely overlooked. In the very first report that Malcolm sent to the Secretary on 25 November 1853, he wrote, '...the terms under which the state of Jhansi was held under us, precluded, in the opinion of government, the Raja or his widow from making any adoption to the prejudice of the paramount power'. He went on to add that '...I do not consider it probable that government will forgo its right to resume this State, I trust that I may be allowed to assure her that she will be allowed to retain all the personal property of her late husband, and the palace situated in the town of Jhansi, and that such an allowance will be made for herself and the old adherents of the family as will maintain them in comfort and respectability during the remainder of their lives'. His final suggestion was that the state of Jhansi should be incorporated with the districts in Bundelkhand, then under the charge of Captain Erskine, commissioner of Jabalpur.[24] The final verdict on the Rani was very close to this proposal.

J.P. Grant, the officiating Secretary to the Government of India, prepared a long note on Jhansi. He described the circumstances under which the present issue of adoption was raised and the past history of the province. It also responded to Lakshmi Bai's reference to Orchha, Datia and Jalaun in her first letter. In this two-part argument, the first underlined that the rights of the ruler of Jhansi had been that of a Governor of the state dependent on the Peshwa, rather than 'of a chief possessing a proprietary right in the soil'. In deference to the 'fidelity and attachment', shown by the late Subedar Sheo Rao Bhao, the British acknowledged his grandson, the ruler in 1817, Ramchandra Rao, 'his heirs and successors, hereditary rulers of Jhansi'. When Ramchandra died without a natural heir in 1835, it was once more the British administration that decided who his successor should be. On this occasion, the right of adoption was set aside in favour of Gangadhar Rao, the younger brother of the deceased Governor. The disinclination to recognize adoption went further back than Dalhousie's time. In 1837, Sir Charles Metcalfe wrote a Minute on this issue, particularly in regard to the chiefs of Bundelkhand. The Minute said that regions which owed their existence to a gift by a sovereign or paramount power would have to accept that 'the power which granted, or the power standing in its place, would have a right to resume on failure of male heirs'. Jhansi fell in this category, and the British were well within their rights to 'resume' its territories as they had done in other instances, he felt.

The cases of Orchha and Datia were different because they were Rajput states that had always been independent of Marathi rule—with them the British had signed separate treaties. Jalaun was ruled by an independent Marathi family. In 1832, on the death of the ruler, the widow had adopted a son who was recognized, but since his death in 1840, the state had been restored to British control. Grant argued that in 1832, the adoption was recognized as a measure 'best for the public good'. But this did not signify that it was granted as a matter of right or that it 'can be claimed as a right in the case of any other state'.[25] In short, the argument was that Jhansi had been a dependent state, first of the Marathis and then of the British, and whatever the decision of the British government, it was above question.

Dalhousie wrote a long thirteen-page explanation, perhaps one of the longest on the subject, before the final verdict on Jhansi was published in the Minute, dated 27 February 1854. This was written ten days before and was somewhat differently argued.[26] Gangadhar Rao had left no heir 'of his body' and there is 'no male heir whatever of any Raja or subedar of Jhansi who has ruled since the first relations of the British Government with that state were formed'. The boy who had been adopted was a very distant relation and could hardly be said to belong to the family. And adoption 'by any man when he is almost in the last agonies is liable to suspicion. It is in the present case more than usually so for it was well known beforehand that the Raja had never contemplated making an adoption.'[27]

He then went on to trace the history of Jhansi and its relationship, first with the Peshwa and then with the British. His conclusion was three-fold: there was no male heir of the late Raja; the late Raja was never expected to adopt and that the British had not acknowledged a previous adoption.

The British government's refusal to acknowledge adoption thus rested on precedent, general principle and a particular rule laid down for successions in Bundelkhand. There was, however, a more pragmatic reason for wanting to appropriate this territory. Jhansi would not give the British any material benefit but it lay in the midst of other British districts, 'the possession of it as our own will tend to the improvement of the general internal administration of our possessions in Bundlecund'. It was also a region not known for prolonged peace and quiet, largely because of the presence and the indomitable spirit of the Rajput landholders. Since Jalaun had already lapsed, it now made for a very compact district and hopefully a more settled one from what it had lately been. The Governor General agreed to Malcolm's proposal regarding the provisions to be made for the Rani of Jhansi.[28] The other members of the Board, J.A. Dorin, F.J. Halliday and J. Low, unanimously approved Dalhousie's verdict.

5

Dethronement

J.W. Dalrymple, the Under-Secretary, sent Dalhousie's Minute, and specific instructions to Malcolm on 7 February 1854. Malcolm, in turn, wrote a short proclamation in Urdu for distribution in the Jhansi territories on 13 March. His longer instructions to Ellis regarding steps to be taken were written in a letter dated 15 March. He dispatched the letter the same day, and it reached Jhansi in the afternoon. The proclamation briefly said that the Governor General in Council had 'declined to confirm and sanction the said adoption'. The principality was, therefore, to be governed by the British government under the present charge of Major Ellis and all subjects should consider themselves under its authority.[1]

Ellis decided to call on Lakshmi Bai the following morning, 16 March. There was a kind of a foreboding as Ellis walked up the stairs to the large hall at the end of which the Rani sat behind the curtain. Without much ado, Ellis read out Dalhousie's Minute and Malcolm's proclamation. There was a hush as the significance of the verdict sank in. According to Mahasweta Devi, the silence was broken by the Rani's firm statement, '*Main Jhansi nahin doongi.*'[2] It is unconfirmed if her famous declamation was made then or to John Lang. As the news spread, gloom and sorrow spread across the town. It was the day of Holi, the spring festival of love and abandonment. The people did not play with colours that day—and since then Holi is not celebrated in Jhansi as a remembrance of the tragedy of the year 1854.[3]

D.V. Tahmankar describes how distressed Lakshmi Bai was on hearing the verdict. Her first reaction was one of intense anger. She was 'white with rage' but did not wish to make a scene before Ellis. Instead, she listened to him and thanked him for all his concern. No sooner had he left than she 'dismissed her ministers and attendants, shut herself in her bedroom and wept bitterly. "That day", it is recorded, "she did not touch food or drink." Late in the afternoon she got up and began to pace the room like an angry tigress.'[4]

After handing over Malcolm's letter to Lakshmi Bai, Ellis was to take charge of the state and send copies of the proclamation to different parts of the district. He had to disband all regular troops in the service of the former Raja. Malcolm promised to apply to the central government for funds to pay the soldiers two months' salary. Till the money arrived, he was asked to pay out of the Raja's assets. He was also asked to reinforce military forces in the forts of Jhansi and Kurehra.[5]

The Governor General in a separate Minute instructed that the Lieutenant-Governor of the North-Western Province (NWP) should be informed of local administrative arrangements as Jhansi fell within his jurisdiction.[6] Grant wrote to William Muir, secretary to the government of NWP on 31 March, seeking the Lieutenant-Governor's 'opinions' on the subject.[7] Muir's reply was dated 18 April. Jhansi was placed under the superintendent of

Jalaun, Captain A. Skene. Together, Jhansi and Jalaun were to be under the supervising authority of the divisional commissioner of the Sagar and Narmada territories, Major W.C. Erskine. A deputy commissioner was to take directions from the superintendent, and both were under the command of the commissioner. Major F.D. Gordon was appointed to this post.[8] Sir Robert Hamilton took charge as the agent Governor General for Central India, operating from Indore.

Malcolm later wrote separately to the Rani specifying the provisions made for her, including her residence, her pension, the personal property of the Raja, the discharge of servants, the debts of the Raja and a list of those who were to be pensioned off. When Ellis showed this to the Rani a month later, she refused to accept it.[9]

Standing over the inner wall of the Jhansi fort overlooking the outer rampart on its eastern side, one faces the crowded bazaar of Jhansi, its meandering streets clogged with shops, people and traffic. Nestled in its midst is the Rani Mahal, the palace where Lakshmi Bai lived for two years before moving back to the fort one last time.

It was a modest structure of three storeys, in the typical style of a north Indian haveli. A solid iron gate opened to a corridor with wide seats on both sides and an open courtyard with a neat flower garden and fountains. The 'palace' was built as a quadrangle surrounding the courtyard. On the ground floor, a long corridor ran all the way through with rooms at the back. All living quarters were on the first floor. There were long halls, one leading to the other, with wide windows and arched doorways. The rooms at the four corners were smaller and had two doors, one leading to a narrow staircase and the other to another corridor and then to a second set of halls. In front of the rooms overlooking the courtyard ran a balcony, partly covered. In the tradition of all Bundela architecture, the walls of the rooms were decorated with frescoes in rich colours and elaborate designs.

Compared to the palace in the fort where the Raja lived and died, this was quite a humble dwelling. Under the new rule, Lakshmi Bai was supposed to move here, since the fort was to be taken over by the British. This must have been a difficult relocation, but she did not object to shifting and moved on 7 March 1854. What she refused to give up was trying to change the stand of the British government on gratifying her husband's last wishes.

The only allowance that Malcolm was ready to make was that the adopted son was permitted to inherit the private property of the late Raja, with the Rani as legal guardian. He promised to apply to the government for permission. In a separate letter written on 31 March 1854, the Secretary granted Lakshmi Bai exemption from the purview of district courts.[10]

Meanwhile, Ellis had to make sure that all former retainers of the Raja were paid and discharged. He was also asked to submit a statement of expenses which, till 1853 had to be met from the Raja's funds.[11] Ellis visited the Rani on 19 April specifically for this purpose. Reporting his visit, Ellis wrote that 'she seems to entertain an idea that the orders of government in her case are not considered as final'. He asked her for a list of servants whom she would like to pension off, but she refused to give him one. Ellis had also not dismissed the Raja's retainers, and this was a cause for concern.

Malcolm was convinced that it was poor handling on Ellis's part that had given Lakshmi Bai the impression that she could still negotiate with the British and have the orders for the lapse of territory annulled. He felt Ellis should have discharged the Raja's regular men right away and taken all necessary steps for resumption of the estate. Ellis's sympathy for the cause of the Rani did not place him in a favourable light.[12]

From 1854, Lakshmi Bai began to communicate with the British personally, either through letters or by seeking interviews. She did not succeed in changing matters or the British government's decision, but she did leave a mark on all those she met with her wisdom and sharp response. Ellis was the first officer to interact with her regularly, and was clearly struck by the strength of her character. As a government official, he was restrained by protocol from expressing his admiration, but he expressed his empathy even at the cost of earning his senior's ire. Lakshmi Bai was also able to convince others who met her about the justice of her cause.

Malcolm and the others, however, were in no mood to listen. Ellis now advised Lakshmi Bai that she should ask John Lang, a barrister and journalist, to represent her case to the authorities in London.[13] Lang, who was in Agra, was formally asked to visit Jhansi in April 1854. It was a two-day journey from Agra to Jhansi, and Lang must have set out right away, for on 25 April Malcolm was writing to Sir Robert Hamilton about Lang's visit to Jhansi. He was palpably upset with Ellis because the latter had not informed him about Lang meeting the Rani.[14] One can only imagine what his reactions would have been if he had known that Ellis had asked Lakshmi Bai to invite Lang to Jhansi.

Lakshmi Bai, in the meantime, sent her lawyer Kashmiri Lal to Gwalior to meet Malcolm, and hand over another letter addressed to Dalhousie. The agent sent him to Robert Hamilton, who was in Goona. Hamilton let the lawyer know that the decision on Jhansi was final, and nothing was to change it. He, however, assured him that the Rani 'would be treated with every consideration consisting with her rank and position'. In future, if she wished to represent her case, she should do so to Malcolm rather than sending a lawyer to him. The local British officials were clearly in a flap. Robert Hamilton, like Malcolm, was very disappointed with Ellis. He would have had him transferred but for the extraordinary circumstances, in which he feared any change of authority would be unsettling.[15]

Lakshmi Bai's letter to Dalhousie this time was a simple appeal for time. She had appointed a representative who would appeal to the Governor General in person. Till then, she was merely asking him to forestall arrangements that would make 'restoration of the raj a matter of difficulty'. She was referring to Lang. She considered the present measure to be 'an error or an act of arbitrary character'. Within a month she hoped to convince the British government of its folly by proving how loyal the Rajas of Jhansi had always been and how justified she was in seeking Jhansi's independent rule. If at the end, the state was absorbed after all, 'the 5,000 rusty swords worn by the people called its army and its fifty pieces of harmless ordnance will be delivered over to your lordship's agent without any demonstration, save that of sorrow'.[16]

One really wonders if Ellis's only fault lay in his inability to overcome the Rani's resolve not to let go till every possible attempt had been exhausted. Lakshmi Bai was not a person to get swayed in a hurry. She refused to discharge soldiers so long as she hoped she could reverse the decision on Jhansi.

John Lang was the first Englishman formally invited by the Jhansi state since the passing away of Gangadhar Rao. And Lakshmi Bai made sure that he was suitably impressed by the magnificence of the court to be persuaded of its ability to rule independently. She was conscious of the political uses of public spectacle as much of the etiquette and formality that a revered guest deserved. The letter of invitation was written in Persian on gold paper and personally brought to Lang by Lakshman Rao, the diwan.[17] No effort or expense was spared to make sure that Lang's journey from Agra to Jhansi was a stately one. Lang halted for a night in Gwalior at a small but comfortable rest-house owned by the late Raja.

The following morning, he set out in a palanquin that was large enough to be a small room, provided with every conceivable comfort. Lakshman Rao, the diwan and Kashmiri Lal, the lawyer, were his escorts. They all travelled on the same palanquin, together with a butler who carried a bucket of ice to keep water, wine and beer cool. There was even a punkah that was being pulled by a servant who sat outside on the footboard. A pair of strong horses that stood 'seventeen hands high', pulled the carriage. These were French steeds purchased by the late Raja for as high an amount as 1,500 rupees. The minister must have shared this information with Lang on the rather long, tedious journey together.

Around two in the afternoon, they entered the territory of Jhansi to another grand reception. All this while, they had four horsemen as escort. Now there were about fifty, each carrying an immense spear. At intervals, horsemen waited by the roadside and joined the procession. By the end of the journey, there was an entire regiment of cavalry in attendance. They drew up in a garden where a large tent was fitted underneath a clump of trees. This was where the Raja had always received guests. He learnt that the Rani could not come to meet the official in the tent and he would have to go to her palace instead.

This raised a difficulty that the minister broached delicately. Would Lang enter the Rani's apartment leaving his shoes outside? The matter was slightly extraordinary. No one had actually visited the royals in their private apartments, because the Raja met them either in a room outside specially assigned for visitors, or in the tent. No one entered an Indian household with shoes on—and the Rani, despite her public appearances, could not contravene local custom by meeting an unknown man outside her home. Therefore, Lang had to make an exception of the British convention of always wearing shoes and agree to take them off instead, in deference to the Rani. He agreed rather reluctantly, not 'as a compliment to her rank and dignity, but to her sex, and her sex alone'. The bargain was that he could keep his hat on, a gesture considered particularly discourteous among his kind. The Rani had in consultations with one of her Brahmin advisers fixed the meeting in the hour between 5.30 and 6.30 in the evening, for it was said to be the most propitious.

The last bit of Lang's journey was on an elephant that was gorgeously decorated with a silver howdah on red velvet. The steps leading to the howdah of the elephant were also covered in red velvet cloth. While Lang rode on the elephant, the ministers of the court rode on both sides on white Arab horses. Truly impressed at the spectacle of which he was a part, Lang finally reached the palace.

The courtyard was buzzing with crowds of servants and attendants. In the room set aside for the interview, an armchair was placed on a thick carpet on which sweet-smelling flowers were strewn. At the end of the room was the curtain behind which the Rani sat. As soon as the interview started, Lakshmi Bai was extremely candid and upfront about all the reasons she had to complain about. Each time she spoke of one grievance, there would be a chorus of women wailing in the background, almost like a well-rehearsed performance. The Rani wanted Lang to represent her case in Calcutta. The Englishman advised caution and prudence. He told her that it was not quite within the Governor General's rights to change or rescind any decision and that it would have to be referred to London. He also asked her to accept the pension with perhaps a note of protest that the young Raja should be given back his rightful claim.

Lang, by his own admission, was quite overawed by the Rani. By accident or design, her young son drew aside the curtain fairly early in the conversation, and for the rest of the time, they talked face-to-face.

Lakshmi Bai struck the visitor as a remarkable woman, not only in terms of her looks but her personality and her deportment. It was the passion with which she spoke of her conviction and her resolve that perhaps seemed startling, coming from an Indian woman. It was hard not to admire her astute comments and her spirited retort. From six in the evening, the parley went on till two in the morning. Lakshmi Bai's famous declamation was recorded by Lang as '*Mera Jhansi nahin dengee*' (sic). The latter interpreted it to mean that the Rani was determined to resist British occupation. He was quick to explain that it was futile to oppose the British because troops were within marching distance of her city, and any adverse move would simply jeopardize her chances of appeal. Their conversation frequently slipped into generalities, a lot of which was devoted to exchanging compliments. Lang observed, 'If the governor general could only be as fortunate as I have been, and even so brief a while, I feel quite sure that he would at once give Jhansi back again to be ruled over by its beautiful queen.'

This may have been said in a true spirit of gallantry

and graciousness but the English journalist certainly meant something of what he observed, for she was truly an extraordinary woman, who was at once clever, impulsive and polite and could mix in the right degree of womanly charm and strength of character befitting a ruler concerned about the interests of her kingdom, her subjects and her son. Her fluctuating moods, changing from anger to light-hearted banter, her quick temper melting into a frivolous giggle, fascinated her visitor. As a true gesture of royalty, she presented Lang with an elephant, a camel, a horse, two greyhounds, silks and shawls.[18]

John Lang forwarded the Rani's letter to the Governor General, but he was not granted permission to meet Dalhousie personally.

Lakshmi Bai now turned to a few other immediate necessities. She had a huge memorial built in memory of Gangadhar Rao next to the Lakshmi Taal and opposite the Mahalakshmi temple, a single-storey square construction around a courtyard with four doors in the centre of the walls, their shape exactly like those over the Lakshmi temple, rounded and decorative. At the four corners were towers with dome-shaped roofs and a small balcony typical of all Rajput architecture.

Lakshmi Bai was somewhat indifferent to Gangadhar Rao's passion for the theatre and in Verma's novel she was once described as being rather harsh about it. But after Gangadhar Rao's death, she did not want the theatre to languish, even though local production had for all purposes stopped after the patron died. As a mark of respect for her husband, she invited the Gwalior theatre (natak) company to come and perform. The three-day performance was a huge affair attended by hundreds of people. Lakshmi Bai gave all the members of the cast generous gifts.[19] It was her way of bringing back normalcy to her kingdom.

Her daily life too now fell into a schedule. She resumed in earnest her childhood passion for physical exercise and riding, and also began organizing and training a small troop of women, something she could not do while her husband was alive. Her day began with physical exercise in the gymnasium, where she lifted weights and did various strenuous workouts. She would then ride around the city on horseback. Horse-riding was both her forte and her passion, and her knowledge of horses was almost legendary. Every day, she practised different feats that included jumping trenches and riding fast, her body almost parallel to the horse's back. She finished this around 8 am, after which she had breakfast. On some days, she would rest for an hour or two or bathe right away. Lakshmi Bai loved a leisurely, luxurious bath. She used fifteen to twenty vessels of warm water and different varieties of aromatic herbs. The water she used was drained out of the tub through a pipe and collected in a receptacle for other women to bathe from.

Lakshmi Bai dressed in white, finely woven Chanderi[20] saris and sat down to lengthy prayers. Since she wore her hair long, and this was considered something of a sin for a widow, she did a special puja for atonement. It was said she wanted her hair shaved off in Banaras. But the British refused to let her leave Jhansi.[21] She performed three kinds of puja every morning while religious scriptures were recited, holy verses sung, and sacred hymns narrated. The Rani personally kept an eye on every detail, including who the performers were. If, for instance, someone was not in attendance some morning, she made it a point to ask after his well-being.

The rituals took most of the morning. At noon, she had her meal. Around three in the afternoon, she would begin her daily court. Lakshmi Bai received a lot of presents by way of tributes from subjects that she liberally distributed among all her dependents, keeping a few things she liked for herself. On some days, she would dress like a man in long trousers, a headdress and a colourful belt from which hung her sword. 'In this manner, in her tall and fair image, she would look like the Goddess Gauri.'[22]

John Lang and Kashmiri Lal arrived in Calcutta in early June 1854 and submitted the Rani's petition. Lang wrote a short note addressed to the Secretary, C. Allen, introducing himself as the Rani's counsel and requesting him to present the petition before the Governor General. The petition repeated what had earlier been submitted. It recapitulated the terms of all the treaties that the British had signed with the Rajas of Jhansi, assuring them rights in perpetuity. It also described Jhansi's relationship with the British and the circumstances in which Gangadhar Rao had adopted the young boy, consciously and publicly. The Secretary replied to Lang's letter on the 21st, stating without frills that the case had been deliberated on and 'no reason is shewn in that document for altering the just and reasonable decision which the Government of India was led to form'.[23]

Not one to give up so easily, Kashmiri Lal presented another memorandum from the Rani, dated 19 July. This was somewhat differently worded. '...the case relating to the state of Jhansi has been decided in the absence of her mokhtar or lawyer, whereas the regulations of government require the presence of the parties even to a trifling suit at the time of its decision'. Again referring to the instance of Orchha, the Rani requested that the case should be reopened and her lawyer allowed to make a proper representation of the case. She was certain that the state of Jhansi would be restored to her 'after enquiries being held into her right'. If her request was indeed turned down, then her lawyer must be given in writing the grounds on which the state of Jhansi was going to be reclaimed by the British. She also requested that the case be heard and adjudicated in the presence of her lawyer.

The reply, a month later, was brief. The Rani should 'be informed in reply that her requests are wholly inadmissible and that she be further told that the orders for the resumption of Jhansi will not be revoked by the government of India'.[24]

Her final appeal was made to the court of directors, London, on 21 December 1854 on two irrefutable grounds, 'the uninterrupted friendship alliance and mutual good service between the government of India and the rulers of Jhansi for a period of fifty years and that the ceremony of adoption was performed publicly and openly'.[25] She also wanted to know from London if the East India Company had the right to 'seize' the government of Jhansi just because it did not accept the adoption. On what grounds do Indian states cease to exist?

The question she raised was regarding the authority of an English trading company to take such a unilateral stand. Its present policy threatened to obliterate the existence of legitimate rule, and that was grossly wrong. It read like a complaint to the higher authorities in which she wanted to know if the East India Company had the right to take away the treasure of the kingdom and 'pension off' the Rani with a pittance for subsistence. After all, it contravened the terms of the treaty that its government had signed. Finally, in what appeared like a mild threat, she added that the other princes in the neighbourhood were looking upon the fate of Jhansi with concern and disquiet and their subsequent faith or distrust would largely be determined by what the government decided.

Lakshmi Bai's sharp arguments could not have endeared her to the white rulers. The British government in India and in England remained unmoved. Major Ellis was finally replaced in the fall of 1854 for his supposed weakness and political impropriety by Captain A. Skene, who became the new superintendent of Jhansi, with Lieutenant F.D. Gordon remaining the deputy commissioner. Major W.C. Erskine was appointed the agent Lieutenant-Governor and commissioner of the Sagar division, responsible for implementing local policies.

Before his departure in June, Ellis wrote to Hamilton that the Rani wanted the personal property of the Raja made over to her since she was the guardian of his adopted son as long as he was a minor. Ellis had no objection as long as she entered into a written agreement promising to act as the guardian. Hamilton added that she should also provide them with guarantee and security that she would be responsible for the 'proper disposal' of the property. A detailed list of all properties and their estimated value should be made in the presence of witnesses and an attested copy given to the Rani on her taking over the property. Ellis left without executing this. Gordon took charge, and high on his priority list was settling the Raja's property matters.

Lakshmi Bai was adamant. She was not going to give security for what legitimately belonged to her husband and now, his son. She refused to take charge. Hamilton decided to be firm and threatened to sell all perishable articles and invest the money in the interests of the adopted son.[26] Authorities in Calcutta this time were more conciliatory and instructed the agent to hand over to the Rani all of her husband's property unconditionally. It was a minor victory of the Rani's indomitable spirit.

It was also the first of a series of incongruities that she

sought to set right, not always successfully, though. The next two years were very busy for her, for while she was coming to terms with the fact that the kingdom of Jhansi had lapsed, the arrangements and prescriptions meant for her required constant negotiating. She had a long struggle ahead and she worked at it relentlessly.

Robert Hamilton undertook a tour of the entire region under his jurisdiction in late March and early April of 1855. On his arrival in Jhansi, he received a special invitation from Lakshmi Bai to visit her. The durbar room in which Lakshmi Bai received him, he reported, was the 'handsomest and the best apartment' that he had seen throughout his tour. But it was her demeanour and the manner in which she conducted the meeting that astonished the officer most. 'She was seated behind the purdah and conversed freely and directly.' She did not complain about the government's decision in regard to Jhansi. On the contrary, she said that she was 'wholly dependent' on the British and thankful that she had been kept out of the purview of the district court. But she requested that she be placed directly under him, the agent Governor General, and not the district officials who reported to the Lieutenant-Governor. Hamilton promised to forward her request to the Governor General.

'The earnestness with which the Ranee made this appeal was such as to cause her to press forward so much against the purdah, as to enable me, distinctly, to see her and hear from her own mouth what she was saying. I saw too, that she was entirely alone, not a female attendant being with her. She is young in years, and was evidently feeling deeply what she was urging with so much firmness.'[27]

The distant and difficult Robert Hamilton was easily persuaded by the Rani's charm and conviction. He felt since she had been already exempted from local courts, putting her under his authority directly would only be a continuation of the privilege. Lakshmi Bai had even warned that if her dignity was compromised, she would retire to Banaras. Hamilton feared this would upset the local community—also, her going away would 'entail serious loss on the town, in which she was the occasion of a good deal of money being circulated'.

He felt that her request should be considered since she had been compliant and both Captain Skene and Lieutenant Gordon endorsed that '...nothing could be more satisfactory than the way the Ranee conducted herself and the readiness with which she attended to all the requisitions that were made of her'. He asked her to stop appointing and wasting money on agents and lawyers to make representations to the government, advice she readily agreed to. He found out that she had not drawn on her pension and asked her to do so without delay, and once more she seemed compliant. 'I took leave with the usual ceremonies, and was much struck not only with the excellent state in which all the buildings of the Palace were kept, but with the great propriety and completeness of all the arrangements.'[28]

W.C. Erskine, the commissioner of Sagar and Narmada districts in Jabalpur, was strongly against the Rani being allowed to report directly to the Governor General's agent. He believed that the Rani and her advisers still harboured hopes of recovering Jhansi and thus the threat of moving to Banaras was an empty one. She wanted to be under the political agent only to improve her chances of appeal for the restoration of her country to her. Erskine reasoned that Lakshmi Bai had said she was satisfied with the arrangement that the British had made when he met her, and there was no other reason why she would want it otherwise. To make the changes now would compromise the positions of the local officials, such as the superintendent and the deputy commissioner. Moreover, Hamilton was 480 kilometres away at Indore without an assistant in Jhansi. If the magistrate were left with no power over the palace, nothing would deter 'criminals' from taking refuge there, which 'they might and probably would do'.

Erskine's suggestion was that he should be made the agent of the Lieutenant-Governor of the North-West provinces with Skene as his assistant. There was perhaps more than just the matter of the Rani to be settled. Local political ambitions and professional jealousy played a larger role in deciding local political fortunes than is usually acknowledged.[29] In fairness to Erskine, it must be said that he was acting on the basis of a report that Captain Skene had furnished him just a couple of weeks ago. According to Skene, the Rani requested that she be placed under more senior officers. But when he explained the matter to her lawyer that such a change would not affect matters because both he and Gordon were treating her with 'utmost consideration and respect' as her status warranted, she appeared satisfied. In fact, she held two interviews with Captain Skene from behind purdah and assured him that subsequent to the loss of territory, she was '... so far satisfied with the position assigned to her by government that she had no wish to change it, feeling satisfied that her rank will be respected and her interests cared for in every way'. He added that 'these expressions were quite as spontaneous as those made use of in the conversation with Sir Robert Hamilton'.[30] Did Lakshmi Bai really agree or was she misrepresented? Because she repeated her request when she met Hamilton later more than once.

Overruling Erskine, Hamilton wrote to Dalhousie, who was in Ootacamund, suggesting that she should be placed under the agent Governor General. Dalhousie wrote back that he agreed with the proposal and recommended it to Calcutta. When J.K. Colvin, the Lieutenant-Governor, was informed of this, he 'gave a contrary opinion, to the effect that his powers would be lost and so the matter ended'. Lakshmi Bai continued to be under the local officials who were answerable to Colvin in Agra. Robert Hamilton was the political agent of the Governor General for this region.

A far more contentious issue now came up, and this time the Rani was certainly not willing to compromise. The accounts of the kingdom of Jhansi showed that there was an outstanding debt of Rs 36,000 that had to be paid to seven persons. Gordon was of the opinion that these were old debts not incurred by Gangadhar Rao, and therefore should be paid by the government now that the state had been taken over. H.W. Hammond, the secretary, Sudder Board of Revenue, NWP, firmly believed that these were personal debts of the Raja and the onus was on the Rani to meet them. Skene and Erskine could not have agreed more. Correspondence on this started from the second half of 1855. Ayodhya Prasad was the lawyer representing the Rani. She was asked to pay seven persons the amount that her husband owed them. If she did not do so, the amount would be deducted from her pension. Her lawyer tried to prove that such a directive was wholly inadmissible, as some of the creditors had put forward false claims. The Raja had tried to meet as much of the debts as he could. But some had never featured among the creditors, while others like Bhaskar Bheekoje had their accounts settled through the agent. In fact, at present he owed the state some money, but had been refusing to submit his papers.

The second reasoning was that these were not the Raja's personal debts and since the state had been attached, the amount should be paid by the British government. The Raja had during his lifetime paid up as much as twenty to twenty-three lakh rupees. The third argument was that quite a few zamindars owed money to the Raja, who had provided them with loans and bonds. Orchha state, too, owed the Raja money. None of that had been repaid to the Rani. And finally, if these debts were regarded as personal, why wasn't the amount deducted from the property before it was restored to him? After all, the management of the state had been taken over to pay up the debts.[31]

The matter was not easily settled. Lakshmi Bai met Hamilton on two more occasions on this issue alone. She was extremely upset that the British government refused to exempt her from paying old debts and she insisted on moving to Banaras. J.K. Colvin, the Lieutenant-Governor of NWP, worried at the consequences, asked Hamilton to pay the Rani another visit to dissuade her. By now Hamilton could claim a degree of acquaintance with Lakshmi Bai. She talked clearly and cleverly, thus discounting the popular notion that she was a 'mere child, under the guidance of others' and 'intemperate in habits'. The Rani said that the pension that was being granted was ostensibly for the support and maintenance of her position, while the debts were those of the state and she had not contracted them. Forcing the payment on her was tantamount to compromising her honour and respect. Both Skene and Gordon were sympathetic and perhaps even Erskine could be persuaded, but Colvin was 'inexorable'. The meeting ended with the Rani thanking Hamilton and the two parting 'as best of friends', to quote the officer himself.

Several years later, when the mutiny had blown over,

lives made and unmade, and Hamilton retired to his home in Stratford-on-Avon, John W. Kaye began research on what would be the most authentic and thorough work on 1857 by a contemporary British historian. He looked for all those who served in India prior to the event and were in touch with the different people later involved in the uprising. He asked Hamilton about the Rani of Jhansi. 'My impression was that she was a clever, strong-minded woman, well able to argue and too much for many, there was a complete command of patience and temper,' he wrote back. He recalled that she was usually alone during the interviews and in the course of the conversations, she 'put aside the purdah and spoke to me face to face and I had a full opportunity of seeing her for some time'.[32] He reminisced about the first time he had visited her and she had received him in full court, in the presence of her father and other ministers together with Captain Skene, Lieutenant Gordon and Hamilton's assistant. It was a crowded gathering. Rani sat behind the purdah alone. He continues, 'On my second visit a year after, I found the Ranee as before, she expressed herself much hurt by a decision of the lieutenant-governor making her personally answerable to some old debts of the late Raja, she expressed herself strongly and she certainly has been harshly treated in this manner which I noticed to the government.'

Hamilton summed up: 'I found the Ranee very civil and polite, *quite the lady.*'[33] The admiration was real and the description apt. And he was certainly neither the first nor the last. Despite having a close coterie of advisers that included her father, Mama Sahib and Diwan Lakshman Rao and Kashmiri Mull among others, Lakshmi Bai chose to act as her own spokesperson. The interviews she had were carefully conducted so that a series of activities built up to a dramatic moment when the curtain would either be inadvertently drawn or pulled aside by a whiff of wind and the Englishman would be face-to-face with the Rani. The effect was never lost.

Lakshmi Bai had other issues to settle such as the introduction of cow slaughter after the British takeover, in what was the stronghold of Brahmanical culture. Her plea that this should be revoked was dismissed both by Skene and Erskine. The two officers, however, were on her side when it was proposed that the responsibilities of Koneha Bawar and Goora Machia, two villages traditionally assigned for the maintenance of the Mahalakshmi temple, should be resumed. Gordon argued that the grant was specially made for the temple. H.W. Hammond of the revenue department refused to listen. For once, both Skene and Erskine agreed with Gordon. The only allowance that Hammond agreed to was that a sum of Rs 700 should be added to the Rani's pension. The three officers used their clout to increase that to Rs 1,000.[34]

Foreign visitors admired Lakshmi Bai for her unconventionality and non-conformism. They did not expect a young Indian queen to make a case so coherently and forcefully—and when she did, with her unique charm, the officers were fascinated. By the same gesture, the Rani of Jhansi could not have pleased the conservative Marathi Brahmins. And yet she did, and she was being compared not to Lakshmi but to Durga, the goddess of strength. This made her singular and incomparable. Lakshmi Bai put her religiosity to excellent political use and the Brahmins were glad to condone her for her unusual lifestyle as a widow. She was the archetype of a devoted wife, a devout Hindu woman, a patron of the Brahmins and finally the wronged Rani, smarting under the injustices of white rulers and fighting for the cause of her people much like Durga did in Hindu mythology.

Lakshmi Bai did not spare expense, time or energy in following religious ceremonies strictly. They served two purposes: they reinforced the image of the devout, pure widow and they provided means by which she patronized the Marathi Brahmins who were living through times of trouble. Their traditional patron, the Peshwa, ceased to exist, and this community was really hard put to survive, for they knew of no other means of livelihood.

Vishnubhatt Godse's family fortunes were one such instance. His father, uncles, brothers and cousins traditionally performed rituals for the families of rich Marathis to earn their livelihood, that was sometimes supplemented by small plots of land. The decline of these traditionally rich families left Brahmin families such as his with no recourse but to travel frequently outside their homes. The Scindias of Gwalior substituted for the Peshwa's largesse, as did some other rich Marathas settled elsewhere, and so did the Raja and Rani of Jhansi. Godse wrote that Jhansi was second only to Pune in its patronage of the Brahmins and this had a lot to do with his gratitude to the Rani.

Vishnu Godse and his uncle arrived in Jhansi in the fall of 1856. They could not have come at a better time, for the Rani, hoping to ward off danger, had turned to spirituality. Every day, she had a religious ceremony to seek the blessings of the gods for the well-being of her kingdom and the annihilation of her enemies. The Brahmins, as priests, served as crucial mediators in the acts of propitiation. At the Mahalakshmi temple, praises of Chandi, the warrior-goddess, were sung every day. Day-long prayers and charity to the poor and Brahmins sought peace and harmony in the state. In the temple of Ganesh, every day, special prayers were held.

It was decided that a yagna be organized for the sake

of domestic welfare. There was an open clearing next to the fort, ideal for both the pit that needed to be dug and the huge tent for the large gathering. Brahmins from Banaras and other places of pilgrimage in northern India were invited, and a hundred Brahmins were engaged every day for the ritual fire. On the first day, at the time of commencement, all the Brahmins sat in solemn gathering. The Rani, dressed in white, sat with her adopted son on her lap. Lalu Bhao, the chief priest, oversaw all the arrangements, while Moropant Tambe sat a little away with other learned and revered men. It was a four-day affair, after which all the Brahmins were generously rewarded with clothes and money. A few days later, Saptashani and Saptachandi pujas were held within the fort. Fourteen Brahmins had to sit around and recite the scriptures. These ceremonies were out of the ordinary. The chief place of worship, however, remained the Mahalakshmi temple where, every afternoon, an elaborate offering of food was made.

However poorly the British may have treated her, the Rani was certainly not short of resources, for she spared no expense in rewarding the Brahmins. Vishnubhatt was one of the grateful beneficiaries of the Rani's munificence. His description of Lakshmi Bai could not but be adulatory.[35] The pious, deeply religious Rani, reverential to the Brahmins, created an unforgettable impression.

There was, however, a certain self-absorbed preoccupation in what the Rani did in these months. Her domain was restricted to the city of Jhansi both territorially and conceptually, for never in her correspondence did she seem concerned about law and order outside the town. Nor did she ever try to establish contact with her peers. Orchha and Datia were the closest principalities under Rajput rulers. Gangadhar Rao had asked them for assistance during times of trouble and in the process established links with the neighbouring chiefs. Lakshmi Bai saw no reason to keep up correspondence with them, not till much later. She was far more engrossed in trying to negotiate with the British officials for a more reasonable and respectable deal. If she had any outside links, they were with Bithur, through the regular passage of Brahmins travelling to and fro.

She was also not concerned about the state of affairs in the surrounding region. Never known to be timid and acquiescent, the thakurs saw the change in governance as another occasion to resist authority. The portions that went to the British included the parganas Pundwaha, Mhow, Jhansi, Kurehra and Puchore that encircled the city, in which the Rani commanded the lone citadel.

There was something mystifying about Lakshmi Bai, in her unusual lifestyle, her public appearance, her private moments, her carefully orchestrated daily schedule. Her feminine charm, matched by her clarity of mind and strength of character, lent a degree of romance to the character of the queen. Her actions in years to come and her last moments only magnified the degree of enigma that was Lakshmi Bai.

In Fraser's fiction, Harry Paget Flashman overdid his bit. His account is a historical romance. A veteran of the Afghan campaign, Flashman visited Jhansi in pursuit of a Russian spy trying to foment trouble in Jhansi, encouraged by who he thought and described crassly as, 'that brooding old bitch of a Rani scheming against us...'[36] He was convinced that she was at the centre of it all until he set his eyes on her and then all he could exclaim was, 'There was strength in every line of her, too, for all her femininity,' and 'I could only stand speechless before such queenly beauty...'.

The rest of Flashman's account reads like a salacious nineteenth-century novel about the bewildering Oriental beauty with irresistible charm and indomitable strength of character who eventually succumbs to the white man. The surrender is complete; she falls madly in love with him and the graphic descriptions of their amorous relationship and sexual escapades were the making of pulp fiction. What is interesting is that as a person, Lakshmi Bai lent herself to such a portrayal. There was, not too far from where she was, the Rani of Jalaun, who too had lost her regency after the death of her young brother who had been nominated Raja after her husband died without an heir. Like Lakshmi Bai, she was a Marathi-speaking queen. But till the outbreak of the rebellion, she is not heard of and even then was hardly a patch on the Rani of Jhansi.

Lakshmi Bai's charisma wove a spell of wonder on the people of Jhansi and her personal tragedy easily translated into a regional one. 'And they'll (the people) jump if she whistles, for they worship the ground she treads on... she's uncommon kind to the poor folk, and highly thought of for her piety—spends five hours a day meditating...'[37] Lakshmi Bai emerged as the perfect protagonist of the hour—young, beautiful, vivacious, deeply religious but tragically wronged by fate and now by the conquerors. She was the ultimate Indian heroine.

Three years of uneasy calm were dramatically transformed at the turn of the year 1857 and Lakshmi Bai was caught completely offguard. But only for some time. In the hour of reckoning, she emerged the true champion, yet another time.

6

A Rebellion and a Massacre

More than once a week, Lakshmi Bai used to go to the Mahalakshmi temple in a beautifully decorated palanquin with satin curtains intricately worked in gold thread hanging over the doors. Four young women, strikingly good-looking, wearing blouses made of brocade and adorned by expensive jewellery from head to foot, ran alongside her palanquin. The dupattas they wore were either bright green or khaki. They had red shoes on and thick anklets that tinkled as they ran. These were girls from the Marathi land, often bought from good families to Jhansi and trained to be runners from the age of fifteen or sixteen. They had the best of food and clothes. Unburdened with marriage, housework and childbirth, their figures remained lithe and beautiful. In one hand, they carried a flapper, the handle wrapped in gold or silver sheet and with the other they held the handle of the palanquin. The sight of the Rani's procession was indeed splendid.[1]

Vishnu Godse, the young impressionable Brahmin from small-town Maharashtra, often gaped at the stunning spectacle as it descended from the fort, turned left and gradually made for the Mahalakshmi temple. Leading the procession were men beating kettledrums and carrying flags. Around the Rani were soldiers on horses and elephants in large numbers. Godse was somewhat inaccurate in his description that the journey began from the fort to the temple early in 1857. For Lakshmi Bai was still living in the palace in the town. She did go to the temple more than once a week and the townsmen watched the Rani either ride her own horse or the palanquin. She may have made a display of her visit as a political expediency, a show of her presence as queen of Jhansi.

Lakshmi Bai could have had no idea of the impending future till the troubles broke out in the summer of 1857. It started on 10 May, when soldiers in Meerut rose in mutiny, destroyed the cantonment, took charge of the district office and marched to Delhi, leading a trail of mutinies in stations in the north and as far east as Bihar.[2] What followed was the great conflagaration, variously called the Indian mutiny, India's first war of independence or the uprising of 1857.

Whatever her personal grouse may have been, she could not have harboured any thoughts about resisting British authority, since the Newalkar family had always been unconditionally loyal and dependent on the white rulers. At the time of her marriage, Gangadhar Rao's property was being managed by them and they had acted in good faith by reverting governance to the Raja the same year. The loyalty of the family could not be shaken easily. The British government provided the royal family with protection, showing proper deference during their pilgrimage. Gangadhar Rao kept the lines of communication with the British open, more so in times of trouble, such as there continuously were because of the surrounding Rajput thakurs' belligerence.

Under these circumstances, the Jhansi raj was pretty much alone. Nationalist historians have often described at length, somewhat dramatically, how Lakshmi Bai, sullen and aggrieved, was contemplating rebellion. She was said to have been seething in anger, waiting eagerly for the moment when she could avenge the wrong done to her family. Her actions till the summer of 1857, however, were contrary to this image. The letters that she composed so well and with so much thought, if anything, confirmed her faith and trust in British justice. She appealed because she appreciated that the system allowed for such petitions and her own or her advisers' brilliance lay in the manner they made use of the finer nuances of colonial law. These were far removed from any plans of subversion. On the contrary, they underlined her hopes that better judgement would prevail and the British governors would see reason in the demands. These were not acts of rebellion but signs of reconciliation. Surrounded by unhappy Rajput landlords, who had little love for the Brahmin Marathis, it would have to be a very foolish Rani to contemplate and conspire resistance.

The mutiny turned this world awry, and the British were not the only ones caught offguard.

*

About three kilometres away from the bustling streets of Jhansi, on a piece of land that Gangadhar Rao had gifted them, the British built their own colonial-style bungalows with low roofs and whitewashed walls, long covered porches and well-manicured gardens. One of the first houses built for Major Ellis has now been converted into the district judge's office. Others that have survived time and disuse are also used as government buildings. The difference between the two worlds is unmistakable, even today. Wide, tree-lined roads with houses set far back in neat rows are a far cry from the chaotic constructions and narrow lanes in the part that the Indians inhabited.

At the centre of the British quarters was the cantonment. It was initially built for the Bundelkhand Legion that was raised in 1839, an irregular force of infantry and artillery, to which later was added one unit of cavalry for the protection of the region. In 1849, the force was upgraded to regular military regiments, with detachments of all the three units of artillery, infantry and cavalry.[3] Jhansi became the headquarters of the infantry regiment with smaller units of cavalry and artillery. This made it one of the larger military posts in Central India to have all three units of the army. In the cantonment was a star-shaped building with high walls, appropriately called Star Fort. This is where the munitions and treasure were kept.

In 1857, the units posted here were the left wing of the 12th Native Infantry, right wing of the 14th Irregular Cavalry and a detachment of foot artillery. These troops were raised and trained elsewhere; most of them being from Delhi, Uttar Pradesh and Bihar. The Rajputs of Bundelkhand, despite their martial spirit and tradition of war, seldom joined the British army. The British characteristically attributed this to their 'predatory habits'.[4] The comparison was clearly made with the Brahmins and Kayasthas of Awadh in Uttar Pradesh who joined the British Indian Army in large numbers. One major difference often overlooked lay in the nature of the two kingdoms. Awadh, a huge, prosperous monarchy that emerged as the regional replacement to Mughal power, provided the local community with patronage and alternate sources of employment. The much more modest Jhansi ruling family largely depended on men brought in from the Deccan, without raising local contingents. Thus, the Rajputs never had the opportunity to join a local army and they were unlikely to make a new beginning with the British.

The Indian soldiers in the cantonment lived away from the town and the townsmen in their barracks. But occasionally they broke away from their closed world of order and discipline to visit local shops in the bazaars.[5] In their time off they wandered through the lanes of Jhansi or participated in one of the many religious festivities organized by the Rani. Theirs was a different world from the 'sahibs', even though they belonged together.

The sprawling bungalows of the British officers, both civil and military, took up the larger share of the cantonment. Captain Skene, the superintendent, and Lieutenant Gordon, his deputy, were the seniormost civilian officials. Captain Dunlop was the commandant of the infantry regiment and Lieutenant Campbell was in charge of the irregular cavalry. There were other British and Anglo-Indian officers in the military and the civil establishments. Most of them lived in Jhansi with their families, a total of fifty-five.

Warnings had been sent to all stations in India, the alarm sounded and officers told to be careful from the time that soldiers mutinied in Meerut and Delhi in May 1857. British officers in Jhansi, however, were confident that soldiers of the 12th Infantry and 14th Cavalry would remain loyal, and that there was little cause for worry, even though some precautions were taken as a matter of course. In late May and early June, for instance, Jhansi fort was equipped and a few of the officers began spending nights there. What followed was worse than a nightmare.

Fifth June was like any other hot, sultry, summer's day. At around three in the afternoon, Debi Singh, Naurang

Singh, Jai Singh and Jaidin Singh, soldiers of the 12th Infantry raised the alarm that robbers had attacked the Star Fort and all of them must hurry to defend it. Quite a number of soldiers, believing this to be true, loaded their guns and rushed there. Men from the artillery joined them too. The British officers were alerted almost immediately. Captain Dunlop and Lieutenant Taylor, his adjutant, rushed to the Star Fort. As they came close to the fort to talk to the soldiers inside, they were fired at. The British officers were left in no doubt about what was really wrong. But they still hoped that they could talk to the soldiers and either clear their confusion, or pacify them. With that intent, Skene hurriedly scribbled a petition and went to the Star Fort so that he could read it out. Just as he reached the fort and was about to read the petition, the soldiers fired at him. He was forced to leave hurriedly. Lieutenant Campbell, commanding the cavalry, went to the soldiers' lines, ordered the whole unit to assemble and marched them to the Star Fort. They found two guns mounted over the ramparts of the fort and, as they came closer, a musket shot was fired. Campbell was forced to take his men back to their quarters. In an emergency meeting, Skene and Gordon decided that all British officials and their families would have to be evacuated from the cantonment and taken to the Jhansi fort, and its defences immediately be reinforced.[6]

Their first concern was to ensure the safety of the women and children. Skene moved his wife and two children to the fort around four in the evening. Skene, Gordon and Andrews joined them an hour later. Skene sent for the other wives and the rest of the children. By six, all the British civilian officers and their families were inside the fort. The servants were sent back to the houses to fetch food for everyone.

Dunlop and Campbell were the only men who opted to stay back in the cantonment, hoping to negotiate with the soldiers whose loyalty had never wavered before. Dunlop was certain that a handful had been 'corrupted' and most of the others, even if carried away, would soon relent. They calculated there were around fifty soldiers with two guns occupying the armoury and the treasury.[7] In fact, after rushing to the fort following the alarm, some infantry soldiers had returned to their quarters. Late in the evening, news arrived that the left wing of the 12th Infantry stationed in Nowgong had mutinied.

Gordon came out of the fort to meet Dunlop and returned around eight in the evening. Gordon then wrote a hurried note to Hamilton in Jabalpur. He was terribly distressed. All arms and treasure were in the hands of a few soldiers who could easily be overpowered, but the situation was so sensitive that a single wrong move would provoke the rest of the soldiers to revolt. The British made contacts with a few Rajput landlords in the neighbourhood who were 'profuse in their offers', which was somewhat comforting since they had quite a number of strong, fighting men. Urgent missives for help were sent to Gwalior and Kanpur, but Gordon and Skene were not very hopeful of support. It did not seem from the letter that the officers in Jhansi were even aware of what had happened in Kanpur, the day before.[8]

Gordon and Skene also sent appeals to the Rajas of Sampthar and Orchha and would have also sent for help to Datia had the Raja not died recently. The letter composed in Jhansi had no mention of Rani Lakshmi Bai or any assistance sought from her. Hamilton, while forwarding this note to his seniors in Calcutta, commented on Gordon's complete disregard of her. He was among the officers not too ill disposed towards Lakshmi Bai.

Skene and Gordon may have thought of the independent Rajput landowners because they were more resourceful than the lapsed Marathi states of Jalaun and Jhansi.[9] With Dunlop, Taylor and Campbell still doing their rounds in the cantonment, and most of the other soldiers back in the barracks, there descended a strange calm over Jhansi.

When did Lakshmi Bai get involved? Accounts abound regarding her role and degree of complicity in the outbreak of the uprising. It is difficult to recreate the exact sequence of events for we can only piece together statements made by Indians and the British before the official inquiry commission set up after the revolt. Their remarks about the Rani had more to do with their anxiety to disprove their own culpability or to prove a preconceived notion right than give an unbiased account. The Rani and her court had nothing to do with the mutiny of the soldiers nor were they consulted prior to the uprising. A few days before, there had been a letter from Delhi, stating that the Indian regiments of the Bengal army had revolted and if the soldiers in Jhansi did not join them, they would be considered outcasts.[10] If this was indeed true, then it is also likely that the news would have spread to the bazaar and reported in the Rani's court. In any case, it is unlikely that she and her courtiers had not heard of the mutinies in the north.

It is, however, improbable that Lakshmi Bai counted on the military insurgence as her great moment of redemption. Around 1 or 2 June, however, Lakshmi Bai made a formal request through her lawyer Ayodhya Prasad to Major Skene that she should be allowed to recruit soldiers for her own security. The superintendent felt it was unnecessary for the Rani to have her own army, and her application was turned down.[11] None of Skene's correspondence survived, and therefore there is no way to verify the Indians' testimony. On 5 June, Lakshmi Bai was in court in the afternoon when trouble first started, and news reached her soon after. The mutinying soldiers, however, did not come to town that evening.[12]

By the next day, there was no doubt what the sepoys intended to do. The morning, however, broke like any other. Gordon visited his bungalow and had tea before returning to the fort. He met a few commissioned and non-commissioned officers, and spoke to them about the defiant soldiers. A little later, Dunlop and Lt. Taylor, along with some cavalry soldiers, went to the Star Fort once again and posted pickets at some distance, with strict orders that no one should communicate or send food to the mutineers. This was a little after noon. A soldier from one picket fired first at Taylor and as soon as he did so, there was another shot from the fort. Taylor went to another picket when a soldier from the first picket called out, 'Don't let him go', and another shot him in the head, while yet the third one speared him in the shoulder. Capt. Dunlop, who was on foot, was shot down next.[13] Two havildars or junior non-commissioned officers and one soldier were also killed because they were with the British.[14] As soon as the gunshots from the infantry lines were heard, the cavalry soldiers became restless. News reached that one officer and two clerks, all British, had been killed. There was no stopping the sepoys now. They fired at Campbell, who succeeded in escaping and rushed towards Star Fort.[15] Lieutenant Turnbull of the survey department, who was now the only British official left outside the fort, ran as fast as he could to reach it. He climbed up the hill and not being able to reach the gate, clambered up a tree close to the wall. He was spotted and shot down.[16]

As the situation worsened, Skene and Gordon sent word to Lakshmi Bai for help on the morning of 6 June.

By now, the Rani and her advisers knew and had even witnessed what was happening in both the forts. Accounts, however, differ regarding how she responded to the British appeal. According to Mrs Mutlow, the only British person to escape from Jhansi, Lakshmi Bai sent about fifty of her own men but subsequently withdrew them.[17] Sheikh Hingun Huqqabardar, Gordon's private pipe-bearer, recalled later that the British officers had first asked the Rani for four elephants.[18] Meanwhile, rebellion spread fast and wide. By late afternoon, the entire station was up in arms, the soldiers having been joined by customs, police orderlies and the jailer Bakshish Ali and his guards. Bakshish Ali emerges as the principal perpetrator of violence against the British.

Vrindavan Lal Verma has an interesting anecdote in his novel to explain why Bakshish Ali harboured such intense hatred for the British. About a year back, he had been insulted and physically kicked by Skene in front of his subordinates and from that moment, had been waiting for the hour to take revenge.[19] The rebellious government officials broke into small parties. Some set the officers' houses and offices on fire, while others set the prisoners loose. They also opened the outer rampart of Jhansi town to the cry of 'Deen ka jay' or victory of religion. Lakshmi Bai placed extra guards over her palace gate and shut herself inside. Gordon sent a second appeal for help the same day. But the mutineers threatened to kill her and set her palace ablaze if she complied with his request. Her guards deserted their posts and joined the mutineers. The chaos and the confusion on the streets were for everyone to witness with horror. Soldiers, residents, men of the bazaars and the ordinary residents ran frightened up and down the town. The administration had obviously come to a standstill.

It could not have been an enviable situation for the Rani.[20] Fifty-five men and women were now besieged in the fort. All of 5 June, Skene and Gordon's servants kept making trips to the fort from the town, getting provisions for them. After the outbreak on the 6th, it was impossible to ferry supplies any more. The rebellious soldiers refused to let anyone enter the fort or offer assistance. It was now becoming increasingly evident to all those who were inside the fort that without some alternative arrangements, they would not survive. Behind the gates of the fort, they piled high stones and rubble to prevent for as long as possible an outright breach. On the 6th afternoon, when men were on a rampage in the lines, a few infantry and cavalry soldiers made the first attack on the fort. This was expected, and the strategy of defence had been worked out.

The landlords of Kurehra, the only ones to respond to the appeal made by the British for help, had sent about forty men to resist the mutineers. These men were posted at the lower wall of the fort. The British officers stood over the middle wall and the Indian retainers together with the women were inside the third wall. The mutineers had one large gun with them that they placed outside the main Rani Darwaza and started firing. The Kurehra men and the British returned fire, and dispelled the attack. The British also got news that the rebels had detained all the Indian officials who had been supplying them with provisions, such as Neeladhar, the kotwal, Nuthoo Singh, the jamadar orderly and Madar Bux, the jamedar. They next seized the kamdar of the Kurrera force and threatened to kill him if his men were not withdrawn. It called for a lot of persuasion from the British to hold the Kurehra men back for they were ready to leave, not willing to face the wrath of the soldiers. The commotion continued through the night of 6 June.

Soldiers resumed their attack on the Jhansi fort from the small hours of the morning of 7 June. Sometime the night before, they dug out two guns that belonged to the royal family and had been buried for the past three years. The first incident inside the fort took place the same morning. Captain Burgess, also of the revenue department, had had his tent pitched inside the fort for quite some time, together with some of his Indian assistants. There were two brothers serving him, one of them being his jamadar. On the morning of 6 June, the brothers said that they wanted to go out because they would rather be shot down than die of starvation inside the fort. One of them started clearing the barricade when Burgess shot him dead. His brother immediately retaliated and cut down Lieutenant Powar, who was standing close by, with his sabre. Burgess killed him too. This fray proved just how vulnerable the British were inside the fort. It also turned out to be the day of reckoning.

All through this, Lakshmi Bai was willy-nilly both physically and symbolically at the centre of activities. The rebels now went to her for help and demanded that she pay them money or provide them with 1,000 men. She did not have so many retainers, but some of her own men must have told the soldiers of the buried guns, which were immediately dug out.[21] All her private servants and guardsmen were in constant touch with the soldiers and must have been in full sympathy with them.

The news that Lakshmi Bai had sent help to the soldiers worried Skene and Gordon. They knew that if they could reach her, they could clarify matters. Nothing in their actions showed that there was anything but complete trust and faith in the Rani. The deputy superintendent wrote a letter and threw it over the wall to one of her servants. 'Don't fire, give this letter to the

Ranee.' Hingun was told by Gordon's cook that he had written to Lakshmi Bai that it was her 'Raj, and she and other Gentlemen would go where she liked'. She sent back a quick reply that was read out for all to hear. 'What can I do? Sepoys have surrounded me and say I have concealed the Gentlemen and that I must get the Fort evacuated and assist them; to save myself I have sent guns and my followers; if you wish to save yourself, abandon the Fort and no one will injure you.'[22] Gordon replied that they had no carriage by which to travel. But this time Lakshmi Bai did not reply. In a desperate attempt to reach her, three British officials, Andrews, Purcell and Scott, disguised themselves as Indians and sneaked out of the fort. Even in that short distance, they were recognized and killed by men surrounding the fort, most of whom were Lakshmi Bai's guards.[23]

The mutineers recommenced attack with greater reinforcements around ten in the morning. A raging battle ensued. Captain Burgess was an excellent marksman and shot down as many as twenty-five men before he got a bullet in his head. The kamdar from Kurehra still held by the rebels asked his men to withdraw. This left one of the walls close to the Ganesh Darwaza completely unguarded. The mutineers scaled the wall and advanced to the gate. The British were able to resist the assault at least for that night. Gordon shot several of the mutineers down, though he could not prevent the breach.

On the morning of 8 June, as Gordon was looking down a window at the ruptured wall, he was shot in the head and died. The rest of the men and women looked with shock at his limp body as it fell inside. There was now very little they could do but surrender. Skene consulted the others and all agreed.[24] What followed was one of the most horrifying incidents of the Indian mutiny. Skene opened parley with the mutineers. The Indian soldiers promised the British safe passage out of the fort, provided they surrendered themselves and their arms. Skene readily consented to this. But no sooner had they emerged from the fort than they were seized by the crowd, tied and taken to Jokhun Bagh, a clearing a few kilometres away from the fort. They were separated into three lines, 'one comprising all adult males, another of adult females and a third all the children. Then commenced the horrid massacre, the daroga of the jail first raising his sword and killing Skene. All hands were raised and an indiscriminate slaughter took place, the males were despatched first, the females next, and the murder of children closed the brutal scene.'[25]

Descriptions of this macabre act, given by various men claiming to have been present, were more or less the same. Sheikh Hingun is slightly more graphic. The men were bound but not the women. The servants were led about thirty paces behind the British. 'When Europeans arrived at the Jhokun Baugh, all men, women and children were killed with swords and spears by the Nujeeb's and Ranee's Sepoys by directions of the Sepoys and Sowars who afterwards joined in the butchery themselves. Bakshish Ali and his men first tied their hands. Bakshish Ali himself first killed Skene with a sword; Sepoys and Sowars then asked Rissaldar for his orders regarding us servants. He said, "Let them go where they like; we have had our revenge on those from whom we wished to take it."'[26] Apparently, the orders to kill British men and women were given by Kale Khan the rissaldar or the seniormost Indian officer of the cavalry, one of the men who organized the resistance against the British. The bodies of the Europeans lay exposed for two days in the Jokhun Bagh before the rissaldar ordered them to be buried. Gordon's body was brought down from the fort and buried with the others.

The sequence in which these events unfolded does not matter. All European men and women in Jhansi were dead, a handful in battle, the rest in this most brutal manner. Who was responsible? Pir Zahur Ali was the only person who said that the Rani was personally present during the assault of the fort and the final killing. There is no other source to corroborate his statement, and even to the British who were later investigating the incidents it was evident that Lakshmi Bai had nothing to do with the decision of the mutineers to cut people down. Lakshmi Bai did not leave her palace till after the mutineers had left and some of the wild confusion simmered down.

But there was no way in which she could have been unaware of what was happening. Even when British officials were taken to Jokhun Bagh, be it from the main gate or the Ganesh gate, both in the south-east, they were visible from Lakshmi Bai's palace just below. She would not have been able to prevent the massacre even if she wanted to, but it is extremely unlikely that she had no inkling of the general mood of the people. This is where the complicity of her men becomes crucial. How deeply was her immediate coterie implicated? How did they get involved in soldiers' affairs? The manner in which Lakshmi Bai was later identified with the rebellion in Jhansi and the reason why the British refused to believe anything she said in her own defence to prove her innocence, was because her advisers and the men close to her were totally in league with the mutineers.

And this was especially true of her father, Moropant Tambe. Let us read the depositions once more. The only one to hold Lakshmi Bai directly responsible for the outrage was S. Thornton, the deputy collector who was at

Mhow at the time of the outbreak at Jhansi and his letter to W.C. Erskine, the commissioner, dated 21 August 1857, was largely based on hearsay and interpreted in terms of his own prejudice. 'It is the general impression that the mutineers after killing some of their own officers and plundering the town, were going off, and it was only at the instigation of the Jhansi Ranee with the object of her obtaining possession of Jhansi state that they attacked the Fort the next day together with the other armed men furnished by her... For this act the mutineers (are) to have received 35,000 rupees in cash, two elephants and five horses from the Ranee. She has now raised a body of about 14,000 men and taken out two guns which were formerly buried within the Fort and of which nothing was known to our officers.'[27]

There are many glaring inaccuracies in his statements. To begin with, the Rani did not have many armed retainers except a few that the British allowed her for her own safety. Lakshmi Bai was in no way related to the mutiny till the persistent request of the soldiers forced her to comply.

One person, however, who is mentioned in practically every statement and thus difficult to ignore is Moropant Tambe or Mama Sahib, the Rani's father. Sahabuddin, Skene's cook said that on the first day of the mutiny, 5 June, some men from the town plundered the superintendent's house and carried away two boxes to Bakshish Ali's house and two to Moropant Tambe's residence. On the morning of 7 June, as Sahabuddin was returning from the fort, having supplied everyone inside with provisions, he was arrested by Chunni, a relative of Jharu Kunwar and taken to 'Mama Sahib, because I had supplied the officers with food. Mama Sahib ordered his men to take me to jamadar Lall Bahadoor and the

rissaldar to be murdered or to be blown from a gun.' He
was confined for a while and then released.[28]

Sheikh Hingun, however, does not mention Moropant
at all, but repeatedly says that those who fought bitterly
against the British were the Rani's guards. It was on the
evening of 6 June that the sepoys went to meet the Rani
and asked her to post her guards around the fort so that
no one could come out. That her guards did so meant that
she conceded to their demands, under duress or otherwise.[29]
Here again, one must be careful in reading too much into
it because the Rani's guards were just a handful and could
not have made much of a difference.

Madar Bux was the head of orderlies attached to
Gordon and thus senior in rank to others. According to
him, he was employed by the British officers to establish
contact with Indian officials in the police and revenue
departments, like the tehsildar and the shirustadar. He
also seemed to have been in the midst of the fray. His first
observation was that a large number of men who had
arrived in Jhansi from outside were assembling at the
Rani's palace. Like others, he also found the Rani's
guards and sepoys deeply mixed up with the mutineers.
He was present when the tehsildar Ahmed Hussain tried
negotiating with the leader of the cavalry over the release
of the Europeans. The latter asked the tehsildar to write
to the British that they would not be hurt if they
surrendered. Madar Bux was asked to take the letter to
the fort. As he came close to it, the Rani's men refused
him permission to enter. He went to the Rani's palace to
seek permission and was met by Mama Sahib, Lakshman
Rao and Lalu Bakshi. They sent an escort with him and
he was able to take the letter to Gordon. Madar Bux was
then asked to take the deputy superintendent's letter back
to the Rani. He once again gave it to Mama Sahib who

carried the letter to the Rani, who in turn sent it to the rissaldar or the man leading the cavalry. The answer that the Rani sent to the British was in reality drafted by the cavalryman. He corroborates that the Rani's men were present at Jokhun Bagh during the massacre and were among the chief perpetrators.[30]

The Bengali in the customs' collector's office, the most cogent in his description of the events, said that the mutineers had threatened to kill the Rani and set fire to her palace if she sent any assistance to the British and she was left with very little to help with since her guards had all joined the rebels. According to him, Andrews, Purcell and Scott disguised as Indians had actually reached the Rani's palace but she had not even deigned to meet them. They were then dragged out of her palace and killed. The mutineers once more warned the Rani that if she did not help them, she would be killed. She agreed to provide them with men and two guns that had been buried in her husband's time.[31]

In Pir Zahur Ali's recollection of the uprising two years later, Lakshmi Bai had helped the mutineers with provisions on the very first night. She was also said to have been personally present when the fort was attacked. There is no doubt that Pir Zahur Ali was eager to ensure that his deposition upheld what the British already wanted to hear. It made perfect sense to condemn the already damned, as Lakshmi Bai was.[32]

Lalu Bakshi's is the only account that talks of Lakshmi Bai being aware of the impending trouble and of wanting to raise soldiers. He also mentions that the rebels had come to seek the Rani's assistance soon after the uprising and it was true that she was under severe pressure to come to their assistance. It also confirms other testimonies that her guards and soldiers had joined the uprising.

It is evident that all these statements were made to exonerate the person who was testifying from any involvement in the mutiny. All of them, however, agreed on two things—the soldiers' actions had no connections with the Rani. If she had been cautious or wary, as any astute leader should be, it was because of the uprisings elsewhere that she must have known of. But the mutineers in Jhansi had no prior links with her. She was even hesitant to help them and did so only under threat. The mutineers, however, came to her palace on 6 June, to seek her support and consent. The same cannot be said of the members of her immediate court. Most of them were in close touch with the leaders of the mutiny either willingly or as strategy for survival. Here Moropant Tambe certainly was more active than the others. This makes his daughter suspect too. Lakshmi Bai must have known everything happening in the fort that was so close to her palace. But personally she had nothing to do with the killing of British men and women. How have the biographers interpreted the actions of the Rani in those three days?

For months, according to Vrindavan Lal Verma, Tantia Tope and Lakshmi Bai, together with a close group of confidants, had been scheming to overthrow British rule. Tantia Tope had toured the entire country in north India assessing the level of willingness and preparedness of the local rulers and soldiers to resist British rule. Lakshmi Bai knew of the letters that the Indian soldiers of the British army had received from cantonments in the north. She had sought permission from the British officers to raise her own army. She was waiting for the army to arrive when the mutiny broke out in Jhansi on the evening of 5 June. When Gordon came to her for help, she asked him to bring all the women and children to her palace. They were escorted to the Rani's palace but later removed to

the fort at the direction of Skene.[33] British records do not
mention this. In the next two days, the Rani made sure
that the British were provided with adequate food. She
sent her three companions—Kashibai, Sundar and
Mandar—with chappatis. She told them of her plans.
Once her army was ready she would disarm the British
and keep them imprisoned in some safe refuge. She
repeated that her war was with the British men, not
defenceless women and children. What followed was
totally against the moral principles of the Rani and when
the leader of the mutineers came to meet her after killing
the British, she did not hesitate to rebuke them. She
agreed to pay them money so that they could leave Jhansi
and march to Delhi. Otherwise, they would have plundered
the town and the people would have suffered.

There is one glaring flaw in Verma's argument.
Describing the moments before the build-up to the mutiny
in Jhansi, he says that, 'in reality, because of the Rani's
strict vigilance, there was no uprising in Jhansi before
time'.[34] The clear suggestion here is that Lakshmi Bai was
in control and that, together with Nana Sahib and Tantia
Tope, masterminded the movement. If she had really been
in charge, why did she not prevent the massacre? The
mutineers made it very clear what they intended to do
when they shot dead all British officers outside the fort—
and Dunlop inside it too. Why would anyone have believed
that they were going to be merciful and kind to the others
just because they had surrendered?

In Verma's novel, the massacre is briefly mentioned,
almost as if to have it out of the way. Bakshish Ali,
recalling the ignominy he suffered at the hands of Skene,
provoked a cavalryman who announced to the others that
Kale Khan had ordered the British to be killed. Just one
sentence was devoted to the most serious incident in

Jhansi that was to determine its fate and that of its Rani. When Kale Khan arrived, there was blood all over and he demanded to know on whose orders the British had been killed. Bakshish Ali admitted that it was done at his bidding and that the Rani was oblivious of this. Kale Khan looked visibly disturbed and warned soldiers that they should not in future act without explicit instructions from seniors. Kale Khan proceeded to meet Lakshmi Bai who was extremely disapproving of what the soldiers had done. 'Are you going to establish independence and the rule of the Badshah with acts like these? Is this what you had been taught?'[35] This reads as if the British were massacred almost by mistake and at the behest of a faceless, insignificant cavalry soldier, all the leaders being quite above suspicion.

It does not seem plausible, and that is exactly how the British construed the affair in Jhansi. After all, like the massacre in Kanpur, this was the most heinous of crimes committed by the Indians against the British. And the most brutal reprisals were set aside for those involved. Regarding the Rani, it was difficult for the British to arrive at any conclusive decision. If she had indeed been the leader of the uprising, as some of her admirers claim, then she was complicit in the scheme of having all the British men and women killed. If she had not been involved, as she herself claimed to British officials, then the mutiny must have taken her unawares and she was a victim in the hands of soldiers—not a pretty picture for the nationalist biographers of Lakshmi Bai.

Mahasweta Devi's historical account of the Rani realistically describes her concern. As the mutiny raged around the palace, 'the doors of Rani Mahal were then closed. Dependent relatives, maids and servants all crowded around the Queen; she reassured them, and with an

anxious, apprehensive heart kept waiting for news'.[36] The
final massacre takes up a short paragraph. Several
horsemen came with Rissaldar Kale Khan's orders to kill
the British and Bakshish Ali took the lead, as the people
of Jhansi looked on horrified and unbelieving.

The mutineers went to the Rani's palace demanding at
least three lakh rupees. 'The Queen had no other choice
and was forced to hand over jewellery valued at one lakh
rupees, from her *khasgi daulati*, in order to save herself
from imminent danger.'[37]

Vishnu Godse recalls rather inaccurately that Gordon
went to the Rani one day before the uprising had been
planned for and pleaded with her that since their days
appeared to be numbered, it was time she took back her
kingdom. Lakshmi Bai rudely turned down the request,
with the retort that if she did assist them, the sepoys
would kill her. She was quick to remind him that things
would not have gone so wrong had they not repulsed her
earnest request to let her have her rightful claims to the
kingdom of Jhansi. She curtly told him off and said the
British would have to fend for themselves. This is a
mistaken impression because there was no date fixed for
the uprising, and even if there had been one, the British
officers were unaware of it. It is evident from all official
correspondence that if anything, the officers in Jhansi
were confident that their men would remain loyal despite
provocations.

Secondly, Gordon had no personal interview with the
Rani or else he would have mentioned it in his letter to
Hamilton, which happened to be the last from the district
office of Jhansi. And even if he did have a meeting,
Lakshmi Bai was too astute to be so bluntly rude. In
Godse's account, the rather long paragraph on the
encounter with the Rani is followed by a brief one of five

sentences that sums up the uprising in Jhansi and the massacre that followed.[38] After the mutiny, the soldiers went to the Rani's palace and acknowledged her as their ruler. 'We will obey your orders and receive our salary every month from you,' they promised.[39]

Om Shankar Asar, who in his long serialized account of Lakshmi Bai and her Jhansi, devotes pages to how badly and unfairly the British had treated the Rani, barely mentions the uprising and the massacre.

S.N. Sinha, the modern scholar, in his biography of Lakshmi Bai, goes to great pains trying to absolve the Rani of the crime attributed to her. Was she or was she not an accomplice in the plot to kill all British men and women after they surrendered? He quotes British historians who have rather groundlessly blamed her for both the rebellion and the massacre. He cites from different depositions to prove how unreliable they are in regard to the observations they make about the Rani and her movements in those few days of confusion. Sinha observes in regard to one deposition: 'The account given by the unnamed Bengali attached to the customs collector's office was based on hearsay as he himself admitted that he was behind bars.[40] Yet two pages later, Sinha writes, 'The unnamed Bengali, though a critic of the Rani, admits that when Gordon solicited Rani's assistance, "the mutineers threatened to put her to death and to set fire to her palace in case of her compliance"'.[41]

If Lakshmi Bai, Rani of Jhansi, was responsible for masterminding the rebellion and taking up leadership of it, then there is no way in which she can be absolved of responsibility for the crime. Even if she had not been responsible for the massacre, she did nothing to prevent it, making her culpable in the eyes of the government. This was precisely the line of thinking of the council in Calcutta that dispatched counter-insurgency forces against her, dismissing all her pleas.

The reason Indian biographers are reticent to talk about it is because logically it becomes difficult for them to assert her leadership of the movement and her innocence in the crime, in the same breath. If she had been innocent, the entire movement had taken her by surprise and that she had to manage her kingdom for the next eleven months was an accident. On the other hand, as an embodiment of Goddess Durga, she could never be involved in the grisly murder of innocent children and women. British retaliation and the subsequent counter-insurgency measures could then be depicted as further instances of British injustice.

The British biographers, on the other hand, spend a large portion of their narrative on this most critical event. For it was the massacre and the responsibility of the Rani, in either commanding it or not preventing it, that determined how they assessed her in posterity. Sir John Smyth had to resolve whether Lakshmi Bai 'had to ride with the tide whether she wished to or not', or if 'she showed a callous disregard for the fate of her captors', or worst still, if 'she had definitely approved of their murder'.[42] This is what he had to say by way of conclusion: Lakshmi Bai was extremely upset at the injustice of the British towards her interests and her son's legitimate rights and therefore, it is difficult to judge if she 'ordered' the massacre or 'condoned' it. 'I think that it was not in character for her to have ordered it—nor do I think the evidence supports the fact; but she may well have condoned it from sheer sense of self-preservation'. Could she have saved the Europeans? Smyth thinks yes, or perhaps that she knew about it when it was too late. His final verdict is that 'I myself come down on the side of the Rani, partly on the grounds that I think it was out of character, and partly on the evidence, which I feel bears out her innocence of actual complicity.'

Antonia Fraser, in *Boadicea's Chariot*, infers that 'It is inconceivable that the Rani encouraged this piece of wanton mayhem. Leaving aside her actions at a later stage, the Rani in these first days of mutiny at Jhansi rightly considered the sepoys to be a frightening force outside her own control, and indeed outside anyone else's.'[43]

To Indian scholars, it was Lakshmi Bai's subsequent actions, her valiant resistance to British forces and her death fighting them that created the image of an undying heroine and a martyr. For the British biographers, her complicity or her innocence in the ghoulish act decided if she were to be compared to Joan of Arc or Jezebel.

7

Legendary Heroics

Late in the evening of 8 July, the city of Jhansi heard to the beat of drums the proclamation, 'The people are God's, the country is the King's (Padshah's) and the two religions govern.'[1] The mutineers did not intend to stay in Jhansi, for their chief purpose was to reach Delhi and instal an alternative order that would replace British rule. But as long as they were in Jhansi, Lakshmi Bai had little freedom. William Kaye, in the course of his investigations to write the most detailed account of the mutiny to date, came across a piece of information that he wasn't able to include in his book but is found in his scribbled notes on the mutiny. The soldiers met the Rani and her officials on the evening of 8 July. They demanded one-and-a-quarter lakh rupees from the Rani that she was both unwilling and unable to pay. The soldiers drove a hard bargain. Either Lakshmi Bai paid up or they would offer the throne to Sadashiv Rao Narain, who had earlier staked a claim and was still very keen on it. She was left with little option but to pay, which she did after hard bargaining, reducing the amount to Rs 15,000.[2]

The soldiers eventually left for Delhi on the evening of

11 July. As soon as they did, Lakshmi Bai had a second decree read out: '*Khalq khoda ki, mulk badshah ki, raj Lakshmi Bai ki* (the people are God's, the country is the Emperor's and the rule is Lakshmi Bai's)'. So she finally became the Rani of Jhansi in the true sense, but under circumstances that would have outraged the Newalkars.

One of her first acts was to write to the British commissioner, Major W.C. Erskine. Gangadhar Dangee and Bhowani, two 'hurkaras', or couriers, reached Jabalpur late in the evening of 11 July with her letters hidden inside their walking sticks. It had taken them over two weeks to cover the distance of 200 kilometres between Jhansi and Jabalpur. The country from Jhansi to Sagar, a little north of Jabalpur, was in a state of complete anarchy. They were robbed of their money and clothes. Erskine received and read the letters. In the first, Lakshmi Bai expressed her deep regret at the murder of the Europeans by faithless, cruel and violent government forces. She had been unable to help for want of resources, money or soldiers, she wrote. They had later come to her to extort money, which they did and 'said that as the Ranee was entitled to succeed to the Reasut, she should undertake the management since the sepoys were proceeding to Delhi to the King'.[3] This may have been her subtle way of reiterating her family's claims to the throne of Jhansi.

However, she was quick to add in the second paragraph that she had always been totally dependent on the British. Keenly aware of her vulnerability, the soldiers sent word through the Indian officials of the revenue and police departments that they would blow up her palace with guns if she did not comply with their demands. She had no way of communicating with the British, being completely surrounded by the mutineers, but as soon as they left on the evening of 11 July, she wrote her first letter to the commissioner. Meanwhile, she sent 'parwanas', or instructions, to all district officials to remain in their posts and perform their duties as usual. She was merely holding fort till the British returned, she said.[4]

In the second letter, dated 14 July, the Rani urged the British government to send her forces and money, without which it would be impossible for her to hold on much longer. The Rajput landlords all around were reoccupying their forts, or garhis, that the British forces had earlier disarmed. They had also resumed their old practice of plundering the country. Lakshmi Bai had no money to recruit soldiers, nor did she have the means to raise funds. The mahajans refused to lend money in times like these and she had had to sell her personal property to put together a minimum of resources to be able to hire a few men for keeping up a form of government both in and outside the town.[5]

Erskine wrote back that he was trying his best to arrange for troops for Jhansi and that there was to be a new superintendent. Till such time as reinforcements arrived, 'I beg you will manage the district for the British Government, collecting the Revenue, raising such Police as may be necessary and making other proper arrangements such as you know the Government will approve and when the Superintendent takes charge from you, he will not only give no trouble, but will repay you for all your losses and expenses, and deal liberally with you.'

He enclosed a proclamation with his seal and signature in Persian and Hindi that was to be circulated:

> *Be it known to all people residing in the Government District of Jhansee, that owing to the bad conduct of the soldiers some valuable lives have been lost, and property destroyed, but the*

strong and powerful British Government is sending thousands of European soldiers to places which have been disturbed, and early arrangements will be made to restore order in Jhansee.

Until Officers and Troops reach Jhansee, the Ranee will rule in the name of the British Government and I hereby call on all, great and small, to obey the Ranee, and to pay the Government Revenue to her for which they will receive credit.

The British Army has retaken the city of Delhi and has killed thousands of the rebels, and will hang or shoot all the rebels wherever they may be found.[6]

It was the Rani's admission and Erskine's endorsement that persuaded S.N. Sen, in the authoritative, well-researched work on the events of 1857 to believe that there was nothing 'clandestine' in her statement that she had been under threat of violence and whatever she had done was in the best interest of the people and the British government.[7]

Even while these letters were being exchanged, there was the immediate situation in Jhansi to grapple with. Lakshmi Bai and her small court spent sleepless nights to ensure that chaos did not prevail. One of her first measures was to raise men to protect the town and the surrounding district, both being open and vulnerable to all forms of disorder and confusion that lack of regular governance brings about. Indian soldiers of the British army who had not accompanied the rest to Delhi and could not go home, readily joined local potentates who offered work and a salary.

Aman Khan, for example was originally from a village near Agra and a sepoy in the 12th Regiment Bengal Native Infantry who did not want to follow the mutineers to Delhi nor had any reason to go home. Instead, when he heard of the recruitment in Jhansi to the Rani's service, he decided to join her. He was offered a salary of four rupees a month. There were some like him and other local residents of Jhansi, a total of 100 men engaged by the court to start with; the numbers grew substantially. Within a short time, around eighty disbanded soldiers of the Scindia's contingent who had been posted in Asirgarh in the south arrived in Jhansi and were recruited by the Rani. There were 500 cavalry soldiers too who had either stayed back or had come from other stations. They had at least five or six rissaldars among them, and 300 mercenary soldiers from the north joined her army.[8]

Lakshmi Bai came to depend upon her two able lieutenants Raghunath Singh and Jawahar Singh. The first was her diwan, or finance minister, and the second the landlord of Katili, who commanded her soldiers.[9] Both of them were Bundela Rajputs of Jhansi and powerful landlords in their own right. They were instrumental in inducting as many as 500 mounted Bundela soldiers into the Rani's army. It is unknown when and how these two men joined Lakshmi Bai's close circle of trusted and faithful men. But they proved fiercely loyal and passionately devoted to their queen. They were one of the reasons why the Bundelas in Jhansi and Lalitpur in the south supported Lakshmi Bai.

In these months from July till the end of the year, Jhansi remained singularly secure from utter political disintegration. While all the major cities of the north such as Delhi, Lucknow, Allahabad and Kanpur witnessed desperately fought battles of competing orders, British forces had still not invaded central India in 1857. And in this region, the administration of Jhansi was most successful in maintaining an element of stability and control. This feature and its strategic location attracted a stream of men looking for employment.

According to Aman Khan, there was a total of 30,000 men in the town and in outpost duties at the end of 1857. The figure appears somewhat exaggerated, but the numbers must have been substantial.[10]

Thus, for all purposes, Lakshmi Bai became the effective ruler of Jhansi from the summer of 1857. Credit may not be due to her for reaching there on her own, but she certainly stayed in control for the next one year in rather adverse circumstances.

Barely had she finished writing to Erskine when Sadashiv Rao Narain offered the first resistance to her new government. Sadashiv had appeared in Jhansi to put forward his claims before the mutineers and, as we have seen, helped the latter strike a bargain with the Rani. Instead of returning to Parola, he captured the fort of Kurehra, forty-eight kilometres west of Jhansi, and gathered around him 300 men from the Puar clan, who had been the chief abettors of the Rajput protest of the 1840s and had little love for the Bundelas supporting the Rani. The local government officials had until then managed to stay on in Kurehra, and since Lakshmi Bai was ostensibly ruling for the British and with their mandate, they were expecting support from Jhansi. Sadashiv Rao now drove them out and appointed his own men instead. He also levied taxes on the people, assumed the title of Maharaja and proclaimed that he had seated himself on the throne of Jhansi at Kurehra.

It took Lakshmi Bai a while to retaliate. She needed time to mobilize her troops, for which she required funds that were running short. She asked the local moneylenders for support and then decided to mint money for local circulation. Having gathered sufficient strength, she sent her army under the command of Jawahar Singh to take on Sadashiv Rao's forces in Kurehra. It was a brief skirmish, and the outcome was evident even as the conflict started. Sadashiv Rao fled to Narwar, further south into the Sagar territory. Realizing what he was up against, he eventually made peace with Lakshmi Bai and joined her rule.[11]

One of the first measures that the reinstated British government did as an act of retribution was to draw up for each region of rebellion, the names of men most guilty of crime. They were ranked according to their culpability. The most guilty, who had been directly responsible for the death of British men and women, were punished by death without trial. Rewards were announced for apprehending them. In Jhansi, Bakshish Ali and Moropant Tambe were ranked on top and an award of Rs 2,000 was to be given to anyone who helped in their capture. Next were those who would be tried, and Lalu Bakshi was among this category of offenders. Trials continued for years and threw up a huge amount of documents, which are crucial sources of the history of the movement. In the course of these trials, after all, the days and months of the uprising were reconstructed, the actions replayed, the chief actors identified.

Lalu Bakshi in his trial had to make sure he did not give away his one last chance of escaping punishment. In his confession, thus, he repeatedly stressed that he had nothing to do with the Rani. He admitted that the Rani had asked him to recruit forces because there were certain 'indications' two or three days before the outbreak. There were some inconsistencies in his statement. He claimed that he refused to raise men for the Rani until the British approved. 'Three days after that, the disturbances took place,' is what he said during trial. He continues, 'Then I reached home and the disturbances began four *gharis* after.' At midnight, the mutineers went to the Rani and asked for Lalu Bakshi and Jharu Kunwar. Lakshmi Bai gave them up, and the soldiers took the two men away as prisoners. They were taken to Lakshmi Bai's palace and that is where they remained.[12]

Madar Bux was called upon to give evidence in the same trial. He was the jamedar or head of orderlies attached to Gordon. His deposition in connection with the uprising has been given credence. He mentioned Lalu Bakshi as being among the close confidants of the Rani and responsible for handing him over to the mutineers, who beat him up. Madar Bux was later called to give evidence at the trial of Lalu Bakshi.

According to him, Lalu Bakshi had actually written to the neighbouring Rajput landlords asking them to come to Jhansi as 'a disturbance must be created'. The men gathered on the occasion of a religious ceremony or Sat Narain Ki Katha, and used the opportunity for discussing more urgent matters relating to Jhansi. Those who participated included Lalu Bakshi, Lakshman Rao, Bholanath Mutsarrif and representatives of several landlords. Madar Bux said that he had warned Lalu Bakshi and Lakshman Rao against impropriety but they feigned ignorance. 'Remember that the British rule is so widely extended that none dare raise his head. How can you do this then?'[13] Madar Bux was doing his best to prove his loyalty to the British government. He, however, corroborated Lalu Bakshi's statement that the latter did implore the British officials to grant him permission to raise soldiers. Gordon eventually allowed only fifty men.

Madar Bux was caught by the sepoys on 6 June and taken to their lines, where he found both Lalu Bakshi and Jharu Kunwar in consultation with Bakshish Ali. Madar Bux was employed to carry letters from the mutineers to the British and the Rani. By his own admission, he was carrying the letter the rissaldar (Kale Khan) made the tahsildar of Jhansi write—that the British could leave the fort without the fear of interception. Madar Bux stayed on in Jhansi for the next four months. Lalu Bakshi remained in the service of the Rani. When Sadashiv Rao threatened Jhansi, Lalu Bakshi tried to get in touch with him but his letter was seized and he was brought back and imprisoned by the Rani. Subsequently, he was reinstated.[14]

Lalu Bakshi certainly had more information than the others about the Rani and her activities immediately after the rebellion. He could also have been a double agent.

Even though Sadashiv Rao was decisively repulsed, Lakshmi Bai realized that these were really dangerous times. She wrote to her neighbours, the rulers of Orchha and Datia, describing the incidents that had thrown everything upside down in Jhansi and asked them to take steps to ensure that disorder did not spread too wide. She was really asking them to keep the Puar Rajput landlords under check.

Bihari Lal, a representative from Orchha, was present all through the turmoil. Baldeo Pandit from Datia came later. She met them in her palace, in her usual place behind the curtain, in the presence of the members of her council, among whom Lalu Bakshi was present.

Some time after the British were killed, Lakshmi Bai thought it appropriate that she should return to the royal palace in Jhansi fort. The entire premises were cleaned and the exact place where the British had lived and thereby 'defiled' was specially purified with river water and cow urine. Then, on a day regarded suitable by the astrologers, Lakshmi Bai moved back to the palace and her legitimate home. She was now indisputably the Rani of Jhansi and made sure that she did not fail her people and did equal justice to the responsibility entrusted to her by the British. She ordered the resumption of the manufacture of guns, cartridges and gunpowder and took up the task of the ruler in great earnest. In Godse's words, 'For nearly eleven months after the return of the kingdom of Jhansi to Lakshmi Bai, it felt as if British rule had ceased to exist in the whole of northern India.'[15] Lakshmi Bai displayed incredible maturity and leadership when she successfully re-established regularity and order in the middle of complete anarchy. There were mutinying soldiers in the city while the administrative machinery was still not in place. As if this were not enough, she had to contend with contesting claims over her territory by local potentates in the neighbourhood. North of Jhansi, around Kalpi, a substantial territory yielding fifty-six lakh rupees was occupied by Tantia Tope.[16] In the south, in Lalitpur and the whole of the Chanderi, the news of the uprising in Jhansi led the thakurs to rise up in arms everywhere in complete defiance of the deputy commissioner, A.C. Gordon. The thakurs collected their forces in large numbers and started to plunder. Chief among them was the Bundela Raja of a small principality called Banpur. Gordon's predecessor Hamilton, in the wake of troubles, had asked him to come to Lalitpur to take charge of the town. They suspected that instead of supporting the British cause, the Raja assumed leadership of the Bundela thakurs and occupied strategic locations and their surrounding forts.[17]

If the Bundela thakurs' conduct disturbed Lakshmi Bai, she had more important matters to attend to. Ignoring

her overtures of peace and cooperation, the Rani of
Orchha sent her army on 10 August to reclaim lands that
her predecessors had lost to the Marathis. North-east of
Orchha and Jhansi, in the Doab of the two rivers, Dhasan
and Betwa, they overran Mhow, Pundwaha and Gurotha,
which were parganas or smaller administrative units
comprising a district. They plundered the moneylenders
and prosperous farmers and burnt down villages if there
was any resistance. The Rani of Orchha maintained that
she was holding these regions in the interests of the British
government against the rebel Rani of Jhansi.[18]

Lakshmi Bai was acutely aware of her helplessness.
Past animosities between the states of Orchha and Jhansi
had come to haunt her at this most critical juncture. Not
to be left out, her neighbour in the north-west, the state
of Datia, invaded her territory too. The consequence was
complete pandemonium. The powerful Puar thakurs in
turn grabbed what they could, while the forces of Orchha
and Datia continued to storm the countryside. The Rani
of Jhansi's army was unable to do better than put up a
weak resistance, at least in the first few months. The
Orchha force came dangerously close and occupied Burwa
Sagar on 3 September 1857. As feared, the Orchha army,
led by their minister Nathe Khan, laid siege upon the city
of Jhansi itself.

The Rani had very little time to get her forces together.
Her army was too small to rally round and beat the
invaders. The 1,000-odd soldiers, some professionals, most
irregulars, were inadequate. The Rani and her council
members took frantic steps to beat back these invaders
and save her country from being completely devastated.
Yet, why were her actions misconstrued by the British
officials later so that the Rani of Orchha became the
friend and the Rani of Jhansi the foe? Why were her

actions condemned as anti-British and not those who attacked her territory?

The reason was the allies she made and the enemies she was forced to fight. In neither had she any choice. The Puars of Jhansi had always fought the government with the tacit support of both Datia and Orchha with whom they had matrimonial links. They rarely let go the opportunity to take advantage of the weakness of the Jhansi throne. In 1857, it was only natural that they should invade the territory. The Rani of Jhansi required assistance and could only look south to Lalitpur where the Bundela Rajputs now were willing to help Lakshmi Bai, perhaps because the Bundelas in Jhansi had become her allies. Affairs in Lalitpur and the district of Chanderi in 1857 had changed the equation in a manner the Rani could not have anticipated. A.C. Gordon, the deputy superintendent of Lalitpur, was certain that Mardan Singh, the Raja of Banpur, was deeply involved in the Rajput uprisings despite his professed loyalty to the British. Lakshmi Bai sent word to the Banpur chief asking him for help, and he came to her assistance almost immediately. He was also instrumental in brokering a temporary ceasefire among the warring states. Lakshmi Bai also wrote to the commissioner of Jabalpur again. Erskine wrote back saying that British forces would be sent to Jhansi, to determine the culpability of all the parties concerned, and that corresponding action would be taken.

The aggression, meanwhile, forced her to take immediate steps. Lakshmi Bai personally led the battle, with her own forces and the men provided by Mardan Singh. Nathe Khan was defeated and was forced to withdraw the siege of Jhansi.[19] A spy of the Gwalior state, however, reported that the Orchha forces had pulled out and encamped close to Jhansi city, with the intention of gathering more troops and attacking the Rani once more.[20] The British report, uncorroborated as it is, hinted at a larger network. Writing to Edmonstone, Secretary to the Government of India, officiating agent of the Governor General of central India Lieutenant-Colonel H.M. Durand observed, 'The Nana through his vakeel Tantia Tope, is taking advantage of the conflict between Jhansi and Tehree Ranees and intriguing with a view of forming a party in Bundelkhand, and obtaining that which he stands in want of, money.'[21]

The British had no doubts about the ulterior motives of Orchha, either. Yet, at the time of judgement, while the Rani of Orchha escaped unscathed, Lakshmi Bai was condemned as a rebel. The Rani of Jhansi did not have much of a case as far as Calcutta was concerned. While Erskine was willing to grant her the benefit of doubt over her direct responsibility for the uprising and the massacre of the British, the men in the capital refused to give her a hearing. Erskine even wrote to Calcutta that the Rani was certainly innocent of the crimes in Jhansi. When he forwarded the letter to Calcutta, the response was anything but favourable to the queen. Responding on 23 July, Edmonstone wrote, 'In respect to the Ranee I am to state that though His Lordship in Council does not blame you for accepting, in the circumstances in which you were placed, her account of her own proceedings, and sentiments, and entrusting to her the management of the Jhansee Territory on behalf of the British Government, yet this circumstance will not protect her if her account turn out to be false. From the account supplied to Government by Major Ellis, it appears, that the Ranee did lend assistance to the mutineers and rebels, and that she gave guns and men.'[22]

The massacre of the Europeans was undoubtedly the

worst crime that the rebels could have been guilty of and anyone even remotely associated with it deserved death as punishment. Some of the men among Lakshmi Bai's coterie were implicated. What made it impossible for her to vindicate her actions was the involvement of her father Moropant Tambe. In the months following the uprising, Lakshmi Bai's independent manner only corroborated their worst doubts about the extent of her involvement and responsibility in the uprising. Once more, it was her associations that made her plea for innocence appear somewhat dubious. In her confrontation with the neighbouring states, the first ruler to come to her aid was Mardan Singh, who in all the reports on Lalitpur is described as the chief of the Bundelas who gained control of the districts as soon as the British were forced to flee.

North of Jhansi, British officials evacuated stations soon after the mutiny in Jhansi and the district was . effectively in the hands of Kesho Rao of Gurserai, the chief of an important family in the region. In the process, he replaced the Rani of Jalaun, Tai Bai. In October 1857, Tantia Tope led the mutineers of the Gwalior contingent to Jalaun. Both Kesho Rao and Tai Bai were ready to hold parleys with him. Tantia Tope was, however, offended by the Gurserai family and helped Tai Bai back to power. When the British arrived to reclaim their authority, Kesho Rao was termed a friend and Tai Bai the foe.[23]

It would have been very difficult for Lakshmi Bai to convince the British that she was not in touch with Tantia Tope. She could not have stopped Tantia Tope's actions, but she could not plead ignorance of the events.

Was her culpability completely contrived by the British? She was not guilty of masterminding the rebellion but once the British governance had been replaced, she represented the alternative order that the rebels endorsed.

Her complete command of the situation made her suspect in British eyes for, as they reasoned, she could not have done so without the support of the insurgents. And in this they were right, for the mutineers and the rebels chose her to stand in for them while they moved on. The trust they reposed in her made her one of them. She could not have symbolized both order and its subversion, and the British in Calcutta knew her from her correspondence and her determined stand. They arranged all the pieces of the jigsaw puzzle to construct an irrevocable image of the rebel Rani who had been aggrieved by British measures against her husband's kingdom. She was spirited enough to fight for it and ambitious enough to hope for its recovery. The uprising offered her the opportunity to take charge and consolidate her control. Her friends and allies were all fighting to resist British return. How could she be any different?

Detailed plans of marching upon central India were being made in Calcutta. Jhansi was marked as one of the chief towns that the rebels held and the counter-insurgency forces had to relieve.

8

The Gathering Storm

The British agent's office in Indore was untouched by the uprising, but that was little consolation for the British officials there, for they lived in constant terror that the rebellion might spread. News that filtered in was frightening and invariably exaggerated. Bundelas in Lalitpur under Mardan Singh had reclaimed their lands and their forts. In Jhansi, three local rulers were at war and the countryside had been laid waste. After the massacre, Jhansi was a dreaded town. Robert Hamilton had left for England before the outbreak and was replaced for the time being by Lieutenant-Colonel H.M. Durand as the officiating agent. His observation in October 1857, that Jhansi and the surrounding areas, 'the original source of great evil, were in the blazing state of insurrection',[1] was therefore not unexpected. From Indore, the situation appeared quite desperate. Durand feared that if matters were not corrected soon, the region in the south, more or less peaceful, would be threatened by a similar blaze.

The Rani of Jhansi, though professedly ruling Jhansi on behalf of the British government, was for all practical purposes acting on her own. She was still under a cloud over the killings in Jhansi. On the other hand, her dispute with her neighbours confirmed British suspicion that she was trying to strengthen her rule and that the uprising had fortuitously given her the opportunity that she had been negotiating so hard with the British for—the right to rule over her husband's kingdom. Her regular contact with Mardan Singh did her no good in the eyes of the British for, as we observed before, the Bundela Raja was already a condemned man. The British deputy commissioner A.C. Gordon had no doubts that he was at the centre of the thakurs' rebellion, playing a double game with the British while promising to protect their interests.[2]

Mardan Singh and Lakshmi Bai were in regular touch. When and how this connection was established between the Bundela chief and the Marathi Rani is hard to say. He visited Jhansi to settle her differences with the neighbouring Rajput state of Orchha. Even though both were ostensibly trying to restore peace and order in the hope of returning the region to the British, the latter had stopped listening. Drowned in the mass of people celebrating the end of foreign rule, the Rani of Jhansi and the Raja of Banpur became, in British eyes, inseparable.

Bundelkhand turned out to be a theatre of action for quite another reason. With the fall of each town in the north, rebels crossed the Yamuna and gathered here in the hope of resisting the British army one last time. Tantia Tope was already in Kalpi on the Yamuna in October 1857 and there was a regular traffic of people and soldiers from the north. Reports reaching the British camp said that Lakshmi Bai was employing most of the men who came from the north, mutineers and rebels. Nobody explained the circumstances in which she was forced to do so. Conditions remained unchanged for the rest of the year; while British forces in the north were fighting hard to defeat rebel armies, their government worked overtime to draw up plans and strategies for retrieving regions still lost to them. Bundelkhand fell in the second category. In January 1858, Calcutta was informed, 'The Ranee of Jhansie continues to rule Jhansie. All disaffected and mutinous men that go to Jhansie are kept by the Ranee. Buksheesh Ali, the late Jail Darogah of Jhansie who was at the bottom of the whole mutiny at that place with about 50 sowars and as many footmen (all mutineers) has taken refuge with the Lady—The whole family of the Darogah has been for sometime protected by the Ranee.'[3]

Bundelkhand was completely cut off from British reach and this report was filed from as far as Indore, 300 kilometres away, by A.N.G. Wick, the Bheel agent and political assistant in charge of the Residency. It said, 'Although the news of the total defeat of the rebels at Cawnpore and that of the advance of the British forces has been received by the Ranee she seems to entertain no fears. The Thakoors all persuade her that Europeans are not to be found in India, and by giving about such reports they serve their own ends, and make the Lady pay them thousands of rupees.' It added that Bakshish Ali, the jail daroga, asked Lakshmi Bai if she would fight the British forces. She was categorical that she would return all the districts to the British as soon as the officers returned. Ali and his brother moved south to Banpur and were employed by the Raja.

Mardan Singh was in Jhansi till 6 January, trying to make peace among the warring states. Having failed in his mission, he went back to his town. Unlike the Rani of Jhansi, he had little hope of being pardoned. Two reactions are attributed to him. First, 'If arrested he does not expect to escape hanging. This being his impression, he says it is much better to die than to be hanged by the hands of a sweeper.' Second, 'He seems to be desirous of surrendering should his life be spared, and a promise given to that effect.' Meanwhile, forces of Jhansi and Orchha continued to fight and the Puars in the northern part of Bundelkhand continued to run riot.

The report was confusing and contradictory. Was Bakshish Ali employed by the Rani or was he not? Wick seems to suggest both. The standard British interpretation was that all local Indian rulers at the time of the mutiny, except for the very obviously loyal ones, played what it called a 'double game'. This meant that the rulers wished to be independent and acted for the purpose too, but did not have the courage to say so openly and thus affirmed their loyalty to the British.

Attached to this report was a translation of Lakshmi Bai's letter to the agent in January 1858, by which time Robert Hamilton was back in the saddle. Forwarding both, Hamilton wrote a short covering letter to C.R. Strachey, clarifying that Lakshmi Bai's letter 'reached me by a Hurkara, but to which I have given no reply'.

Thus, Lakshmi Bai received no answer to the letter that she wrote in right earnest some time around the middle of January:

To narrate all the strange and unexpected occurrences that took place during your absence from India, is a painful task. I cannot describe the troubles and hardships I have suffered during this period. Your return to India gives me a new life. I take this opportunity to give you a brief statement of my history. At the time when the British forces mutinied at this place and plundered me of my property, and when the Chiefs of Datia and Orchha commenced their career of coercion and rapine I lost no time in writing to the British Officers... and gave them detailed information as to the state of the country. Some of the bearers of these letters are missing, others being plundered before reaching their destination came back to Jhansi, those that were sent to Agra returning, stated that they succeeded in sending the letters within the Fort of Agra through a Bheestie, that their life being not safe they did not wait for a reply. Major Ellis informed me that my letters were referred to the Officer that was acting for Captain Skene. I got a letter from the Commissioner through the Chief of Gurserai dated 23rd June stating that I should take charge of the district. Another communication from the same officer dated 10th June in reply to my three letters was also received, it referred me to his former communication in which a proclamation putting me in charge of the District was said to have been enclosed. On the 29th July I wrote back in reply stating that I had not received the proclamation.

She described how the rulers of Orchha and Datia invaded and occupied territories in Jhansi, threatening the town itself. She sent copies of the letters from the British commissioner, conferring on her the custody of their district to Nathe Khan, the commander of the Orchha forces, who chose to ignore them. She wrote once more to the commissioner, who promised in a letter dated 19 October that he would personally visit Jhansi to examine the conduct of all, high and low.

She continued:

In the mean time I tried my best by selling my property, taking money on interest, collected a party of men and took steps to protect the city and to meet the invading force. The enemy by firing guns, matchlocks and rockets (bombs) did much mischief, and killed thousands of precious souls, my resources failing I wrote on the 20ᵗʰ September and 19ᵗʰ October for reinforcements. After two months the besieging force retired to a village Koma situated about three miles from Orchha. All the districts that were formerly occupied by the Chief of Orchha are still in his possession. In the same manner Rani of Datia still holds all the districts that fell into her hands, the authorities at Orchha and Datia do not give up these places, the Troops sent to reoccupy them meet with opposition. (sic)

Under these circumstances I can never expect to get rid of these enemies, and to clear myself of heavy debts without the assistance of the British Government.

The Commissioner seems not prepared to move for my help as he states in his letter dated 9ᵗʰ November that the services of the British Troops for the present are required at his quarter. As these short-sighted individuals seem unmindful of the British supremacy and do their best to ruin myself and the whole country, I beg you will give me your support in the best way you can, and thus save myself and the people who are reduced to the last extremity and are not able to cope with the enemy.[4]

Meanwhile, she had Jhansi to protect. Lying strategically at the crossroads where a number of routes criss-crossed, it witnessed constant movement of people, both former soldiers and civilians. Soldiers moved south to Jhansi from Kanpur; they came from Gwalior in the west; others came looking for work knowing that the Rani was at war with her neighbours and would be requiring men. Figures varied: some 400 rebels stayed on since the mutiny in the summer of 1857, while 600 arrived at different times from various destinations. There were around 1,000 soldiers both from the infantry and cavalry.[5] In the midst of this, Lakshmi Bai, after September 1857, was constantly fighting and had to replenish her resources. She built a well-trained cavalry and made arrangements that three to four maunds of gunpowder were produced and stored in the fort every day. In addition to the four old guns, five new ones were manufactured.[6]

These measures had little to do with her affirmation that she did not wish to fight the British. These were defensive steps to save Jhansi. There was near mayhem in the region around Jhansi and it would have been unwise of the Rani not to defend her territory. Some of her former officials wanted her to take a stronger stand against the British. Lakshmi Bai refused and asked them to leave. They went west to Datia and found alternative employment. But she continued to keep in contact with Mardan Singh. Late in January, a son was born to the Raja and Lakshmi Bai sent jewellery and clothes as presents for the newborn through the hands of her trusted servant.[7]

What began to disturb her from the end of 1857 was the utter silence of the British government to all her appeals and letters. She waited till Robert Hamilton returned; after all, she had met him several times and they were on fairly friendly terms. But when he did not respond either, Lakshmi Bai began to fear the worst: that the British did not believe her. In their strict demarcation of 'those for and against the State', despite her best intentions, she feared she would be placed in the second category. She sent her lawyer, Bhaia Dewan, to the British commissioner in Sagar. 'It is given out that should this Wakeel who has gone towards Seepree be treated kindly, the Ranee will in no way oppose the British forces. She will pay obedience to our Government and return all the districts now in her possession while on the contrary should the British officer show displeasure she will fight to the last.'

Something else was happening in Bundelkhand completely outside Lakshmi Bai's control and which had no connection with the queen. The town of Kalpi in Jalaun, overlooking the Yamuna, was emerging as the alternate centre of resistance from the time Tantia Tope moved there in October 1857. The chiefs of other states in Bundelkhand, except Jhansi, and leaders of the mutiny now began a resolute drive to mobilize support and galvanize defiance one last time in the south after Delhi and Kanpur were taken by British counter-insurgency forces.

From the end of 1857, there began a frequent exchange of letters, notices and proclamations. They reached Jhansi, of course, and even though none were addressed to the Rani, they caused her some consternation. For the language used was very provocative. The Nawab of Banda wrote to the rulers of the surrounding states of Shahgarh, Chattarpur, Rewa, Bijairaghogarh and to Nana Sahib. His letter to the Raja of Shahgarh was fairly representative of the nature and purpose of letters exchanged:

After expressing my desire to see and consult with you, which is so intense that the pen cannot describe, I have to state that after the destruction and flight of the infidels who were enemies to the religion and customs of every one, in and from

> *almost all the towns, the Emperor's rule has, by
> divine mercy, been established and several Princes
> have declared themselves for the Emperor, and
> fought memorably to protect their religion and
> destroy the enemy. Maharajah Sreemunt Nana
> Sahib Bahadoor began the praiseworthy act; and
> though evil tidings have lately been received, still
> the Sreemunt Sahib Bahadoor aforesaid has taken
> courage and is reported to drive away the enemy.*[8]

In the same series of letters was his mail seeking help from
the Nana Sahib:

> *After paying my respects and obeisance, I beg to
> inform you, that some time ago I forwarded to
> you a letter by the hands of the trustworthy and
> confidential Madho Rao Punth, informing you the
> state of affairs here, and requesting you to send
> troops, Artillery, Ammunition and money, of which
> I have not been honoured with an answer,
> notwithstanding the lapse of a long time. Now the
> real fact is that this Government was supported
> only by pension, which has now ceased and the
> District of Banda being in the centre surrounded
> on all sides by the territories of the Bundelas,
> troops and money are necessary to retain
> possession of it. But this Government is in want
> of both. The Bundelas have accordingly surrounded
> the District and some have advanced with their
> troops to a short distance from this, I am unable
> to drive them away owing to want of means. If
> now, you send me assistance agreeably to my
> request, I can take possession of the Pergunnahs
> of Banda...which belongs from time immemorial
> to the family of Peshwa (i.e.you)...*[9]

The purpose of these letters sent during December 1857 and January 1858 and the urgency with which they were composed were to persuade anyone unsympathetic to the cause. They were appeals and exhortations regarding the need for action to eliminate the enemy such as the infidel British rulers were. Religion offered a practical and rhetorical device for forging unity among different peoples against a common adversary.

From January 1858, these letters became more urgent and more frequent as frenetic activities were afoot in the rebel camp with different leaders trying to coordinate their efforts. Time was running short. Tantia Tope regularly sent reports to Nana in Bithur, keeping the latter abreast of his plan of action. There was a small state in the district of Hamirpur called Chirkhari whose ruler remained staunchly in favour of the British government. Tantia wrote, 'The Rajah does not wish to side with us, as he relies very much on the strength of the English.'[10] He decided to invade the fort of Chirkhari so that when British forces marched, the rebel army would not be distracted by a possible attack from the rear by an accomplice of the enemy.

The justification for such actions was not one of a struggle for power but safety of faith.[11] Circulars and proclamations urging those undecided to join used the strong, persuasive idiom of religion. It was a war fought to defend the faith of the Muslims and the Hindus that was being defiled by Christian rule:

> 'God has provided you with bodies for the performance of His sacred rites, these are revealed to all by their religion and are stringently enjoined upon all. God has created you, Oh Rajahs, for the destruction of the destroyers of your creed;...'

The circular goes on to list all the transgressions that the English committed as 'perverters (sic) of all men's religion'. Missionary activities had deliberately defiled both Islam and Hinduism as had government measures against practices such as the 'forcible' marriage of widows and abolition of the practice of sati. The British had also prohibited adopted sons from inheriting thrones which are 'the stratagems by which the Europeans deprive us of our thrones and wealth, for instance I refer to Nagpore and Lucknow'.[12] The letter thus urged that Hindus in the name of Ganga, Tulsi and Salikram, and Muslims by the name of God should:

> *join us, in destroying the English for their mutual welfare. Let not this opportunity pass away. Know Oh people! You will never have such another. Since letters are considered to be the half of a meeting it is hoped that the contents of this letter may be considered and replied to.*[13]

This last letter was printed by Moulvie Syed Kutab Shah at the Bahaduri Press in the city of Bareilly and copies of this were circulating in the bazaars of Jhansi from where Hamilton's men picked one up. He sent this with Lakshmi Bai's letter to him and his regular weekly report to Calcutta. When such a letter was archived, it was passed off as Lakshmi Bai's proclamation, whereas she had nothing to do with it.[14] This was certainly not the language that she had ever used in regard to the British. It may have been a mistake or deliberate labelling.

Lakshmi Bai's cause was lost. And she was beginning to realize it.

While the northern towns were in the process of being reoccupied, the British government had to expeditiously make plans of reoccupying Bundelkhand. Calcutta could not afford to spare either soldiers or commanders, and turned to Madras and Bombay. What they required was a competent commander to match the skill and dexterity of John Nicholson, Henry Havelock, James Outram and Colin Campbell. The man called upon to take charge was a fifty-six-year-old general who had recently been honoured in the Crimean War for his astute handling of diplomatic affairs as the British envoy at the French headquarters. Sir Hugh Henry belonged to the well-known Rose family of Strathnairn in Scotland that could trace direct lineage almost uninterrupted for 600 years. And in all these years, the family preserved the tradition of calling their first-born son Hugh. Rose started his career in the army at the age of nineteen and was soon after posted in the East and served equally well as a military commander and a shrewd diplomat in such sensitive areas as Syria and Turkey. He was selected now for India for his experience in balancing military task with tact and sensitivity.

Hugh Rose reached Bombay on 19 September 1857 and immediately started working on the operations in central India. He had to march from Bombay in the west, right across the entire stretch from Indore to Kalpi, defeating rebel forces and reaffirming British rule on the way. Once Bundelkhand was reoccupied, Rose would cross the Jamuna and meet with the rest of the British forces in Kanpur. He was to command a division that was named Central India Field Force with two brigades, the infantry from Bombay under Brigadier C.S. Stuart and the 14th Light Dragoons under Brigadier Steuart stationed in Sehore. The plan was that while Hugh Rose marched from the south-west, a corresponding division from Madras commanded by Brigadier General Whitlock would start out from Jabalpur and march east towards Banda to set up links with eastern Bundelkhand and Allahabad. Rose formally took office on 17 December 1857 in Mhow, the small military town that was to serve as his headquarters.[15]

Once in Mhow, General Rose received his first detailed briefing on the situation in Bundelkhand. The news was grim. Mutineers and rebels were strongly entrenched in scattered pockets all the way north. A wide expanse of rugged, uneven territory, with hill forts, offered perfect cover for local insurgents. Soldiers of the 31st Native Infantry had mutinied in Jabalpur, the capital of the Sagar and Narmada division. Just a little north, Sagar, the town that stood close to the southern borders of Bundelkhand, was surrounded by armed thakurs, and Major Erskine with a handful of loyal soldiers was finding it very difficult to hold on. Lalitpur and its environs were under the Bundela Rajputs. And finally, there was Jhansi— regarding which reports were contradictory.

The initial plan was that General Whitlock would relieve Sagar while Rose marched straight to Lalitpur and then to Kalpi but Rose calculated that it would be another two months before the Madras contingent arrived and Sagar could not be left undefended. He therefore decided to detour, march a little to the east and rescue Sagar.

Hugh Rose left Mhow on 6 January 1858 and reached Sehore from where, leading the second brigade, he started on the 16th towards his first destination—Sagar. Sir Robert Hamilton accompanied him. Forty kilometres west of Sagar on the Bhopal road, which Rose had to follow, was a village called Rahatgarh, overlooking the river Bina. South-west of the town stood a hill surrounded by thick forest. Over the sharp incline of the hill was built the fort of Rahatgarh that had suddenly come to life after some years of being abandoned. In 1857, the Nawab of Amapani had occupied the fort with the assistance of the neighbouring peasants and thakurs. This is where Rose made his first assault.

The men protecting the fort had no doubt about the difficult battle ahead. Sufficient food to provide for more than a thousand men and women for a year had been stored inside it.[16] British forces laid siege to the fort. In a strategic move, Mardan Singh attacked the British force from behind. The Bundela chief foreclosed the option of reconciliation for he was convinced that the British would never condone him. The battle lasted three days and the fort was eventually forced to surrender to the British army. The rebel forces now took a stand across the river Bina in the midst of a thick forest. They were chiefly Afghan and Pathan mercenaries led by Mardan Singh. The British defeated this resistance rather easily. Moving a little to the east, Rose occupied Sagar on 4 February.[17]

The next stop for Hugh Rose was Jhansi, and he now concentrated his energies on marching there. On the way, he received news that some rebels had gathered in the fort of Garhakota, between the rivers Betwa and Dhasan. He overtook the fort on 15 February and drove the rebels up north.[18] The army returned to Sagar on 17 February and halted for four days to gather replenishments for what threatened to be a difficult campaign with the impending onset of summer in central India. Major Boileau and some sappers and miners were kept behind at Garhakota.

This was Rose's strategy. He made sure that there was a contingent of British forces at all the small forts that his army conquered, so that the rebels would not recapture them and disrupt British links with headquarters.

Just as soon as the British forces marched from Sagar for Jhansi, large rockets were seen to shoot up into the dark sky from the centre of the city. 'The enemy had evidently had their spies in our camp, who were now telegraphing the departure of our troops to their friends north of us,' recalled Thomas Lowe, the biographer of Rose's campaign.[19]

The crucial factor in the counter-insurgency campaign was to keep the channel of communications open so that

Rose would have proper information on rebel strength, their entrenched positions and their weaker spots. News from Jhansi was becoming more and more difficult to gather since the town was completely cut off. After every battle and each setback, soldiers moved north, perhaps to go to Kalpi, but Jhansi was invariably their first halt. Indian officials were now filing news from Datia and Orchha. They could not get any closer to Jhansi. The courts of Datia and Orchha were, relatively speaking, bereft of rebel forces, while Jhansi was swamped and Rani Lakshmi Bai lost in the crowd of mutineers and rebels.

None of this escaped the Rani's calculations. She was acutely aware of just how exposed her situation was. She received regular intelligence of the battlefields in the south. This was perhaps one of the most difficult times that she had had to face and the test of her leadership depended on just how well she coped. Orchha troops were still encamped in Mau-Ranipur and had to be driven back to their country. One of the Rani's trusted servants came back with the news that Mardan Singh was defeated and possibly injured during the blockade of Rahatgarh. The envoy she sent to Sagar to meet the British commissioner had still not returned. Before she could garner her resources, soldiers poured into town, driving the residents into a state of panic. Jhansi could not afford to let go of her people, least of all the merchants and the bankers. And yet she was finding it increasingly difficult to hold them back. A large contingent of soldiers waited outside the city in early February.[20] The figures, as always, varied from 500 to 2,000. Lakshmi Bai was still uncertain about what the British made of her claims that she was ruling in their interests. If they did not believe her, then she would have to fight. She was astute enough to realize how impossible the challenge of confronting British forces was going to be. Therefore, till February, she continued to 'profess' that she did not intend to fight the British.[21] This, however, did not stop her from making preparations. She ordered six guns to be manufactured and saltpetre brought from Gwalior. Eight gunners of the former Morar regiment were specially called in from Kalpi to take charge of the artillery and to supervise the production of cannon balls. Given her close association with forces in Kalpi, Lakshmi Bai was unlikely to make a case for herself.

Meanwhile, the Rani closely watched every move of the British army. She called her close confidants for discussions. Her immediate circle included her father Mama Sahib, as he was called in court, Diwan Lakshman Singh and his son Gangadhar Singh, Kashinath Hari, Lalu Bakshi, Diwan Jawahar Singh and Raghunath Singh, the commanders of her army and a few thakurs of the neighbouring estates. They chalked out a plan of action and the strategy of defence for the town of Jhansi.

The use of artillery was to be the best means of defence for the fort and large amounts of money and efforts were spent on the manufacture of new guns, maintenance of old guns and restoration of disused ones. Raghunath Singh reported that the fort accumulated enough gunpowder to last three months of battle. Lakshmi Bai began to train her women attendants to operate guns. Even if they were not engaged in the front, they would be indispensable as back-up support. She confided this to Raghunath Singh.[22] Training and practice started in right earnest. She also asked her men to gather sufficient food grains.

Lalu Bakshi was sent to Banpur with 2,000 men and two guns for providing succour to the Bundela chief.[23] Meanwhile, news kept pouring in about the British march and British success.

Lakshmi Bai was miserably alone and undecided. Most of her immediate advisers wanted her to fight, but she was not convinced. One of her early advisers, lawyer Ayodhya Prasad, who was the chief officer liaising between Lakshmi Bai and the British officials, had retired and was settled in Gwalior. Lakshmi Bai now sent word to him, requesting him to come to Jhansi. He refused, replying that Lakshmi Bai was following the advice of a council of which he did not approve. He was staunchly in favour of supporting the British.

The Rani was left all on her own. All the intelligence reports that Rose received said that the Rani was making every preparation to resist the British. All she was doing actually, even as late as February 1858, was trying to keep her Jhansi from being invaded by the Orchha troops and the town slipping into complete chaos.[24] It was alleged that Lakshmi Bai always provided for the rebel soldiers who escaped the battlefield and moved north. This signified that she was in sympathy with them. But what could she have done?[25] If she refused them, she would earn their ire, in addition to having the Orchha troops breathing down her back. What she feared most was that if she did not supply them with food, they would go on a rampage of the town. She could not let that happen to her people and her home. So she made the best of a bad situation. She let those who wanted to move north continue while others she recruited for her own security. British intelligence reports filed from February 1858 interpreted the Rani's actions as those of a rebel determined to resist. One dated 14 February said that there was going to be a great gathering in Kalpi under the leadership of Nana Sahib. 'Jhansee is supposed to be under the Peshwa and every one going to join him passes through that place without molestation and is furnished with supplies.'

Logically, the first part of the statement cannot be deduced from the second. Not resisting rebel forces did not make the Rani a rebel herself. Nor did it make Jhansi a part of the Nana's dominion. The weekly narrative on the Jhansi subdivision compiled in Allahabad also dated 14 February was short and succinct:

> Sir R.N.C. Hamilton has forwarded a translation of a letter from the rebel Ranee of Jhansi professing her loyalty in general terms. Having regard to the part which the Ranee has played it is not the intention of the Governor General to notice this letter at present.[26]

Ganesh Lal, the Indian superintendent based temporarily in Datia, described the Rani's actions on February 1858:

> The Baee of Jhansi no doubt is preparing herself to fight against us. She has filled the Jhansi fort with supplies, ammunition, good large old and newly-made guns etc. She is very bold since the return of Tehree forces from Jhansi without success. She is clearing and cutting down all the trees etc. around the fort and around the walls of the town. I think these, her preparations, will become of very great use to us but I am sorry that the notorious woman does not allow a single soul of the poor subjects to go out and therefore all of them will suffer for nothing. The troops here, about 2,000 men with four guns, have been made to station outside the wall of Duttiah town. I do not place much faith in many of them as they are connected with some others who are employed in Jhansi; however, the old army and their officers are fit to place confidence.[27]

Lakshmi Bai was now condemned as the notorious woman and the rebel.

About the same time, a proclamation issued in the name of the Peshwa began making its rounds of the region. 'The Chief of Chirkhari did not come to terms with this government nor did he embrace the course of religion, that infidel having no regard for religion is prepared to fight.'[28] Such pronouncements gave a religious rationale to rebel actions, thereby not only consecrating them but by the same argument making supporters of the British cause religious and moral dissenters. 'The Chief sides with the English against the supporters of faith. Therefore, he declared that everyone should consider him as an English man and send him to hell.' There was little choice in this; either they had to be for the faith or against it.

It is doubtful if Lakshmi Bai could hope to negotiate any halfway house. She concentrated instead on building up her strength for the impending contest with Orchha. She sent troops and guns to Mau-Ranipur and asked the residents of Jhansi for contributions towards meeting the expenses for the protection of their town.[29] Gunpowder continued to be heaped and stored in the fort in huge quantities.[30]

In the first week of March, Jhansi troops were eventually able to uproot the Orchha army occupying Burwa Sagar. The report that was officially sent ran as follows: 'Orcha is besieged by the Jhansi rebels, so is Burwa Sagar. The Orcha or Tehree troops were completely defeated at Mau-Ranipur, losing great many men, all ammunition supplies... The rebels burn and plunder villages in the Tehree districts and intend to take all the principal forts. Deserters from Shahgurh and Banpur, and mutinous sowars and sepoys with guns daily join these rebels. Some insurgents are coming from Chirkhari.'[31]

All British reports carried the datelines Datia or Orchha, which were friendly states. In her action against the invaders of Burwa Sagar, Lakshmi Bai had in reality taken on a British ally.

9

Desperate Manoeuvres

Lakshmi Bai chose to ignore the gathering storm and instead concentrated on giving her people confidence and a sense of normalcy and routine. In keeping with royal traditions, she celebrated her army's victory in Mau-Ranipur by firing a five-gun salute in the city. But the battle, which was little more than a skirmish, was not enough to obscure the imminent danger. Some not-so-brave men packed their belongings and left with their family for the safer refuge of Gwalior, where the Scindia was an unwavering supporter of the British. Lakshmi Bai now tried hard to stop people from being afraid, for widespread alarm was the last thing that the town could afford. Instead, she decided to divert the attention of her people by organizing the 'haldi-kumkum' ceremony.

This was indeed a masterstroke in political tactics. For the ordinary residents, the times seemed to be normal, with the Rani in charge. Haldi-kumkum, or 'turmeric-vermilion', was an annual ritual that all married Marathi women followed in spring. Lakshmi Bai decided to organize the ceremony in the royal palace inside the fort rather lavishly.

On a Friday in early March, married women from all castes and communities were invited to the fort. From two in the afternoon till nine at night, hundreds of women came for the offering. One hundred women were engaged to distribute turmeric, vermilion powder, flowers, sandalwood paste, sweets, and in small silver bowls, soaked gram, betel leaves and nuts, all symbolic of good fortune to women and long lives to their husbands. Huge quantities of flowers and sweets were given away and women dressed in their finery forgot they were living in uncertain times. The rich flaunted their expensive palanquins while the humble came to admire them. In the royal court, a tall throne measuring as high as the ceiling was built to instal the image of 'Gauri', the goddess of beauty, as her loving subjects called her. Steps leading to her throne were filled with gifts and the best samples of Jhansi's arts and crafts.[1] It was a huge public spectacle staged for the political intent of assuring people that things were fine, and just as they should be.

Festivities over, the Rani returned to her responsibility, which now was to keep vigilant. Villagers were asked to light a fire to indicate the route that the British army was taking. Lowe described what it looked like, 'A mile or two ahead of our force, on an elevated piece of ground, a bright beacon was blazing out and then some seven or eight hundred yards in advance of another of this another burst up in flames, and as the column marched on and on, another and another bright fire shone out of the dark masses of jungle on the different hills, first on our right, then on our left, until the morning rendered them useless.'[2] The tension on both sides was palpable.

Unknown to Lakshmi Bai, Robert Hamilton sent a brief report on the situation in Bundelkhand:

The rebels are now occupying Mau Raneepur, and Burwa Saugor, and have abandoned on Orchha itself, after burning five villages and levying exactions on the people. Their object now seems plunder, and they have burnt Chirkharee, and demanded 5 lacs from the Rajah, who is besieged in his Fort. They have sent a demand of 7 lacs from Chutterpore where they threaten next to visit.[3]

Lakshmi Bai's forces, who drove the invaders away, became interchangeable with Tantia Tope's army besieging Chirkhari.

Chirkhari was attacked in late February and by the evening of 1 March, the fort to all purposes had capitulated to the rebel force. The victorious soldiers from here moved to the south to assist those braving British guns.

Hugh Rose halted at Sagar for four days to repair his guns. This gave Mardan Singh, the Raja of Banpur and his ally the Raja of the neighbouring state of Shahgarh something of a breather and some time to plan alternate strategies. They gathered their Bundela men and took up strong positions along the entire stretch from Sagar to Jhansi. The terrain was difficult and offered natural cover in the low hills and scattered forests. Conflicting reports about Mardan Singh's moves came trickling in the British camp. 'The Raja of Banpore is at Palee; regrets of what he has done—extremely desirous of being pardoned, being driven to despair, resolves to fight.'[4] The British, however, chose to ignore this message. Meanwhile, a feverish movement of soldiers and men in the region south of Jhansi threw major challenges to Hugh Rose. For even if they occupied the rebel forts, they were unable to prevent the soldiers from escaping and scattering.

After Garhakota, Rose learnt that the march was going to be tough because of the passes and narrow passageways that ran between low hills. The hills that rose straight from the ground blocked the view of those trying to cross them while providing excellent cover to the others trying to prevent them from doing so. All the way north from Garhakota to Jhansi was such a hilly region, dotted with passes and small forts. At the centre was the somewhat larger town and fort of Malthone. There were two most difficult passes, one at Narhat just below Malthone and the other at Madanpur.

Hugh Rose routed the rebel army by a cunning stratagem. He was informed that the rebels were concentrating their defence over the pass of Narhat. There were close to 10,000 men under Mardan Singh. Rose decided to feign an attack on Narhat while the main army fought through the relatively weaker defence over Malthone. The plan worked exactly as he had intended. Even though they had some initial success, the men were beaten back and the British army set out for Banpur on their way up north.

They started on the morning of 9 March. 'The villages we now passed were all deserted,' Lowe recalled, 'a few half-starved oxen and pariah dogs appeared their sole occupants... The town of Baunpore was almost as deserted as the villages we had passed on our march.'[5] Rose reached Banpur on 10 March and Robert Hamilton read out proclamations that the territories of the 'Rebel Rajahs' of Shahgarh and Banpur were confiscated.[6] A little to the east, the first brigade of the Central India Field Force under the command of Brigadier C.A. Stuart captured the fort of Chanderi on 17 March.

It did not take long for news to travel that despite their best efforts, the Rajas of Banpur and Shahgarh were defeated and that the British army had breached the defences over the passes of Narhat and Madanpur. The defending rebel army scattered; some arrived at Jhansi, beaten and dispirited, some went north to join Tantia Tope.

Lakshmi Bai's reactions at this time became crucial. All British sources say that even then the Rani did not wish to fight the British and wanted to settle for peace instead. Indian historians dismiss this and state that she was determined to resist the counter-insurgency forces and had thus begun making preparations in earnest. Her last letter to the British agent, however, was testimony to her circumspection rather than bravado.

The first two weeks of March proved to be the real test of Lakshmi Bai's judgement and ability to take charge. She tried her best to stop the residents of Jhansi from panicking and made announcements in the town that no one should leave. The gates were specially guarded to prevent people from moving out. But what could not be prevented was news and reports of wars all around. They were mixed. The Orchha troops had been beaten back; the Raja of Chirkhari defeated; and the army of the Rajas of Banpur and Shahgarh routed. All three battles were fought for different purposes and with different actors. Jhansi had been invaded by Orchha and her actions against the latter were in defence. The rebel army from Kalpi conquered Chirkhari for being a British ally. It was an offensive plan of action in which Lakshmi Bai was not a participant. In a recent account of the uprising, her actions against Orchha have also been interpreted as that against an ally of the British state. Contemporary British officials must have thought the same. It is puzzling why they were so keen not to believe her and equally eager to prove her guilty of rebellion. Her only fault was that she was unable and unwilling to stop soldiers stopping by in Jhansi.

By March, the total strength of armed fighters in Jhansi had grown substantially to an estimated 15,000. There were 6,000 men under the thakurs, 1,200 men led by Munsaram Gujar, 800 under Udit Singh at Pichore, 1,000 men at different outposts, 2,000 soldiers defending the city and 4,000 that had fought the Orchha army at Burwa Sagar. There were twelve old guns, both small and large, that had been repaired and made functional and eight new ones made, making a total of twenty. Four of these were still in Burwa Sagar but the rest were in the town.[7]

Soon after the debacle at Madanpur Pass, Khurshed Ali, the son of Bakshish Ali and the eldest son of Mardan Singh, arrived at Jhansi with the information that British troops had invaded Chanderi. Soldiers who fought for the Rajas of Banpur and Shahgarh against Rose's force arrived at Jhansi fuming that the Bundelas had deserted them during the battle over the Madanpur Pass and left them to fight alone. They said they would never take service with the Rajas even if they were paid one rupee per day per person. Despite the Rani's best efforts, this kind of news put the people of the town in great unease.[8]

Lakshmi Bai spent long hours in the court, deliberating and dispensing justice, leaving nothing for the next day.[9] The chief of Banpur sent a letter to the Rani, advising her to make peace with the British. The early victories of Hugh Rose proved the superior strength of his men and arms. The court met again. Kashinath Hari and Lalu Bakshi advised that Jhansi should make peace with the British. Gangadhar Rao, after all, had given the state of Jhansi back to be governed by the British for some time. This was a strong argument and was likely to persuade the Rani.

But Lakshmi Bai's father Mama Sahib and Lakshman Singh's son Gangadhar argued that the kingdom should not be given up easily, since a lot of effort had gone into claiming and defending it.[10] Such disagreements and debates in the court continued into the wee hours of the morning. On the night of 14 March, the court was finally called off at three in the morning, without any agreement. Lalu Bakshi and Kashinath contended, 'The English are masters of the country; no one ever made any thing of fighting with them...Submission will be better.' The counter-argument was, 'Our lost kingdom has been recovered with infinite difficulty; it were now unbecoming to surrender it save upon death in fight.'[11] It was pragmatism versus passion; practical sense against patriotic fervour.[12]

Nothing in the reports disclose what Lakshmi Bai made of these conflicting views. In all likelihood, true to the nature of an astute ruler, she reserved judgement and instead busied herself in preparations for the future. She knew she had very little time. The son of the Raja of Narwar, a small principality in Gwalior state, who had been repulsed by the Gwalior army, arrived in Jhansi on 14 March. Lakshmi Bai supplied him with necessities. He was on his way to Kalpi in order to join Tantia Tope. The following night, Mardan Singh arrived at Jhansi close to midnight with 2,500 cavalry and infantry soldiers. The Rani provided for the Raja's needs and comforts, while his men spread out to the neighbouring villages such as Lohar, Khairar and Babina.[13]

Reports were often inconsistent. Some said that Lakshmi Bai always provided for everyone who passed her town just as she did before; others reported that she had become more wary and quite often asked soldiers to march straight to Kalpi without halting at Jhansi. Meanwhile, Jhansi had to be protected and Lakshmi Bai made all appropriate arrangements. Perhaps she realized that the option of reconciliation was gradually fading. Six guns facing south were placed on the wall surrounding the city and houses that stood on the fringe were ordered to make provisions for accommodating troops when required. Lakshmi Bai continued her regular routine that included vigorous exercise and inspection of her soldiers, both men and women. On one of the routine marches, Lakshmi Bai asked the assembled group if they would fight the British or opt to withdraw. They pledged to fight till death in order to defend their country and their Rani.[14]

To gather together her scattered forces, Lakshmi Bai recalled all her soldiers and commanders. Doolaju and Ganeshju, two thakurs of Kairwa who had been guarding Mau-Ranipur against Orchha, returned to Jhansi with 2,000 soldiers and two guns. Despite these steps, the Rani made sure that she made no move to precipitate confrontation. When the killadar of Talbehat arrived on the evening of 14 March, the Rani asked him to leave at once.

On the eve of the battle with the British, and in the context of a realistic assessment of what the likely outcome would be, officers of the Rani's army demanded that they be paid two months' salary in advance. This was not easy. By March 1858, the treasury was empty as in the past few months there had been practically no collection of revenue and the reserve had been spent. The only source of earnings was what could be raised from the people in the city, which was also why traders and merchants were strictly forbidden to leave.[15] Spies and news-writers were on a round-the-clock vigil to keep the court informed about the movement of British troops. Soldiers took up positions along the city walls; the residents vacated their houses and in some instances even provided for their food and supplies.

Meanwhile, all around Jhansi in the north, west and east, forces were gathering in anticipation of the march of counter-insurgency troops. There were significant numbers of armed men in Gurserai, Mau-Ranipur and Jaitpur. As far as the south was concerned, the whole of the Lalitpur district that Mardan Singh controlled was back under British rule.[16]

On 17 March, the court finally decided that Lakshmi Bai should for one last time try to establish contact with the British through correspondence. It was also decided that Mardan Singh, who had fought the British, and the son of the chief of Narwar, who had rebelled against Gwalior state, an avowed ally of the British, should be asked to leave Jhansi, for their presence would never allow Jhansi and her Rani to prove their neutrality amidst rebellion. The two men had directly or indirectly fought with the British and were deeply implicated in acts of insurgency.

All the above news was described in the intelligence report of 16 March. If it is true, as seems likely, because Mardan Singh did leave Jhansi to join Tantia Tope, then some of Lakshmi Bai's daring was certainly compromised by her hardheaded assessment of the situation. According to the news, Lakshmi Bai wrote a letter addressed to General Hugh Rose and sent it to the agent for being delivered. Her messenger Kishan Prasad wrote back to her from Sagar that he would seek an appointment with Erskine, the British agent, and deliver her letter. Meanwhile, news got around and the owners of houses close to the town wall refused to let soldiers in.[17] The courier returned on 18 March saying that he had handed over the Rani's letter to the agent but the latter had nothing to give him in response.

It did not take long for the information to spread that

the Rani was trying to negotiate peace with the British. Hasan Ali Khan, a rissaldar in command of the cavalry, and one of the former sepoys in the British army, together with his other colleagues, now met the court officials. They said they had taken service with the Rani because they assumed she would fight the British. But if she intended to make peace with them instead, they requested that their arrears of pay be met so that they could move on, for they knew once the British army marched upon Jhansi, these men would stand little chance of being pardoned. One year into the movement, there were little illusions and even less of ideology. Everyone was engaged in working out the best strategy of survival.[18]

As the town waited in apprehension, people defied court orders and started leaving the town. Some of the court officials moved their families and treasure to safer places. There was an estimated 7,000 people left behind in Jhansi, of whom close to half were soldiers and Bundelas. Lakshmi Bai was evidently in a quandary. Her senior advisers counselled that she settle for peace; the soldiers were determined to fight. And the success of British forces so far left no one with any doubts about what the outcome of their invasion of Jhansi was likely to be. As a perceptive and sensitive ruler, Lakshmi Bai could only dread the intensity of British retaliation and how difficult it would be for the people. If she had had thoughts of compromise and peace, they were not those of cowardice but practical judgement.

The second brigade of the Central India Field Force arrived at Simri, one day's march from Jhansi. Activities suddenly had to be hastened and the highest alert sounded. In panic, the kotwal, or chief of police in the town, tried to escape but was arrested by the soldiers and brought back. News arrived that Tantia Tope, leading four companies of about 30,000 men, was heading to defend Jhansi. Kashinath, one of Lakshmi Bai's advisers, felt that the messenger sent with the letter to the British agent should be recalled. The Rani of Jhansi knew she had to prepare for battle.

In the British camp, news of rebels gathering in Jhansi alerted the army that the combat would be intense and difficult. 'The nearer that Force approached, the greater became the interest and excitement, for it was well known to all that the enemy was there in great force, and had made grand preparations for our reception,' recalled J.H. Sylvester.[19] It was also a place where the British men, women and children had been brutally murdered. As Kaye described it, 'hatred to the English name had been illustrated by acts of the most wanton barbarity'.[20] Lakshmi Bai had no chance to prove otherwise. The British army was marching for vengeance. But a slight change in the route may have changed the nature of the battle.

While he was in Sagar, Hugh Rose had drawn up detailed plans for the conquest of Jhansi according to which he was to reach the vicinity of Jhansi by 20 March. He was delayed by one day because the second brigade that invaded Chanderi had still not arrived and the general had to wait lest it required assistance. The same day, Hamilton and Rose received two letters from Calcutta. One was from the Governor General's office and the other from Colin Campbell, the commander-in-chief. Their letters instructed the commanders to divert their course, move east and offer support to the Raja of Chirkhari who was besieged by Tantia Tope's army. It was a political scheme to save an ally and a loyal follower, a move that would offer enticement to the local people to change their outlook towards British rule.

Military circumstances, however, had to override

political stratagem. Rose was encamped only twenty-two kilometres away from Jhansi. 'If he were to retire from Jhansi, the Rani and her people would feel that they had won a moral victory; and 11,000 rebels and mutineers would let loose upon his line of operations and upon that of Whitlock.' Perhaps, Lakshmi Bai would have been given another chance to prove that she was ready to make peace.

But fate had something else in store for her. Despite the order, Hugh Rose in consultation with Robert Hamilton decided to continue with his plans of invading Jhansi for the news he had was that he could never reach in time to relieve Chirkhari. On the other hand, if he attacked Jhansi, Tantia Tope would in all likelihood abandon Chirkhari to come to the Rani's rescue, and the purpose would be served. This proved to be quite prophetic.[21]

The Jhansi court learnt of the advance of the British troops to Simri on 20 March. The next day, Hugh Rose, with the remaining forces joined the second brigade. Meanwhile, a small contingent of cavalry was sent from Simri to survey the surroundings, for Hugh Rose had no proper information on the topography of the town and the fort. The cavalry encountered about 100 armed Bundelas trying to enter the town and cut them all to pieces. The British had arrived.

In a last-ditch effort, the court tried to parley for peace. On the morning of 21 March, as her men spotted stray British soldiers in red and blue jackets, the queen and her advisers sat down to write what was to be the last letter to the British agent, stating that they were ready to start talks. Even before the letter could be concluded, the first sign of siege appeared as British troops surrounded the fort. Gangadhar Bhaia ordered fire. The battle of Jhansi began.

10

The Siege

After marching through large stretches of barren, uncultivated land, the British found Jhansi a welcome contrast. A sprawling town, manicured and orderly, it was like a haven amidst the wild. From a far distance, the fort stood tall and imposing, with the sheer drop of cliff on its north-western side. The wall encircling the town showed signs of being recently repaired. Guns were mounted on this outer wall and several were positioned on the inner wall of the fort. One round tower that the British called a 'white turret' inside the fort seemed as if it had also been restored, as the whitewash was in stark contrast to the other erections along the ramparts.[1]

Hugh Rose had no detailed description of the fort or the town of Jhansi and was forced to send out several exploratory marches to determine the strength of rebel defences. This took a couple of days, in which a thorough study of the fort was also made. The strong outer rampart made of granite that fell sharply on the west and the south looked as if it would stand up to flank fire. The wall on the south ended in a mound. Apart from the guns on the wall, a ditch twelve feet deep and fifteen feet broad made of solid brickwork protected the fort. On the eastern side of the fort was the city, sprawling and busy.

There was no easy way to breach the fort. A wall that measured six to twelve feet in thickness and eighteen to thirty feet in height encircled the city. Rose sent two flying camps of cavalry under Majors Scudamore and Gall to keep watch on the town gates and to stop if possible all movement to and from it. After several inspections, the British concluded that the best strategy would be to first capture the mound that overlooked the southern side of the fort. They concentrated their assault on the knoll in order to dislodge the rebel forces there and make the first breach. They had to wait till 25 March for the 1st Brigade to arrive from Chanderi. Meanwhile, firing on the mound was commenced.

The Rani's forces retaliated with regular firing both from the white turret and the southern gate. It was evident that the guns were under a first-rate artillery officer, who had under him at least two companies of well-trained soldiers. The rest of the people, both men and women, served the artillery. The firing was incessant, British forces receiving shot for shot. They were surprised to see the Rani's well-trained women's unit actively working in the batteries and carrying ammunition. From another side, the Bundelas fired under a black banner that flew high against the clear summer sky. Robert Hamilton's estimate was that there were around 10,000 soldiers, Bundelas, hired mercenaries and former sepoys of the Bengal army altogether inside the fort, with thirty to forty guns. There was every indication of a determined and gritty resistance. But they had no post outside the city.[2]

British forces could thus occupy and surround the town. Their strategy was to get as close as possible to the fort and keep firing from the outside till one section was breached—the rest would be easy. They targeted the mound that overlooked the southern part of the town.

The Indian account of these events was somewhat different. It is said that the moment she heard of the defeat of the Rajas' forces at Madanpur, Lakshmi Bai became worried, for she knew it was only a matter of time before the British army would reach Jhansi. She began to prepare for the contingency, every move and each step well thought out.[3] Lakshmi Bai ordered regular prayers and offerings at the Mahalakshmi temple. She wrote to Rao Sahib and Tantia Tope for assistance. 'In this manner, the brave woman, without being afraid, with peace and astuteness was preparing for the battle in the city.' In Godse's version, on reaching the outskirts of Jhansi, Hugh Rose sent a rider with a letter for the Rani. The Diwan brought the letter to Lakshmi Bai, who hastily called her council to read it with her advisers. Rose invited the Rani to come and meet the general in person with eight of her close confidants including Lakshman Rao, Lalu Bakshi and Moropant Tambe. There is no mention of this letter in the accounts of Hamilton, Rose or Pinkney. Godse writes that the letter stated that no one else should accompany them and they should be unarmed. The council was already resolute in its decision to fight the British army. The meeting was simply to decide what the Rani should write in reply.[4]

In a rather theatrical description of the scene, Vrindavan Lal Verma narrates how all the members of her inner circle including landlords and chiefs cried out in one voice: 'We will fight. We will die for our Jhansi and for our Rani.' 'Whatever money and wealth we have we will give them up for the fight for our own land.'[5] Lakshmi Bai sent her reply: 'You don't mention why you have called us nor is there any assurance that there is not going to be a fracas there. According to royal protocol, only Dewan Lakshman Rao will go to meet you in the company of armed guards. I am a woman and it is not possible for me to go. It is your decision after this.'[6]

What followed was the British siege, which began in right earnest from 23 March.[7] News reached the British camp that the Rani was very worried and had moved to underground quarters in Jhansi fort. According to the British account, she refused food and water on the first day of the attack.[8] Four British cavalry units were first sent to clear the town. This proved harder than anticipated, because the soldiers defending it hid behind houses and fired from street corners or unseen positions at the invading army. The British were unable to clear the town. They instead focused on frontal attack. Batteries of British infantry and artillery began their assault. Two eighteen-pounder guns were fired in order to breach the wall of the fort; two ten-inch mortar guns aimed to demolish it; two eight-inch mortars targeted the mound and one eight-inch howitzer was placed over the adjacent wall and the city. Rose identified thirteen rebel batteries in the town and the fort.

The eighteen-pounders proved very effective and the white turret was destroyed in a couple of days. On 28 March, as mortars from the British guns fell inside the fort, five maunds of gunpowder were blown up and the British were informed that about forty men lost their lives. The soldiers in the fort continued to resist till the first crack was made in their defence on 30 March. For eight long days and nights the troops had maintained continuous firing. Just as soon as some damage was done by British fire, it was hastily repaired and shooting resumed. When parapets were wrecked, women were seen fixing them. 'Notwithstanding the damage done to their fort and the works upon the wall, their vigilance and determination to resist abated not an iota; on the contrary, their danger appeared to add to their courage.'[9] The Rani of Jhansi was, according to the British account, seen every evening making her rounds among the soldiers, inspiring them with her presence and words of courage.[10]

The British army would have continued the breach and overtaken the fort on 31 March, but for a diversion.[11]

Hugh Rose had for some time been hearing of Tantia Tope's plans, that he was gathering his army somewhere north-east of Jhansi with the purpose of marching south in aid of the Rani and her besieged army. On 30 March, Hamilton informed Rose that Tantia Tope had reached Burwa Sagar, two kilometres south of the river Betwa, intending to cross the river and attack the British army from the rear the following morning. In order to pre-empt this move, Rose wanted to engage the enemy before it gathered ground, so that the soldiers would have to fight with their backs to the river. He marched the 2nd Brigade east, taking up position on 30 March at the fords that overlooked the river and the point at which Tantia Tope would have to cross the river. He did not cross that day or night. Rose returned to the camp in Jhansi, leaving outposts to keep vigil on the fords. On the evening of 31 March, Tantia Tope's forces were seen crossing the Betwa in large numbers. They encamped on the western bank of the river at sundown and lit a large fire, an ingenious way of sending messages to the Rani's forces. The signal was rightly read and responded to with 'salvos from all the Batteries of the fort and city, and shouts of joy from their defenders'.[12] Tantia Tope acted on definite information, which by Rose's admission was not wrong, that British forces were scattered and engaged in separate sieges all around the town and the fort. Tantia Tope hoped to destroy the camp and thus deprive the British of their base.[13]

The battle at Burwa Sagar commenced at 6 am on 1 April, with heavy firing from Tantia Tope's camp. Hugh Rose planned to attack them at the point of their weakest defence as he had always done, but this time he found they had covered the ground well. Intense fighting took place for the entire day, Tantia Tope and Hugh Rose alternately overpowering one another. In the end, the better strategy of the British and the adroitness and initiative of their junior officers forced Tantia Tope to retreat. The action took place over an area that stretched twenty-two kilometres in length and six kilometres in width. Despite a valiant fight, Tantia Tope lost up to eighteen guns and a few hundred men. He was forced to retreat in two divisions, one moving towards Kalpi in the north and the other to Mau-Ranipur down south-east.[14]

Contrary to what the army in the fort had hoped, the siege of the town and fort of Jhansi continued even while action took place at Burwa Sagar. The rearguard action was not strong enough to weaken the British assault. On 2 April, there was a lull. Rose made sure that in the midst of all distractions, telegraph connections between Jhansi and the surrounding areas were set up, to be constantly updated on the activities and movements in the rebel camps scattered across the region.

All through the night of 2 April, British forces prepared for the attack on the town of Jhansi that was to be both by escalades and frontal strike from the twenty-four-pound howitzer positioned to overlook the fort. On 3 April, three main assaults were conducted on the ramparts of the town, on the left at the southern wall, in the centre and the right by scaling the wall. The British made their first breach by breaking down the postern gate, but they found the entrance blocked. They were able to enter eventually through a small opening. The right attack was not successful, but the 3rd Bombay Sappers entered town from the breach made in the centre. Once inside the town, British units pressed on through the streets, striking back at the defenders hidden in the houses.[15] The besieged force hurled missiles, earthen pots filled with powder and logs of wood at the invaders. What followed was a furious battle that raged 'from street to street, from house to house, and from room to room and the defenders fought like tigers'.[16]

One strong battery defended the Rani's palace. They were overtaken by the 3rd Hyderabad and European contingent. Located in a crowded part of the town, the palace was guarded by men who took positions in the neighbouring houses and kept up continuous firing. 'When even the courtyard of the palace was reached, it became apparent that resistance had only begun. Every room was savagely contested... From chamber to chamber the enemy were driven at the point of bayonet. At length the palace was gained. The opposition, however, had not even then entirely ceased. Two hours later it was discovered that fifty men of the Rani's bodyguard still held the stables attached to the building.'[17] While the battle over the palace was on in full force, Rose took possession over a large part of the town. It was a hard fight, often hand-to-hand combat, fought with desperation on both sides.

The British occupation of the Rani's palace, so bravely defended, pretty much determined the final outcome of this hard combat. The spirit and resolve of the men fighting to defend their land flagged, and they knew it was only a matter of time before they would have to give up. An English Union Jack made of silk was found in the Rani's palace. It had once been flown high and with pride by the Maharaja of Jhansi Ramchandra Rao after seeking a special favour from the British to do so. Now soldiers of the counter-insurgency force hoisted the flag over the palace as a sign that the British power over Jhansi had been restored.

The loss of the palace and the town was a great blow to the morale of the people fighting so hard to protect them. In the tradition of a true Indian warrior, a soldier in the Rani's army cut down his wife and then killed himself. Two other mercenary soldiers also killed themselves and a woman who was with them by jumping into the well.[18] Death was the honourable choice preferred over the possibility of falling into the hands of the conquerors.

The army in the fort, however, was not ready to give up. It attacked a British cavalry unit on the west of the fort. Rose immediately sent reinforcements from the camp. Even though beaten back, the Rani's men occupied the high rocky hills adjoining the fort. The strategy was to cause a diversion for the British army. It was an intensely fought battle over the ridge of the hill and the British lost many soldiers including a young lieutenant.

It was a long and hard day of battle that ended with the British making some more inroads.

The next day, Brigadier Stuart and General Rose set out to occupy the rest of the city. Major Gall of the flying camp scaled one of the gates of the fort and captured the gun, making their first breach. The defenders fought hard and fought bravely. They barricaded houses in the city, gardens and woods around it. The British stormed houses but the Indian soldiers continued to fight from the passages and vaults that lay hidden inside. The British won eventually, though not without suffering casualties. It was another long day of determined fighting, often hand-to-hand.

Godse describes the scene inside the town in those fourteen days. The British army was seen advancing and tents appeared, dotting the horizon. Spies brought back news that, compared to the number of tents, there were few people visible. From the time the British army appeared, Lakshmi Bai began inspecting the defence arrangements regularly. Jhansi's strength lay in her strong fortification that ran around the town and her fort. Lakshmi Bai personally went around the skirting walls, arranged and improvised security measures.

The day after the British army arrived, a small unit of cavalry tried to make a breach in the wall. The intrepid artillery of the Rani's army beat them back. There was only one place along the wall of the city that could be breached but very few residents knew about this. Someone among them must have sneaked this bit of information to the British because the third day, the invading army found the opportunity to set up a barricade. In the early hours of the morning, when it was still dark, British guns began firing. It was the fourth day and battle began in right earnest. Lakshmi Bai was now extremely upset. What the British informers said was not true for she was not distressed at the thought of fighting but suffered because of betrayal. She now began working around the clock, keeping vigil and personally overseeing measures. In the later popular narratives about the Rani, including Verma's novel, the traitor was identified as Dulhaju, one of her advisers.[19]

The British fired constantly and relentlessly on houses and shelters of the people who turned helpless victims of the wrath and fury of the conquering army. Cannon balls fell, houses crumbled, men, women and children died buried in the rubble. Lakshmi Bai arranged for water to douse fires but they were far too many and too frequent.

She, however, was able to provide alternative shelter and food for those rendered homeless by the devastation. At night, the cannon balls soaring up in the sky made an awesome sight and, as people watched in wonder and trepidation, fell over them.

The defenders knew that the British had very powerful field glasses through which they could keep a constant watch on what was happening inside the town and even in the fort. They targeted the Shankar temple because it was next to the well from where everyone inside the fort collected their water. Several men and women gathered to collect water died when firing started. Only after the gunmen at the fort retaliated by firing at the British did they stop targeting the water source. On the seventh day, just after noon, the arms factory opposite the palace went up in flames as a huge cannon ball fell on it. The whole fort was shrouded in a cloud of smoke. When it cleared, they found thirty men and eight women lying dead.

The eighth day of battle was very intense. There was continuous firing day and night and the noise and confusion inside the town became unbearable. People could hear nothing but cannon fire and see nothing but smoke. Unknown to the British scribe, it was Lakshmi Bai who kept constant watch and in the fashion of a true commander, looked into every detail. Wherever she found resistance slacking, she made alternative provisions immediately. She was somewhat distraught because no relief army had till then come from Rao Sahib and Tantia Tope. Her council advised her that to make sure assistance would come soon, she should propitiate the gods and the Brahmins. A hundred Brahmins should be asked to pray at the Ganesh temple. Arrangements were immediately made for what would be the last religious rite performed by Rani Lakshmi Bai in Jhansi. After the ceremony, an exhausted Lakshmi Bai lay down for a while in the royal hall of the palace. In her dream she saw a young, fair woman with a high forehead, covered in pearls, and wearing a red sari, throwing cannon balls till her palms turned black. She turned to Lakshmi Bai and said, 'Even I am throwing cannon balls.' The Rani woke up with a start and told everyone around her about the dream, about how Durga, the goddess, was on their side.[20]

Instead of losing heart, the commanders gritted their resolve to fight harder for Jhansi after Tantia Tope's defeat. She had never been dependent on the Peshwa's forces, nor would she need them now, the Rani assured them, and led them to fight with fresh energy and fortitude. Lakshmi Bai was now truly the commander-in-chief of Jhansi.

The town of Jhansi was encircled by a wall with several gates, the principal eight being Orchha, Datia, Sainwar, Bhander, Lakshmi, Khanderao, Onao and Sagar.[21] Cannons were placed on the ramparts of the fort and the outer walls. Lakshmi Bai ordered that there should be constant vigil day and night by commanders. At night, to give them some relief, women took over. Sometimes, they even fought side by side all through the night and a good part of the day.[22]

It was the twelfth day of the British attack. Lakshmi Bai had not rested in the past couple of days from her constant watchfulness, stirring men and comforting women inside the fort. Her artillerymen were doing excellent work. Then she was told that a few guns had suddenly fallen silent. She immediately sent special rewards for the artillery soldiers and promptly, the guns started booming again. She inspired by her example and her idealism, and by incentive. All the while, British firing continued relentlessly. Despite her best efforts, Lakshmi Bai could not prevent people from panicking. There was a great deal of fear and much consternation.

That evening, there was suddenly a loud explosion inside the fort. As people ran to find out what the matter was, they discovered that the large house decorated and covered with glass and mirrors had been shattered. Four men were killed and several injured. The loss of lives and instances of personal tragedy seemed endless. People ran for shelter in the basement of the palace, which appeared to be the only building that could withstand the firing. Godse, who worried about his own safety, recalled that he could not stop admiring Rani Lakshmi Bai for constantly making rounds by day and night. That evening a spy informed the Rani that the British were running out of ammunition and that they intended to withdraw by the end of the following evening. Lakshmi Bai was delighted and after many days was able to sleep with relief.

She was, however, woken up in the middle of the night with the alarming news that the gun placed over the southern rampart had fallen silent and the British forces, taking advantage of that, had succeeded in their first breach. Before long, infantry soldiers scaled the wall of the town. The British entered Jhansi. They opened all the gates to let in more soldiers. Lakshmi Bai was visibly disturbed by the turn of events, but only for a while. She jumped up and, carrying her sword, led the mercenary soldiers out of the fort gates to fight the invading army. A lot of them were killed and the rest retreated. One of her elderly generals, Nana Bhopatkar, advised Lakshmi Bai that she should return to the fort because the British soldiers had started firing from tops of trees and roofs. Her army now returned to the fort and shut the gate.

General mayhem followed as the British soldiers slaughtered indiscriminately, set shops and houses on fire and plundered and destroyed with a passion and frenzy that the residents had never witnessed. The soldiers would storm in, carry away all that was of value and leave. If anyone dared resist them, he was cut down. There were instances when the first set of soldiers took away all valuables and the second lot, not finding anything in the house, killed the owner as an act of vengeance. Nothing of this was ever reported in the official correspondence that Hugh Rose or Robert Hamilton sent to Calcutta, or their admiring biographers recalled later.

Halwaipura, a prosperous neighbourhood, was ablaze in the hot April sun. Lakshmi Bai watched in silent horror as her beloved capital turned into rubble, and men and women wailed in anguish and pain while gunfire continued to spell havoc.

As the Rani, Lakshmi Bai felt responsible for her people's suffering. They were paying for her sins. She called her confidants and said that she wanted everyone to evacuate the fort. She would alone set all the gunpowder on fire in the fort and die so that her capital was saved from further destruction. Nana Bhopatkar counselled her once more. Committing suicide was a crime that would further add to sins and alleviate nothing. If the gods willed the destruction of Jhansi, it was beyond human endeavour to stop it. Instead, she should leave town and join up with the Peshwa in the north.

Lakshmi Bai conceded to his better judgement. She spent the whole day preparing to withdraw. She made sure that all the Brahmins were paid handsomely before being sent off and the rest of the people were evacuated from the fort. Late in the evening, she changed into a pair of trousers and high boots, and tying her ten-year-old adopted son to her back with a dupatta, mounted her favourite white stallion named Sarangi.[23]

The following morning, Rose woke up to rather unexpected news. Lakshmi Bai, the Rani of Jhansi, accompanied by about 300 Afghan mercenaries and twenty-five riders, had escaped from the fort on the night of 4 April. Rose immediately sent detachments of the 14th Light Dragoons and 3rd Light Cavalry after her. They were able to intercept a group of cavalry that had been with the Rani, but Lakshmi Bai and her son got away.[24] A few men of a picket of the 86th Regiment went up to the gate of the fort and found it open. Firing had stopped and there was complete silence. They entered it cautiously and to their surprise found that it was absolutely deserted. Thus, rather unexpectedly, the British gained control over the fort of Jhansi. Brigadier Stuart, his staff, Colonel Lowth and the men of the 86th Regiment marched from the palace to the fort, walking up the pathway leading to the gate, looking at the wrecked town lying silent below. 'They then planted the colours in the Queen's name, with three times three, on the square tower.'[25]

The whole of 5 April was spent in occupying the fort of Jhansi, the ultimate bastion of Lakshmi Bai's strength. The estimated loss of lives at the end of that day was around 3,000 men fighting on Lakshmi Bai's side and 229 on the British. The siege of Jhansi was the longest and the hardest in Hugh Rose's campaign, even though the concentration of forces here was less than in later battles.

11

The Chase to the End

When facts are fuzzy, stories are born and legends grow. The sensational escape lent itself to multiple renditions. The most popular Indian version that is still narrated to tourists visiting the fort is that Lakshmi Bai tied young Damodar Rao to her back, jumped from a particular spot in the fort and fled. A plaque fixed to the wall indicates the exact location. The spot overlooks the palace and the crowded town. It would have been indeed a very imprudent measure to jump from there for she was bound to land in the most visible and congested neighbourhood. Om Shankar Asar discussed at length the impossibility of anyone undertaking that feat, saying it was too high for any horse to jump and land on all fours with two riders on its back.

The interesting point, however, is the manner in which this story came to be a part of history. Godse, when narrating the Rani's departure from the fort, writes that after chanting 'Jayshankar', Lakshmi Bai descended from the central part of the fort and, riding through the town, left by the gate in the north. In fact, according to him, the residents stood by to pay obeisance to their Rani for the last time.

This too seems inaccurate for the obvious reason that she could never have avoided British surveillance, unless soldiers in that camp helped her—as has been suggested too.

After all, Rani Lakshmi Bai was always an elusive figure about whom British soldiers fantasized. 'The dauntless bravery of the Ranee was a great topic of conversation in camp.' During the siege of the fort, men thought they could see her sitting under an awning on a square next to the tower, monitoring actions. 'Reports said she was young and beautiful, and as yet unmarried. Field and opera glasses were constantly directed to the awning in question, over which hung sulkily a large red flag.'[1] She was the archetypal Oriental Indian princess, mystifying, distant and romantic.

Not every British official was equally enamoured:

Ten moons only had shone upon the gory pit in which the seventy-four mangled bodies of our fellow countrymen had been thrown, and the day of avenging had arrived; their spirits had risen up against their murderers, who were now hemmed in on every side, and the voices from the grave were soon to be answered by the deafening roar of cannon and the shouts of vengeance falling with the merciless sword. No maudlin clemency was to mark the fall of the city. The Jezebel of India was there—the young, energetic, proud, unbending, uncompromising Ranee, and upon her head rested the blood of the slain, and a punishment as awful awaited her.

Despite such outright condemnation, Lowe had to admire the Rani for the kind of resistance the men put up under her leadership. It would have been of 'honour' and 'fame' only if she did not have such a sullied past. No one till now had condemned Lakshmi Bai so unequivocally. Lowe was accompanying Hugh Rose on his campaign. If what he wrote represented what the army thought of her, the Rani had no hopes of reconciliation with the British. He rejoiced that they had been able to kill more than 3,000 of the enemy. 'Such was the retribution meted out to this Jezebel Ranee and her people for the heinous crimes done by them in Jhansi.'[2] Thus, a description of how she escaped forms a crucial section in British accounts. Forrest describes how Lakshmi Bai escaped. 'During the night, the really dark night since our arrival, the Ranee's horse had been brought into the fort ditch. Let down from a window in the turret, she mounted with her stepson in her lap, and accompanied by three hundred Afghans and twenty-five troopers, she stole away from the fort.'[3]

The group headed for Bhandere, thirty kilometres north of Jhansi. Detachments of British cavalry were sent in pursuit of them. Lieutenant Dowker was sent to Bhandere. As he rode through the town, he saw traces of the Rani's hasty flight in her tent where the breakfast lay unfinished. He later said he thought he saw a glimpse of the Rani riding her grey stallion accompanied by four attendants. He was fast gaining on her till he was fired at and fell off the horse.[4]

Out in the streets of Jhansi, the people braving British guns milled around her to get the last glimpse of their Rani. When the British found out, they sent cavalry after her but she had ridden far away.[5] The Rani of Jhansi left the capital she was so passionately possessive of and Jhansi never again saw the Rani that made her proud and later famous.

Hamilton wrote, 'On the night of the 4th the Ranee and a large body of rebels made a dash out of the Fort, but were driven back from the direction they first took; they then changed their course and got through the picket towards Bhandere.'[6] Rose's report is somewhat similar, '... that after leaving it, (Jhansi) they (the Rani and her soldiers) had been headed back by one of the picquets (sic) where the Ranee and her party separated, she herself taking to the right with a few sowars in the direction of her intended flight to Bhandere.'[7] None of the descriptions clearly states how Lakshmi Bai managed to elude soldiers of the British army who were all over Jhansi. Even though she made her escape in the dark hours of the night, it was unlikely that there were no soldiers on guard around the fort, which the invading army believed was still strongly barricaded by the Rani's men. In the last few days of combat, fighting had seldom ceased even at night. If the reports are true, then there must have been quite a crowd leaving Jhansi without being offered any resistance from the invading forces—300 men could not be an insignificant number.

Years later, Damodar Rao related that night's adventure to his son Lakshman Rao, who in turn spoke to the writer Mahasweta Devi. According to this account, the Rani, dressed like a soldier, tied her son to her back and rode through the blazing town. She saw the mayhem that the British forces 'like messengers from hell' were wreaking on the innocent people. She reached one of the northern Bhandere gates where a man was waiting for her. She passed a few British soldiers who were on guard together with men from Orchha. They asked who she was and she replied with a heavy local accent that she was from Orchha. They let her ride away.[8] Her followers rode past the soldiers who could not make them out in the dark. By the time Moropant Tambe and Lalu Bakshi left, the moon had risen and they could not go much further.

Lalu Bakshi was supposed to have created a distraction for the British army and taken their attention away from the convoy. Jawahar Singh, leading his 400 men, stood opposing the British army. He lost his life in the struggle.

John Smyth describes how Lakshmi Bai had inadvertently leaked out her decision to leave. Hundreds gathered to bid her farewell and thus alerted the British soldiers. They, however, could not make out exactly what was happening and a 'confused skirmish' followed. In the midst of this, Lakshmi Bai escaped with a few of her close followers towards Kalpi. The British cavalry pursued her for some time but gave up because they did not know who she was.[9] The British too were unable to explain how the Rani managed to hoodwink the invading army.

For the British counter-insurgency forces, this daring act was an outright breach of security measures. Lakshmi Bai not only rode past the soldiers in the town but also travelled all of the 480 kilometres unopposed. The story that did its round in the British camp has been attributed to General Lyster, who was at the time of the battle aide-de-camp to Hugh Rose. The general was apparently very keen on capturing the Rani of Jhansi but did not know how to without invading the fort, which would cause great damage to lives since it was strongly defended.

Rose's plan was to withdraw a picket and leave a gap for the Rani to escape through. The picket was to be withdrawn in the morning so that Lakshmi Bai and her forces could plan the escape the same evening. Rose thus ordered one of the pickets to be pulled out, leaving an opening of about 366 metres. 'In the night we heard heavy firing by the pickets at each side of the gap, firing at the escaping Rani and her followers; but as it was a dark night the firing was at random and no one was hit.'[1] The next morning, Rose was informed of the Rani's flight and a futile pursuit followed. Hugh Rose was, according to Lyster, surprised that 'women who had never been on horseback before could have ridden the distance in such a short time'. Written years later, this account appears somewhat imprecise. Everyone in the British camp was aware of Lakshmi Bai's equestrian skills and even if he were not, it remains inexplicable why he did not take extra security precautions for he himself had laid the trap.

How the Rani of Jhansi escaped, therefore, remains a mystery. But the legends serve their own purpose. The British version credits Hugh Rose with providing her with the opportunity to decamp. The Indian version of her jumping 200 metres and dodging British security were yet more proof of qualities of the intrepid warrior queen who offered future nationalists an image of the strength that the Indian nation stood for. It was the stuff that heroines were made of.

Lakshmi Bai knew she was leaving Jhansi never to return. There was no time for sentiments and emotional leave-taking. She barely had a chance to look back one last time at the town she had tried passionately to defend, a place that had metamorphosed young Manu to the queen of Jhansi. The only person who bid a tearful farewell was Chima Bai, her stepmother and friend. Moropant was hurt in an encounter with the British on the hill next to the fort. He knew the odds were against him and asked his wife to escape with their children. He had little illusion about the fate that awaited him and his first-born daughter, who was born to be queen.[10]

Following the battle of Jhansi, rebels dispersed all over the countryside to the north and east of Jhansi. Here some of them joined the Rajput landlords still up in arms against the British government. Lakshmi Bai headed straight north to Kalpi, where Rao Sahib, the brother of Nana

Sahib and Tantia Tope had set up base. Several others
followed her trail; and there began a continuous gathering
of men and ammunition in this border town. She was
armed with two swords and a pair of pistols and was
accompanied only by four cavalry soldiers. They were
Tantia Tope's brother, the nephew of Jawahar Singh
named Buruju, Mulla Qazi and Wilayat Khan.[11] They
halted at Bhandere for some rest and refreshments for the
young Damodar Rao. Some local friends had arranged a
light breakfast in a temporary tent. They were sitting
around the food when a spy rushed in to inform them that
the British were coming. Lakshmi Bai hurried out, strapped
young Damodar Rao to her back, mounted the horse and
rode without stopping till she reached Kunch.

The British force in pursuit of Rani Lakshmi Bai was
constituted of the 14th Light Dragoons, the 3rd Light
Cavalry and Hyderabad Cavalry under the command of
Captain Forbes. The captain divided his men into small
groups so that they could search the countryside in
different directions. Leading the Hyderabad Cavalry was
Lieutenant Dowkar, who ran into the tent that the Rani
had briefly stopped by at Bhandere. Finding it empty, he
rode on and at the end of the town, found the Rohillas
and soldiers of the Bengal Irregular Cavalry. He fired and
shot down about forty of them till he saw the Rani
straight ahead with only four attendants. Before he could
catch up, he was struck with a sword and fell down. Even
though the British reports briefly mention him being
injured, he was believed to have been cut down by
Lakshmi Bai herself when he came too near her.

Lakshmi Bai arrived at Kunch late at night, having
travelled the whole day. Tantia Tope was already there.
The following morning, the two with four guns and
property worth fourteen lakh rupees started for Kalpi.[12]

Queen Without a Kingdom

Kalpi, 142 kilometres north-east of Jhansi, overlooking the Yamuna, was a trading town, small and pretty. The fort was modest, but strategically perched on a hilltop, with wide ravines serving as natural defence. From about the beginning of 1858, Kalpi began emerging as the alternative to Kanpur, a centre of resistance to British forces, largely because of its location. In February, Nana Sahib, with four regiments of cavalry, eight regiments of infantry and sixteen guns encamped outside the town.[1] Tantia Tope and Rao Sahib followed. After the fall of Jhansi, Kalpi rapidly became the rallying point for everyone opposing the British and intending to make one last stand. The Rajas of Banpur and Shahgarh, and several local Rajput landowners, assembled here. From the end of March, there was constant movement of men and arms across the region between Jhansi and Kalpi. On 19 April, General Whitlock of the Madras Regiment overran Banda and defeated the forces of the Nawab. In the adjoining district of Hamirpur, as the British army regained control, those opposing them withdrew to Kalpi.[2] Lakshmi Bai was among the last to arrive—but once she did, her presence added significance to the gathering.

The leaders now put their heads together to draw up detailed strategies and plans for what everyone knew would be the crucial conflict. There were approximately 10,000 men, soldiers and retainers of the thakurs, both infantry and cavalry, with fifteen guns at Kalpi.[3] Many of Lakshmi Bai's soldiers had already arrived. Officially, Rao Sahib, the nephew of Nana Sahib, was commander of the army, but the Rani of Jhansi and Tantia Tope were prominent leaders, commanding their own retinue of soldiers. Each leader was assigned separate roles and functions. The Rajas of Banpur and Shahgarh were asked to move south to Mau-Ranipur in order to collaborate with the local Bundela and Puar thakurs who were now up in arms against the British in what was a second phase of civil uprising. Lakshmi Bai led 2,000 men 'with two guns under her charge and moved to Murgaon, a village on the Jhansi road, in order to offer Hugh Rose the first line of resistance'.[4]

Several issues had to be addressed. The first was training the soldiers. For not all of them were skilled—even if they were, they had to relearn fighting under new circumstances and under the new leadership. Then there had to be perfect coordination among the leaders. The fortification of the town had to be strengthened. Local support from the people and landed aristocracy had to be solicited and, finally, the exact tactic of fighting the British decided upon.

Their first action plan was to raise barriers so that the invading army could not reach the town easily. All roads within the radius of one-and-a-half kilometres of Kalpi were destroyed and trenches dug to act as obstructions. Pickets were set up around the town, each guarded by 200 soldiers. In the north along the Yamuna, men were posted at all the ghats, especially the ones that were in regular use, to prevent British troops moving from the north. They collected 200 boats at Rajghat and Baluwa Ghat. Soldiers were also posted on the east, south and west, creating a barricade around the town. Strict vigilance was kept on anyone wanting to enter or exit Kalpi. The guards posted there carried out a thorough search of all travellers. To pay for these soldiers and their provisions, money was raised from local bankers and mahajans, the community that remained staunchly in support of British rule all through the uprising. Now they were compelled to contribute to the Nana's cause.[5]

General Hugh Rose could not leave Jhansi till adequate measures had been taken for the safety and security of the town. Given its position, there was every chance that rebels would try to capture it one more time. He marched with the 1st Brigade from Jhansi, finally on 25 April for Kalpi, leaving the town under the protection of the main wing of the 3rd European Regiment, eight companies of the 24th Bombay Native Infantry, 100 Hyderabad Cavalry, three guns from the Bhopal Artillery and half of a company of sappers and miners. Together they formed the 2nd Brigade under Brigadier Steuart. Rose had earlier sent a wing of the 3rd Bombay Light Cavalry to Goona in the south to prevent thakurs and their men from marching on the town from the south.

Those defending Kalpi spent this time in organizing and replenishing their strength. Their first step was to enlist more soldiers. Four Brahmin commanders, Basdeo Pant, Bishnu Pant, Gungadhar Pant and Balwant Rao sent an appeal to all fellow Brahmins of the south to rise to the call of war in defence of religion. The Peshwa was no longer a political figure or patron. His struggle was for defending his religion from being desecrated by the foreign rulers:

*Formerly we served the Peshwa with great zeal
and alacrity in the hope that we might obtain
Jagheers and donations, but now if we all unite
together in the present cause, we will please one
Deity, 'Maha Deo', and preserve our faith. We
hope that all those who have attained the age of
between sixteen years and twenty-three and can
use swords will serve as soldiers in the Regiments
and thereby prosper.*

All those willing to serve were asked to meet a certain
Madari Lal Bakht.[6]

The arrangements undertaken by the forces in Kalpi
were exceptionally meticulous and formalized. Official
directives were sent out to identify men who could assist
and collaborate and, if they were agreeable to the terms,
a formal deed was drawn up. A certain Radha Kishan
Chowbey living in Mathura received, on 17 April 1858,
instructions that he should create 'disturbance' in the
British territory. This was going to be his contribution in
strengthening the government of the Peshwa and in driving
out infidels from the country. Chowbey agreed to do so
and officially conveyed his consent by drawing up a
proper deed in which he promised to raise a body of men,
to provoke people to rise against the British, and pledged
not to claim anything more than what the Peshwa willingly
granted. At the end of the deed, it was notified, 'As Radha
Kishan Chowbey has this day appeared in person and
attested this Deed with his signature, it is ordered that it
be deposited among the records of this office.'[7]

There was a functioning bureaucracy that took care of
all the Peshwa's correspondence that included appeals,
praises, proclamations and reminders. In one
announcement, the chiefs of Bundelkhand were specially
mentioned for their exertion in the cause of the 'Sirkar' or

government. Rao Sahib signed most of these letters and sent such proclamations as the one addressed to the chiefs and talukdars of Kuchwagarh. The region inhabited by the Kuchwaha Rajputs lay to the north-west of Jhansi between the district of Jalaun and the state of Gwalior. The chiefs had sent word that they were ready to help the Peshwa provided they were issued a parwana that assured them of protection and benefits. This letter guaranteed them 'that the more you will display your gallantry on the present occasion, the greater benefit will accrue to you'. The first would be blessings from God for safeguarding the religion, the second would be praise from the Peshwa. As for more tangible gains, jagirs would be granted to those who performed 'meritorious' services.[8]

For the local landlords, bankers, dealers in sugar and merchants, the Peshwa had clear incentives and categorical punishments. In principle, the imperative to join the rebellion was the need to safeguard religion. Landlords who provided men, ammunition and provision were to receive 'credit for the price of those articles in the accounts relative to the revenue of his *Zamindaree*, and also a remission of the whole of the revenue for two years, and afterwards of four annas in the rupee per annum for eight years'. Categories were divided according to the kind of support lent and each of these had a corresponding incentive. Therefore, those who helped only with provisions and ammunition but not men were to be given remission for only one year, not two. Merchants and suppliers of sugar were to receive certificates of honour. Bankers who lent one lakh rupees were to be given a two per cent interest over those who lent Rs 50,000 and these would receive only one-and-a-half per cent. On the other hand, those who refused assistance were to be severely punished.[9]

There were other regular letters and urzees or requests from officers for help. Pandit Vaman Rao, the paymaster employed in Hamirpur, was in need of money to obtain gunpowder and bullocks; thanadar Altaf Hussain of Hamirpur reported what was going on in his territory, as did Khoda Baksh and Khadim Hossein. They were district officials appointed by the Peshwa. One set of papers contained requests for money—Gopal Rao, the news-writer posted at Chilla Tara Ghat required fifty rupees to be disbursed among the harkaras or postmen. Mohammad Ishaq, who was a senior official, reported measures he had taken and the recruitments he had made.

Certain protocols were followed. Thus, when some zamindars demanded reduction of their revenue, it was denied on the ground that they belonged to the kingdom of the Nawab of Banda and thus outside the Peshwa's domain, even though Ali Bahadur was an ally. By sending a copy of these letters, officials regularly kept headquarters informed.[10] An unsigned and undated letter was in the nature of an advertisement seeking information about those who manufacture caps and their composition for the long-barrel guns to be used.[11]

These were some of the papers retrieved by the British counter-insurgency forces once they captured Kalpi and ransacked rebel camps. There was deliberate organization, calculated planning, careful coordination among leaders and men deputed in neighbouring regions. Everything spoke of a determined resistance that the Peshwa's court, which included Lakshmi Bai, Rao Sahib, Ali Bahadur and Tantia Tope, had mustered.

Among the mutiny papers in the India Office Library, London, I found a file on which was written 'Translation of Tantia Tope's orders'. Since his defeat at Burwa Sagar and somewhat ignominious retreat, biographers of Lakshmi Bai have tended to project Tantia as a poor leader and a weak soldier who pales before the spirit and dynamism of the Rani. These 'orders' speak, contrarily, of the singular attention he paid to organization and regulation. They are in the nature of short, terse messages for soldiers taking into account a variety of occasions and contingencies. The measures have close resemblance to British military practices, and yet it is evident that they were drafted at different times. A standard order read:

> Orders by Tantia Saheb—All Commanders, sepoys and sowars are hereby informed that from the date whoever applies for his discharge will forfeit any pay that may be due to him, and will be punished by order of the Court. The Brigadier of Divisions should be very attentive to his duty and not neglect it, and no sepoy should be allowed to go in the city during the night, no noise should be made in the Fort or outside, and no fire should be lighted, and every day at 3 pm Choona Sing and the Brig. Major should inspect the picquets and place them in proper positions. And there should be a muster daily at 10 am and 4 pm and every Brigadier should make a report at 10 am. Every Brigadier should warn the men under his command not to cut down trees belonging to ryots—many complaints have been made—in future if anyone does so he will be punished.[12]

The task of managing men could not have been easy. These orders were compiled over March and April of 1858 and attended to the need for a proper structure to keep the men under control. Quite a significant number among them were retainers of thakurs, never known for discipline in the best of times. The rest were soldiers who had served the British army but since the mutiny had come to assume a kind of licence unheard of in a regular army. There was very little regularity in the composition of Tantia's forces assembled in Kalpi. Steps thus had to be carefully devised to ensure unity, discipline and performance.

First, there was a proper hierarchy. Brigadier majors followed by brigadiers headed the infantry and artillery divisions of the army, which constituted regiments. They were responsible for regular inspection and discipline of the soldiers under them.[13] Next in line were havaldar majors and kote havaldars. Havaldar majors attended the brigadier's office every day to take down daily directives and orders. Pickets set up at various strategic points had subedars, jamedars and naiks who were to report daily to the brigadier's office at ten in the morning. The brigadier major and the brigadier marched only if the entire force was in action.[14] Each regiment in turn had its own commandant and a regimental munshi. It was the munshi who recorded all orders, both of the regiment and those received from the brigadiers' office. There were other officers attached to every regiment such as pay havaldars and drill naiks. A brigadier court was convened both for trying offenders and recruiting new officers. While recruiting new soldiers, one officer and one soldier representing every regiment had to be present. When resolving disputes or trying offenders, maulvis and pundits were present.[15]

The brigadier court was usually busiest in the morning. Pilfering, petty crimes and spying were regular issues that needed to be resolved summarily. A more serious complaint was about a syce or groom engaged by someone rumoured to be a British spy. Every soldier and officer was asked to be on special alert to identify the person. Soldiers were often guilty of taking wood from the official warehouse without permission or of forcibly seizing it from the poor. Anyone found guilty had to pay a fine or do extra drill under the hot April sun. Similar intimidations were made for those who did not attend regimental parade every day.

It was very important that the soldiers set an example of orderliness, cleanliness and discipline. They were strictly forbidden to venture out of the fort, except when on guard in the pickets. No one was to be absent from the fort. No one was to dirty the fort. There were sweepers and bhishtees, water-carriers, employed for keeping the fort clean and providing it with a regular supply of water. Thousands of pots were set aside to collect water and these were regularly replenished. Sweepers and bhishtees were present at all times in the fort. But soldiers and officers were categorically instructed that they should dispose of garbage at a distance of 100 yards and not litter the fort.[16]

Sentries guarded the fort day and night. They were to keep vigil, carrying their guns. Under no circumstances were they to put their guns down. The sentries were relieved twice during their duty hours and the officers regularly inspected the guard both in the morning and at night. Such were the details of Tantia Tope's directions. Any negligence in security measures was severely punished. Among these papers were also messages from Tantia Tope written in the months he spent outside Kalpi. There was one he wrote from Chirkhari, reporting his success against the chief and also informing about developments in the north. In one such missive, he wrote that Ghulam Hydar Khan, the son of Dost Mohammad Khan, the Amir of Kabul, was coming with a large force to assist the rebels against the British.

The Peshwa did not always have cash to pay his soldiers, and frequently promises were made that the arrears would be paid.[17] Everybody was told that all official appeals and pleas should be submitted in writing.

The Peshwa held court every day from ten in the morning, the first session being devoted to military affairs. Lawyers representing the Rajas would meet him between noon and five in the evening.

During Holi, special orders were given out for maintaining discipline. Soldiers were excused from their regular drill and parade but were required to perform their assigned tasks and duties. They had to be extra vigilant because the enemy was close at hand and, therefore, half the soldiers had to be on duty at all times. They were not to mouth obscenities or throw gulal, or coloured powder, on one another. Instead, there was to be a ritual to celebrate and reinforce a sense of camaraderie among the soldiers and between them and their new leaders, Nana Sahib and Tantia Tope. Every soldier was to be offered paan and gulal when they assembled at 3 pm on Sundays. But the commanders had to make arrangements that the fort did not ever remain unattended.

Commanding officers were asked to deal with minor differences between soldiers belonging to different regiments, those who had served the British army and those belonging to the native states. The situation was somewhat tense, as the Peshwa was not able to pay, and he was more than apologetic about it. A lot of the correspondence was about the happenings in neighbouring places, particularly Kanpur. News about Jhansi was yet to be confirmed but meanwhile, commanders were asked to get soldiers ready for the defence of Kalpi. The entire force was to be divided into four divisions—one was to remain in the fort, the second stationed two-and-a-half kilometres from Kalpi on the Orai and Jalaun road, the third on the road going east towards Banda and Hamirpur, and the fourth was to be on the outskirts of the town, ready for assistance to any of the three others. Meanwhile,

Tantia Tope was regularly sending in reinforcements of men and ammunition.

A lot of emphasis was placed on regular parade, roll-calls and muster. The day began every morning with gunfire. Separate rules were laid down for soldiers coming in from other combat zones, such as Jhansi. Those who did not join their regiments in the fort but stayed back in the town were not to be restored to their former employment.[18] As more and more soldiers began to trickle in, commanders had to discern the seasoned military men from stragglers.

A court martial was held on 10 April for the trial of two soldiers, Peetam Singh and Durga Singh, guilty of dereliction of duty and misbehaviour. The sentence passed by Tantia Tope was sent to Nana for his final verdict.

From April, Kalpi became busier. The Raja of Shahgarh arrived on 16 April to the firing of eleven guns in his honour. The first of the contingent was thereafter ordered to take a stand at Chowrasee Gombuz, or Eighty-four Tombs, a medieval relic. The orders that followed were more in the nature of routine measures. There were to be regular parades, and every day, one person would be in charge as the field officer. Together with a few soldiers, he was to inspect the pickets for that day. A picket was composed of one officer, four havaldars, four naiks, one driver, fifty soldiers and sixteen troopers.

The popular belief that Lakshmi Bai took charge of forces in Kalpi, that she rebuked Rao Sahib and Tantia Tope for their negligence, flies in the face of these records.

Unfortunately, the daily notes that give us all the above information stopped short of Lakshmi Bai's coming to Kalpi. Godse describes how she arrived late at night without food, shelter or clothes, and how Tantia Tope hastily made arrangements for her.[19] In Vrindavan Lal

Verma's fiction, Lakshmi Bai was supposed to have been very disappointed to see how badly the soldiers were organized in Kalpi. It was another part, perhaps, of the legend—that the Rani of Jhansi was the only true commander of forces in Kalpi. The notes we referred to earlier speak quite the contrary. If for a festival like Holi, such a strict code of conduct and decorum was laid down, surely the leaders would have taken the trouble of going into details of military management. They were quite different from the characters in Verma's novel, seeking pleasure in song and dance.[20]

Lakshmi Bai formally accepted the leadership of Rao Sahib and actively discussed strategies of resisting Rose's forces. It was decided that they should meet Rose's forces a little ahead of Kalpi. On 28 April, Tantia Tope, Lakshmi Bai with 4,000 men and five guns, and the Rajas of Shahgarh and Banpur with 3,000 men, reached Kunch, thirty-seven kilometres south of Kalpi.[21] All through April, small contingents of soldiers were sent to different places on the route from Jhansi to Kalpi.[22] There were close to 1,000 men in Kunch already, but they had no guns. A little to the east, there were men at Orai and others dispersed around the town, in the shades of trees.[23] A few moved further east to Gurserai, while the Rajas of Banpur and Shahgarh marched south to Mhow. The tactic was to create diversions from all sides for the British march upon Kalpi. Local rulers and landholders, including the chief of Narwar and the rebel thakur Despat of Jheejhan in Hamirpur, and other thakurs of Hamirpur, joined Lakshmi Bai and Tantia Tope. The army in Kunch dug entrenchments all around the town and posted armed troops along all the roads leading to it. If British counter-insurgency forces could be stopped well before they reached Kalpi, the Peshwa's stronghold would be saved and hopes of retrieving Kanpur revived. Three guns were seized from the Rani of Orchha and sent to Kalpi where Rao Sahib defended the fort with 2,000 men and three guns.[24] Before the British reached Kunch, the Rajas of Banpur and Shahgarh moved south-east on Kotra. It was a village on the river Betwa to the south-east of Kunch. The purpose was to attack Rose's army from the rear. As if predicting this move, Rose sent Major Orr with a small unit to pre-empt just this. At the battle of Kotra, the Rajas were defeated and forced to move further south.

In contrast to the time that preparations took for defending Kunch, the battle for the town was short and decisive. Hugh Rose arrived in the first week of May, with the summer sun blazing at 120 degrees Fahrenheit. The general knew that in that heat it was impossible to besiege the town for long. The attack had to be direct, fast and effective. He discovered that while the town was defended strongly on all sides, the north-western side was open. He ordered three columns of soldiers to advance upon the town; while leading the 1st Brigade he moved twenty-two kilometres to the west and then marched upon the town from the north-west. The confrontation took place on 7 May and, after a day's fighting, the defending army was forced to withdraw first from the pickets surrounding the town and then from the town itself. They moved east towards Orai, in order to reach Kalpi. In a gesture of generosity, Rose admitted in his report that:

> *If, on the one hand, the Enemy had retired from Kunch with too great precipitation, on the other, it is fair to say that they commenced their retreat across the plain with resolution and intelligence. The line of skirmishers fought well to protest the retreat of the main body, observing the rules of*

Light Infantry drill. When charged, they threw aside their muskets, and fought desperately with their swords.[25]

British cavalry and artillery, sent in pursuit of the retreating forces, killed 350–400 soldiers.[26] The British army saw the Rani of Jhansi riding back, dressed in a man's attire, her dagger and sword dangling from her belt, a string of pearls dazzling around her neck.[27] This was the image immortalized in historical memory.

All energies were now focused on the last town in Bundelkhand. The fate of the resistance depended on the outcome of the battle in Kalpi. Lakshmi Bai had no illusions about the seriousness of the encounter. She advised Vishnubhatt Godse and his uncle, who had followed the rest of them to Kalpi, to take the boat across the river Yamuna and move north. By that time, she must have known that her father and most of her women companions—with one exception—had died. She was left with Tantia Tope and Rao Sahib, planning the last strategy.

Hugh Rose arrived before Kalpi on 16 May. In a parallel movement, British columns took up position across the Yamuna on the Kanpur side in the north.[28] Deep trenches around the town prevented the invading forces from coming too close.

Kalpi was without doubt the strongest rebel bastion whose defence had been planned in minute detail. There was an underground magazine with several hundred barrels of gunpowder and a huge quantity of ammunition and war-like stores, boxes of cartridges and shells, both of British and indigenous design, and a large number of muskets. In addition to this, engineering tools, surveying and topographical instruments spoke volumes of the organization of the resistance.[29] Four foundries were established for manufacturing eighteen-pounder brass guns, short cannons and nine-pounder guns.[30]

After the battle of Kunch, Tantia Tope and Lakshmi Bai returned to Kalpi to make fresh arrangements. Deep ravines on its western, southern and eastern sides naturally guarded the town. Soldiers from the infantry and artillery regiments were dispatched to cover the ground all around so that they could fire upon the British army hidden behind the protection of ravines and low hills and yet remain concealed from their direct line of attack. Marathi Brahmins were sent to all the villages surrounding Kalpi to inspire people, stir their loyalty for the Peshwa and his fight for the faith. Never known for their allegiance to the British state, the villagers here acted as spies and informers of British movement.[31] The Nawab of Banda, Rao Sahib and the Rani of Jhansi were excellent leaders, and commanded the unstinted loyalty of their forces. Of the three, Hugh Rose rightly felt that 'The high descent of the Ranee, her unbounded liberality to her troops and retainers, and her fortitude which no reverses could shake, rendered her an influential and dangerous adversary.'[32]

Each of these leaders took upon themselves separate assignments. Lakshmi Bai's was undoubtedly the most challenging. Leading 400 cavalry and close to 2,000 infantry, she personally defended the ravines. Rao Sahib and the Nawab of Banda divided the rest of the forces under them. The three of them intended to commence a three-pronged assault on the invading army. Tantia Tope was absent.[33] A well-planned strategy under the guidance of Rao Sahib, Lakshmi Bai and Ali Bahadur was amply supported by their equally strong determination, courage and commitment to the cause. All of this, however, proved inadequate.

The British victory at Kalpi was the ultimate testimony

to Hugh Rose's superb planning, his centralized command and huge support from other divisions. The intense heat and the constant attack from the defending force made the initial going very difficult. Hugh Rose marched towards a village called Gulowli, south of Kalpi on the river Yamuna. His intention was to set up communication with Lieutenant-Colonel Maxwell who was in command of a column of the Bengal army on the Kanpur side across the river. General Whitlock's forces were to march from the east.

Soldiers occupying Kalpi, inspired and stimulated, swore on the waters of the Yamuna that they would drive Rose's army into the river or die. All the while they were trying to draw British soldiers out into the open by keeping up constant fire, hoping the enemy would wilt in the heat of the summer sun. They concentrated their force on the right but, as a ruse, attacked the British on the left.

Hugh Rose covered his heavy guns with a squadron of 14th Light Dragoons and a company of 3rd Hyderabad Cavalry that started frontal firing and drew the rebels out. The units then withdrew gradually, exposing the defenders to the heavy British guns. The tactic succeeded in catching them unawares, causing confusion and many casualties. But the Nana's army made sure that the British never came too close so that they would never know the real strength of the force defending Kalpi. Serious fighting broke out on 21 May, the two armies appearing equally poised. The defending army made a major inroad against the adversaries on its right where Brigadier Stuart was fighting with his back to the wall, unable to withstand the assault.

Even though biographers credit Lakshmi Bai with the leadership and command of the forces in Kalpi, the actual proceedings of the battle suggest that someone with experience in military planning and tactics had been involved in the actual decision-making. The correspondence, earlier referred to, addressed issues that only a person who had served in the army could anticipate. Lakshmi Bai certainly made an exemplary and inspiring leader by virtue of her position, her gender and her single-minded dedication to the cause that she espoused. She could have coached novices in horse-riding and sword-fighting, but it is doubtful if she were capable of strategizing, for that called for a different kind of experience and learning. This still made her the leader who stirred her followers, but perhaps not the commander who worked out the details of the operations.

Some of the defending soldiers came very close to the Indians serving in the British army and tried to induce in them a feeling of guilt for their unwavering fidelity to the alien ruler. But while the British army could be continuously replenished with arms and men, the defenders were limited to what they had. Hugh Rose, despite losses, could carry on the assault, but the Nana's men, despite good tactics and energy, fell back. The British succeeded in making crucial advances into their defences on 22 May and forced the soldiers to scatter, leaving the ravines that encircled the town somewhat exposed. Hugh Rose decided to make the most of the advantage and, allowing his men only a few hours of rest, launched the attack on Kalpi before sunrise on 23 May. It was short and conclusive. By ten that morning, two brigades of the British army captured the fort and the town of Kalpi. Once more, the British were victorious.[34]

While the British were fighting through the labyrinth of ravines, the defending army beat a hasty but well-planned retreat. Lakshmi Bai left Kalpi during the night of 22 May, while Rose was scheming the attack. Rao Sahib and the Nawab of Banda escaped the following morning. Quite a large number of soldiers left for their homes, while others followed their leaders. Since they went away with no baggage, they were able to cover ground very fast, before the British could pursue or capture them. They moved south, took the Jalaun road and proceeded westwards, the only route that the British had not covered.[35] The route they were to follow had been carefully designed. Tantia Tope had left the battlefield early, perhaps to prepare for this contingency. Therefore, even though the leaders and soldiers escaped in small groups, by the time they assembled at the border of Gwalior, they were between 5,000 and 6,000 strong with nine guns.

Rao Sahib and the Rani of Jhansi stopped at a village called Churkhi, twenty-two kilometres west of Kalpi. Forty cavalrymen and only one of the Rani's female companions, Sundar, were with them. They chose not to spend the night there but moved further west to Sravun where soldiers of the former 5th Irregulars and 500 or so belonging to the infantry regiments rallied around Rao Sahib. Lakshmi Bai, in the true spirit of a commander, actively moved among the soldiers. A typical nineteenth-century British account describes the Rani of Jhansi as 'an ardent, daring, licentious woman under thirty, (who) gave spirit and hope to all'.[36] She certainly was ardent, determined and daring but why she should have to be 'licentious' only because she had dared to trespass on male domain, can be explained as a hasty remark prompted by British ire and spleen rather than a deliberate assessment of her character. It also prompted another kind of portrayal of the warrior queen who defied all the norms of Victorian prudence and served the image of a lustful Oriental woman.

The Scindias of Gwalior, belying the tradition of their founder Mahadji Scindia of upholding fiercely and

passionately freedom and independence, had under the
British rule, bartered their pride for security. They were
among the most loyal supporters of British rule and
eventually were handsomely rewarded for resolutely
opposing the Indian rebels. Their sprawling palaces and
properties all over India are testimony to their political
servitude. A visitor to Gwalior, before being driven to the
imposing fort, however, is shown one other place. It is an
enclosed garden, circular in shape, measuring
approximately 1,200 square metres. In the middle stands
the unmistakable statue of Rani Lakshmi Bai of Jhansi,
mounted on a horse in a galloping posture, her right hand
raised, holding a sword. This is the archetypal
representation of Lakshmi Bai, the inveterate fighter, the
warrior queen, the Rani whose last living moments were
on horseback, fighting to preserve what was dearer than
her life—her husband's kingdom for their son to inherit.
She is also the image of Goddess Durga, the slayer of evil.
The site is commemorated as the exact spot where Lakshmi
Bai fell and died on 17 June.

It must have been part of a well-planned design that
if defeated in Kalpi, the rebel force would move to
Gwalior and establish an alternative political base in the
name of the Peshwa. Gwalior was an obvious choice not
only because of its location but also for the fact that even
though the Scindias were British sympathizers, their soldiers
supported rebellion. On 29 May, the Scindia sent an
urgent message to Hugh Rose's camp informing him that
Rao Sahib, Tantia Tope, Lakshmi Bai and the Nawab of
Banda had crossed the river Scind, leading a substantial
number of soldiers ready to march upon the city. Young
Jayaji Rao Scindia sent two regiments and eighteen guns
to oppose them, while he decided to take command of the
rest of his soldiers and guardsmen. The first contest took

place on 2 June at eight in the morning. By ten, one unit of the Scindia's cavalry was beaten back. A message later in the day read: 'His Highness the Maharajah finding himself unable to resist them (the rebel force) and deserted by his troops fled to Agra. The whole of his force joined the Rebels, who have pushed pickets round the City.'[37] Rao Sahib, Lakshmi Bai and their army meanwhile marched into the fort and raised the flag of the Peshwa. Rao Sahib, as the commander-in-chief, however, refused to assume authority.

The Peshwa's force displayed amazing restraint and discipline, quite in contrast to the invading British forces. No one was allowed to indulge in arson or plunder. Only the houses of traitors such as the prime minister and some senior officers who accompanied the Scindia were identified and soldiers were told to pillage them. The rest of the people were assured that the force had come to restore the Maratha Confederacy under the tutelage of the Peshwa. Rao Sahib sent word to Scindia that he should return and take charge of his government, since none of them was interested in power. He gave the soldiers of Scindia's army three months' pay due to them and two months' pay as gratuity.[38]

Meanwhile, a provisional administration was put into place for the daily running of the state. All state prisoners were released and special measures taken to protect the bankers and merchants. About 500 harkaras were appointed to bring in news of the British army. The alternative arrangement was far more appealing to the people and neighbouring landlords than that of the Scindia had ever been. Once order was restored, the leaders settled in with their own troops. The Rajas of Banpur and Shahgarh now joined them. Proclamations were read out that Nana Sahib was the Peshwa, Rao Sahib his deputy and Tantia Tope his diwan.[39]

Despite her singular contribution to military organization, Lakshmi Bai was kept out of political prominence. She may have chosen to remain so herself. But she continued to be an active figure, constantly on horseback, inspecting troops. She rented a house outside the fort and lived with her son and a few female companions. During inspection, she wore army uniform, but otherwise she was in a sari and blouse. She usually tied her long hair and covered it with a scarf.[40] One report said, 'The Rani of Jhansi is always surrounded by 50 sowars with drawn swords, 100 Mewatiees and 1000 sowars and sepoys go (on) rounds in the streets and lanes.'[41] All the leaders chose to live in houses outside the fort or in the camp. Houses of the noblemen were taken for the chiefs to live in.[42]

Meanwhile, the weak-hearted Scindia sent frantic messages from Agra to Calcutta and to Hugh Rose that a force must be sent immediately to Gwalior and it must reach before the onset of the monsoon, for otherwise the rains would make it impossible for the army to cross the rivers criss-crossing the region.

British counter-insurgency forces appeared in the neighbourhood of Gwalior by 7 June. The advance brigade was under Brigadier Steuart, who sent a column under Colonel Robertson to Indurki in Bundelkhand, bordering Gwalior. Hugh Rose followed, crossing the river Pahuj on 13 June. Another brigade led by Brigadier Smith marched upon the town. Tantia Tope and Rao Sahib sent soldiers towards Indurki and neighbouring outposts to prepare for resistance. In the fort, 2,000 troops were being daily replenished with fresh recruits. News reaching British camps said that a number of Scindia's soldiers were deserting the Indian army. Tantia Tope, like before, left Gwalior and proceeded about five or six kos to keep a watch on British forces. The city was left to the Nawab of Banda and the Rani of Jhansi. This was the first instance where, prior to the arrival of Hugh Rose, skirmishes between the defending army and smaller units of the invading forces began. The first combat within the city was reported to have started on 16 June. Heavy firing was heard in the Morar cantonment and near Phulbagh, all through the next day, when Brigadier Smith's force entered Gwalior. Even before any serious battle started, tragedy hit the defending army.

On 18 June, Robert Hamilton wrote a brief message at nine in the morning to Lord Charles Canning, Colin Campbell and E.A. Reade, among others, that 'The Rani of Jhansi is killed. Maharaja Scindia has arrived. Brigadier Smith took four guns in the fight yesterday.'[43]

The longer reports were explicit as to the manner in which she died. Brigadier Smith's forces reached Kotah-ke-Sarai in the early morning of 17 June. There were scattered low hills and passes between there and the city. The defending army set up guns at different points on the mountain overlooking the region. With two infantry and two cavalry regiments under Captains Hicks and Heneage, Smith was able to make a sweep of the ravines and come upon the outskirts of the town, near Phulbagh. A squadron of the 8th Hussars charged at a camp at Phulbagh and forced a rebel camp to retreat.

Lakshmi Bai was present in that camp. The description runs, 'She was seated, says her servant, drinking sherbet, 400 of the 5th Irregulars near her, when the alarm was given that the Hussars approached. Forty or fifty of them came up, and the rebels fled, save about fifteen. The Ranee's horse refused to leap the canal, when she received a shot in the side, and then a sabre cut on the head, but rode off. She soon after fell dead, and was burnt in the garden close by. I may add, that the Brahminee concubine of her late husband, who never left her side, received a long sabre cut in front...The rebels were deeply dispirited by the Ranee's death.'[44]

Godse corroborates the account. Rao Sahib, Lakshmi Bai and Tantia Tope were together when they heard that the British army had arrived and was attacking the Morar forces. The three of them hurriedly mounted their horses and galloped towards the cantonment. Fierce battle broke out between the British and the defending soldiers. Lakshmi Bai was hit by a bullet, but she refused to stop. Then a sword cut her leg and she fell off the horse.[45]

The first apocryphal twist to her death was in Bhawani Prasad's report. As a special agent of the Nawab of Bhopal stationed in Sehore, he used to send regular information to his master. He wrote in the afternoon of 18 June, 'The hand of Nawab of Banda was blown off by a ball fired from the *morcha* of Major R. Another mortar ball hit the Rani of Jhansi on the breast and killed her in the battlefield. The insurgents burnt her body in sandalwood.'[46] In the middle of the battle, it would have been highly improbable, if not impossible for the Rani's followers, however ardent they may have been, to arrange for sandalwood to light her pyre.

Reminiscing about her campaigning experience, Mrs Henry Duberly wrote 'nothing is known with certainty, except that she (the Rani) was killed. Various stories got afloat; amongst others, that she was run through the body by a private of the 8th Hussars, who, as she was dressed as a man in a white turban and crimson tunic and trousers, had no idea that his sword was pointed at the breast of a woman.' The other story, according to Duberly, was that she died of bullet wounds. Sir Hugh Rose had told her that the Rani was fatally wounded in the battlefield. Even as she was being taken away from the grounds, she made arrangements for her own funeral and climbed the pyre herself and lit it with her own hands, in a kind of 'fierce and desperate courage'.[47] Legends about Lakshmi Bai were created in her lifetime and not only by her Indian admirers. Hugh Rose, in his official reports, however, did not give such a sensational description.

There are several versions regarding the manner in which she died. In one, Lakshmi Bai's death seemed somewhat of an anticlimax to the incredible last six months of her life. She died not fighting but from a stray bullet or an accidental sword cut. The attempt to add sheen with a little more romance was to make her death as remarkable as her life. It is said a British soldier threw a dagger at the Rani, hitting her just below her chest. She turned around and killed the man. The rest of the unit was closely pursuing her. She came upon a canal and while trying to cross it on horseback, a soldier struck her with his sword and hurt her thigh. 'Flashing the sword with her left hand, the Rani put an end to him.' She collapsed in a heap and was carried to the house of Baba Gangadas who took her in, washed her face, put Ganga water into her mouth, as is the religious custom. Lakshmi Bai recovered a little and muttered 'Har Har Mahadev' before passing out. A little later, she opened her eyes once more and began reciting in a feeble, barely audible voice, slokas, or verses from the scriptures. Her last words were 'Vasudev, I bow to you.' As the men who had brought her, Raghunath Singh and Gul Muhammad and her adopted son Damodar Rao shed tears, Baba Gangadas said, 'Brightness has no end; it is hidden in every atom. It shines again at the proper time.' The narrative ends rather dramatically: 'The incomparable Rani's body disappeared in flames.'[48] By not mentioning the funeral pyre, the author creates an impression that the body of Lakshmi Bai, the Rani of Jhansi, and the Devi incarnate, had actually vanished in the fire.

Lord Canning confirmed that a trooper of the 8th Hussar killed Lakshmi Bai. 'Shot in the back, her horse balked. She then fired at the man and he passed his sword through her.' Then a rather inconsequential remark on her attire followed: 'She used to wear gold anklets, and Scindia's pearl necklace, plundered from Gwalior. (Scindia says its value is untold) These when dying she distributed among the soldiery, when taken to die under the mango clump.'[49] The Scindia had earlier claimed that the pearls Lakshmi Bai was wearing had been stolen from his treasure. This was a lie because if she had given her ornaments away, there was no way for him to see what her pearls looked like and thus could not have asserted that they were really his. Hugh Rose later confirmed that she was immolated with great haste. Her remains were buried 'with great ceremony, under a tamarind tree under the Rock of Gwalior, where I saw her bones and ashes'.[50] Unless he had her body exhumed, Hugh Rose could not have seen the bones and ashes of the Rani of Jhansi.

None of the British accounts describe the scene of Lakshmi Bai fighting the British army, as the Indian versions do. Parasnis sets the tone in some ways. He writes that Rani Lakshmi Bai and Tantia Tope followed the Marathi tactic of avoiding being shut off in the fort. Instead, they occupied all roads leading to the town. The force was personally commanded by Lakshmi Bai dressed in military attire, leading a small group of hand-picked and well-armed men, being 'constantly in the saddle, ubiquitous and untiring'.[51] Then, over six pages, Parasnis narrates in somewhat epic manner the warrior queen's encounter with the British forces. She fought relentlessly and without a break. Then, on the fateful day, she was separated from her companions and suddenly a soldier put his sword through her chest. Caught unawares, Lakshmi Bai was fatally wounded.[52] Yet, on the same page and in subsequent pages, Parasnis quotes in the footnote how the British officials recorded her death.

Tahmankar debunks official accounts. In his narrative, Lakshmi Bai and her men succeeded in pushing back soldiers of the 8th Hussars under Captain Heneage on the morning of 17 June. 'The Ranee was in the thick of the fight, using her sword with both hands and holding the reins of her horse in her mouth. Suddenly she fell from a carbine shot, mortally.'[53] She died fighting, in the true spirit of a martyr. Robert Hamilton after inquiry reported that the Rani was killed when she along with Rao Sahib and Tantia Tope were watching the advance of the British forces. She was on horseback and was struck by a bullet. She died within minutes, and was carried away, her body cremated almost immediately. Tahmankar's objection to the British versions was that neither Hamilton nor Mcpherson mentions that Lakshmi Bai was fighting when she was hit. On the contrary, both suggest that she was caught offguard and tried to escape on seeing the British forces arrive suddenly. Tahmankar quotes despatches sent by Indian officials of neighbouring Bhopal and Indore in which she was embroiled in severe fighting when she was struck. 'At the time of engagement the lady was present on the battlefield where she received a sabre blow which killed her. All people call her the bravest fighter.'[54]

Mahasweta Devi similarly narrates in some detail the last two days of battle fought primarily by Lakshmi Bai on the Indian side. On the morning of 17 June, she made some special arrangements, almost as a premonition to what was to come. Her own horse was very tired and she chose another. She called her companions, Ramachandra Rao Deshmukh, Ganpatrao and Kashi and spoke to them about the arrangements they should make in her absence. They promised to protect the young prince while the mother was away. Then she softly kissed the sleeping Damodar Rao and left the house.[55] Lakshmi Bai with Raghunath Singh commanded the division between Phulbagh and Kotah. After two hours of intense fighting, despite initial success, the defending side began to show signs of fatigue and retreated till they reached Phulbagh. Here the Rani of Jhansi and her companion Mandar fought side by side, relentlessly. At a critical juncture Brigadier Smith ordered the 8th Hussar to attack. The sudden and rather unexpected attack threw the Indian side into complete disarray.

What followed is history. Raghunath Rao and Mandar separated from Lakshmi Bai and suddenly found themselves in an open ground surrounded by the soldiers of the 8th Hussars. Mandar was the first to be hit. As she cried out, Lakshmi Bai, turned around and cut her assailant down. She then tried to cross the Sonerekha canal but her tired horse would not budge. 'Suddenly she felt a sword strike her forehead, slashing the right side of her head up to her right eye. She tried to stop the bleeding with torn folds from her turban. Despite the blood gushing out in a jet, she struck her horse's belly to make it go onward. Finally, when the horse crossed the Sonerekha, a sudden bullet pierced the left side of her chest. She immediately fell over the horse.'[56]

George Fraser's romantic, fictionalized version embellished the incident. Lakshmi Bai was completely surrounded by British soldiers but she fought hard and she fought without flinching. Suddenly he saw her ride fast out, 'clutching her hands to her stomach, and her head was down. A trooper drove his horse straight into the mare, and as it staggered he sabred at Lakshmibai back-handed—I shrieked aloud and shut my eyes, and when I looked again, she was in the dust, and even at that distance I could see the crimson stain on her jodhpurs.'[57] The outcome of the rest of the campaign was certain after the death of Lakshmi Bai.

In October 1858, Robert Hamilton wrote to Edmonstone in Calcutta that he had been receiving applications from a certain person by the name of Damodar Rao, who claimed to be the adopted son of the Rani of Jhansi. Damodar begged that his life and honour be spared and that a stipend should be settled upon him. Left without shelter and provision, the hapless lad had been wandering the neighbourhoods of Jhansi with a handful of followers. Hamilton issued an order that Damodar Rao and his group should surrender by 15 December. But they did not, perhaps from fear of reprisals. The surviving family members of the Newalkars left Jhansi and chose smaller habitations where they could live incognito, dropping their surnames so that they were not easily identified. Nothing was heard of Damodar Rao for one-and-a-half years more. In 1860, the case of Damodar Rao was opened when the government received a fresh application on his behalf. The British now undertook a thorough investigation to ascertain the true identity of the boy. Inquiries proved that he was indeed Damodar Rao. He was still accompanied by three followers and four unarmed soldiers. They finally gave themselves up in April 1860. The British government had still not decided about the pension he was eligible to receive. The figure suggested was something between Rs 150 and Rs 300 per month. Colonel R. Shakespeare, who had replaced Hamilton, met Damodar Rao. Among other things, the twelve-year-old boy told the officer about the last moments of his mother's life.

The rebels had been in possession of Gwalior for several days. The Rani was living in a separate house. Then, one morning, news arrived that British forces had breached the security and made inroads into the town. Lakshmi Bai rushed up to the terrace of her house and saw the British coming. She quickly got down and mounted her horse, but the invading soldiers surrounded her and 'she received one sword cut on the left hand, and a ball pierced her right side'. The guns from the defending army drove the European away but the Rani fell from her horse, fatally wounded. Her female companion Sundar was also wounded by a sword cut to her stomach. After the British soldiers withdrew, her own soldiers carried Lakshmi Bai and Sundar back to the house, gave her some water to drink, but she died before they could reach any place of safety. Her body was taken to a garden under the fort. Damodar Rao then said that he performed some funeral rites and 'buried the body in a stack of grass'.[58] They dared not light the pyre for fear of being detected by the British army. The next day Sundar died and was buried at the Kotwali in Gwalior. Colonel Shakespeare added that this was the most detailed account he had seen of the death of the Rani of Jhansi.

The file on Damodar Rao is closed with two entries. The first confirmed that the Governor General had agreed to grant Damodar Rao Rs 150 as pension per month for life.[59] While he received a pittance, the already opulent Scindia was duly rewarded for good services. The houses belonging to Nana Sahib and Lakshmi Bai in Banaras were now 'available for bestowal' on Scindia of Gwalior.[60]

For the British office, the case on the Rani of Jhansi was closed. It was the beginning of another story, the story of how those who survived her were lost in the crowd, while Lakshmi Bai passed into legend and lived on.

Epilogue

We will not follow the story of the apotheosis of Lakshmi Bai. In the course of the national movement and more so after India's Independence, the Rani's struggle came to be regarded as the quintessential symbol of resistance that Indians offered to colonial rule. Being a woman, she highlighted the vulnerability of a victim and the daring of a rebel. Her image on horseback with an arm raised ready for combat became iconic and was frequently invoked to stir nationalist spirit. Her life and death were subjects of a wide range of imaginative compositions ranging from folk songs, poetry, novels, paintings, and cinema to even more academic historical studies. Joyce Lebra-Chapman explores the conditions in which the Rani legend was born and evolved, and the multiple forms in which it was expressed. The impression immortalized is the one Subhadra Kumari Chauhan extolled in her poem *Khoob Lari Mardani Jhansiwali Rani*:

> *How valiantly like a man she fought*
> *On every parapet she set a gun*
> *Raining fire of hell,*
> *How well like a man fought the Rani of Jhansi,*
> *How valiantly and well!*[1]

Lakshmi Bai thus finds place alongside other figures like Rana Pratap and Shivaji who fought to safeguard their country. Certainly, her pictorial and literary representation is as popular as theirs are. Yet, reflecting upon her life without being blinkered by the emotions of an Indian nationalist, one is struck by a certain mismatch between the life of Lakshmi Bai and the memory of the Rani of Jhansi. Her struggle before the uprising, after all, was only to get back what she felt legitimately belonged to her adopted son. The British had wronged her just as they had wronged the Begums of Awadh and the Ranis of Nagpur. Lakshmi Bai was not hostile to the British nor did she have any ideological difference with colonial rule. As late as May 1857, when the sepoy mutiny had already begun in the north, Lakshmi Bai was corresponding with British officials and throughout her negotiations she was never belligerent. That is not surprising, as her husband's family owed the kingdom to British military support.

All admiring biographers quote a letter that T.A. Martin, who had been present at the time of the mutiny in Jhansi, wrote to Damodar Rao. It is well worth reading:

> 'Your poor mother was very unjustly and cruelly dealt with, no one knows her true cause as I do. The poor thing took no part whatever in the massacre of the European residents of Jhansi in June 1857. On the contrary, she supplied them with food for two days after they had gone into the fort, got one hundred matchlock men from Kurrura and sent them to assist us. But after being kept a day in the fort they were sent away in the evening. She then advised Skene and Gordon to fly at once to Duttia and place themselves under the Raja's protection.'[2]

At what point did Lakshmi Bai cross over from being the ally to the antagonist? By not believing her and by forcing her to fight, did Erskine and Rose make her a hero? Were they instrumental in her becoming a martyr or in turning her into a larger-than-life figure? Not even the most avowed of her detractors could be so uncharitable. For there is little doubt that in all inclement circumstances, Lakshmi Bai had the extraordinary capacity of appropriating initiative and assuming charge. We have observed how during deliberations after her husband's death, she used her femininity, her charm and her wit to overawe British officials.

That she was equally successful in impressing contemporary Indians is not surprising. After all those years, she was the first ruler of Jhansi to forge collaboration between the Marathis and the Bundelas. The Rajputs, as her biographers tell us, pledged to fight and die for the Rani. They unequivocally accepted her leadership and this could not have been a slight achievement for a young woman who had barely three years of experience in managing public affairs. She had not intended to resist the British but when forced to do so, she easily slipped into the role of the commander and the leader. It is not without reason, after all, that Lakshmi Bai was perhaps the only figure on the side of the rebellion to have won such generous commendation from the British. Hugh Rose went on record that he considered her the 'bravest and the best Military leader of the Rebels'. E. Arnold, while writing an introduction for a play written by Alexander Rogers in 1895 called *The Rani of Jhansi* or the *Widowed Queen*,[3] recalled that he had often 'heard Sir Hugh Rose talk about the brave and beautiful Princess who gave his column' a hard fight. That was what she was, 'brave and beautiful', 'quite the lady' in Hamilton's words. It is little wonder that Indian writers put a halo around her. Writing a biography 100 years after her death, to 'vindicate her name and character' and 'secure for her the historical justice to which she is entitled', D.V. Tahmankar says that she was not revered for her courage but 'as an avatar of the Goddess Kali, come to the mortal world to save the downtrodden Indian from the wicked British'. She was just and generous, 'pure in mind and body—indeed, the holy crusader and the anointed saint'.[4] Her singularity lay in that she easily lent herself to all these different dispositions and was equally convincing in all.

In her different avatars, Lakshmi Bai remains a unique figure, elusive, mystifying, the stuff romance is made of. The best tribute to her was, perhaps, by an English author, Michael White, who called his novel *Lachmi Bai—Rani of Jhansi: The Jeanne D'Arc of India*. The advertisement for this 'Strong Historical Novel' ran: 'The novel shows her in the role of the Jeanne d'Arc of India, depicting with masterly skill the brains, unceasing energy and indomitable courage which enabled her to rouse the native princes to strike a blow for freedom. Her beauty, woman's wit and earnestness of purpose, all make her a most fascinating heroine, both in romance and history.' That was Manu, Lakshmi Bai, the Rani of Jhansi.

Notes

Preface

1. *The Rani of Jhansi* or the *Widowed Queen* by Alexander Rogers; Westminster: (A.Constable & Co. 1895). *Flashman in the Great Game* from the *Flashman Papers*, 1856-1858, edited and arranged by George MacDonald Fraser; (Barnes & Jenkins, 1975).

1. New Beginnings

1. H.R. Nevill, *Cawnpore: A Gazetteer. Vol. XIX, District Gazetteers of the United Provinces of Agra and Oudh* (Allahabad; 1909), 210-211.
2. Ibid., 258-60.
3. Swami Medhasananda, *Varanasi—At the Crossroads.* (Kolkata: The Ramakrishna Mission Institute of Culture, 2003), 109.
4. Sandra B. Frietag, ed. *Culture and Power in Banaras Community, Performance and Environment, 1800-1980* (Delhi: Oxford University Press, 1989), 5.
5. Mahasweta Devi, *The Queen of Jhansi* (Kolkata: Seagull, 2000), 17.
6. Medhasananda, 110.
7. Vrindavan Lal Verma, *Jhansi Ki Rani Lakshmibai* (Delhi: Prabhat Prakasan, 2003), 28.
8. Mahasweta Devi, 18.
9. Vrindavan Lal Verma, 21.
10. Dattatraya Balwant Parasnis, *Jhansi Ki Rani Lakshmibai*

(Hindi translation), (Allahabad: Sahitya Bhavan Limited, 1938), 18.

11. D.V. Tahmankar, *The Ranee of Jhansi* (London: Macgibbon & Kee, 1958), 23.

12. G.S. Sardesai, *A New History of the Marathis Vol.III* (Agra: Sheolal Agarwal & Co., 1982), 487. I am grateful to Dr Mahendra Verma for this reference; Dr Motilal Bhargava, *Jhansi ki Rani* (Aligarh: Bharat Prakashan Mandir, 1964), 19, Tahmankar, 23.

13. Sir Robert Hamilton to Sir John Kaye, 20 March 1862. *Kaye's Mutiny Papers,* Home Misc. Series, *Vol.4,* H/726.

14. Joyce Lebra-Chapman, *The Rani of Jhansi—A Study in Female Heroism in India* (Honolulu: University of Havana Press, 1986), 69.

15. *Parliamentary Papers, House of Commons, Vol.8, 1831-32.*

16. S.A.A. Rizvi & M.L. Bhargava, *Freedom Struggle in Uttar Pradesh* (Uttar Pradesh: Publication Bureau, Information Department, 1959), vol. I, 21-22.

17. J.W. Kaye, *A History of the Sepoy War in India, 1857-58* (London: W.H.Allen, 1875), vol. I., 72.

18. Ibid., 73-74.

19. Tahmankar, 26. Practically all biographers mention this.

20. Tahmankar, 26, Mahasweta Devi, 20; Sir John Smyth, *The Rebellious Rani* (London: Frederick Muller, 1966), 16.

21. Tahmankar, 26.

22. Sir John Smyth, 16-17.

23. Joyce Lebra-Chapman, 16-17.

2. Coming of Age

1. Census of the N.W.P. of the Bengal Presidency taken on the 1st of Jan. 1853 (Calcutta, 1853), Pt. XXIV, Dist. of Banda. From G.J. Christain, letter dated 18 March 1853, 327-328.

2. Drake D.L.Brochman, ed., *District Gazetteer of the United Provinces of Agra and Oudh vol. XXV* (Allahabad: 1909), (1909), 58.

3. *Notes on Bundelkhand, Extract of Political letter from Bengal,* 14 May 1812 (Home Misc. Series, Nos. 11 & 12, 459-511).

4. The practice was called *bhaiachara*. Men belonging to the same clan held land as *bhaiachara* tenure, whereby the proprietors formed a close brotherhood and shared their revenue burden corresponding to their fractional interest in the share. Given how difficult regular cultivation was here, they worked out the custom (*achara*) of flexible adjustments of rights and revenue. The other and often notorious and more powerful of the landlords were the *garhi-band* thakurs. They occupied small forts called *garhi* and held several adjoining villages for which they paid the local king rent at a rate that worked out to be less than a regular assessment.

5. W.H. Sleeman, *Rambles and Recollections of an Indian Official* (reprint, Karachi: Oxford University Press, 1973), 178.

6. Kevin Rushby, *Children of Kali—Through India in Search of Bandits, the Thug Cult and the British Raj* (New Delhi: Penguin Books, 2003), 188.

7. Brochman, *District Gazetteer of Jhansi Vol. XXIV,* (Allahabad, 1909), 180-199.

8. Om Shankar Asar, *Maharani Lakshmi Bai aur Unki Jhansi,* Pt. I, *Dainik Jagaran*, 6 February 2000.

9. S.N. Sinha, *Rani Lakshmi Bai of Jhansi* (Allahabad: Chugh Publications, 1980), 1-6.

10. Om Shankar Asar, 7.

11. Amrit Lal Nagar, translated, *Ankhon Dekha Gadar* (Delhi: Rajpal & Sons, 1986).

12. Om Shankar Asar, 7.

13. E.G. Jenkinson, *Report on the Settlement of Jhansi* (Allahabad: 1871).

14. Lt. F.D. Gordon, Dy Suptd. of Jhansi to Capt. A. Skene, Suptd. at Jhansi, Camp Goonah, 4 February, 1856. *Commissioners of Jhansi Vol.10, File No: 170.*

15. Lt. F.D. Gordon, Dy. Suptd. of Jhansi to Capt. A. Skene, Suptd. at Jhansi, Jhansi, 21 July 1856, *Jhansi Rev. Records (Misc)*, No. 100.

16. *Memorandum on the Political State of India*, 19 February. 1813. Home Misc. Series, Nos. 416, 617.

17. Andrew D'Cruz, *On the Political Relations Existing Between the British Government and Native States and Chiefs Subject*

to the Government of the North-Western Provinces as they
stood in 1840 (Calcutta: 1844), 5.

18. Tahmankar, 16.

19. Joyce Lebra-Chapman, 14.

20. From the Gov. Gen. In Council, London, 16 September
    1835. *Foreign Department, India Political Proceedings.*
    Dispatch from Court of Directors, No. 41 of 1835.

21. Tahmankar, 16. Mahasweta Devi gives a longer title,
    Maharajadhiraj Fidui Badshah, Januja Inglistan, Maharaja,
    12.

22. Ibid., 16.

23. Ibid., 17.

24. M. Ainslie to H.T. Princep, Secy to the Gov. Gen., 6 March,
    1831, 29 March 1831; from Ramchunder Soobehdar of
    Jhansi to M. Ainslie, 28 April 1831, Foreign Misc., No.
    246.

25. Collector of Hamirpur to T.I. Turner, Commr. of Rev.,
    Kanpur, 31 August 1836, COJ Basta No. 73, Box No. 221,
    Sl. No. 9, File No. 123.

26. F.C. Smith, Agent Gov. Gen. Jubbulpore to W.H.
    Macaughten, Secy. to the Gov. Gen., 7 July, 1834, Foreign
    Pol., C. Nos. 1-3.

27. Translation of a letter from Maharaja of Jhansi to the Right
    Hon'ble the Governor General. *Foreign Department,
    Ootacammund Political,* 15 August, 1834, Nos. 40-41.

28. Mahasweta Devi, 13.

3. Marital Bliss, Shortlived

1. Om Shankar Asar, 11; Mahasweta Devi, 14-15.

2. S.I. Fraser to W.H. Macaughten, 24 May 1838, *Foreign
   Political Proceedings,* 17 October, 1838, No. 59.

3. Agent to the Gov. Gen., Bundelkhand, Camp Mahoba to
   Secy. to the Gov. Gen., 10 October 1838. Foreign Political
   Proceedings, 6 February 1839, No. 16; I. Sutherland, Gwalior
   Residency, 9 November 1838. Foreign Political Proceedings,
   17 April 1839, No. 42.

4. S.I. Fraser to W.H. Macaughten, 6 November 1838. *Foreign
   Political Proceedings,* 6 February 1839, No. 16; Mahasweta
   Devi, 15.

5. Om Shankar Asar, 11.

6. Motilal Bhargava, *Jhansi ki Rani* (Aligarh: Bharat Prakashan Mandir, 1964), 16.

7. S.I. Fraser to J. Thomason, Secy. to the Lt. Gov., N.W. Provinces, Agra, Camp Jhansi, 14 March 1840. *Foreign Political Proceedings*, 6 April, 1840. No. 53.

8. Mahasweta Devi, 15.

9. V. Godse, 49; Tahmankar, 20.

10. Verma, 48-50.

11. Like some others, this is an anecdote that cannot be attributed to any source.

12. Drake D.L. Brochman, compiled & edited, *District Gazetteer of the United Provinces of Agra and Oudh, vol. xxiv*, Jhansi (Allahabad, 1874), 13, 1-32; E.T. Atkinson, *Statistical Description and Historical Account of the North-Western Provinces of India*, NWP Gazetteer. Vol. I, Bundelkhand. (Allahabad, 1874), 273-289.

13. V. Godse, 50. He describes Jhansi in the best of terms, and speaks very highly of Jhansi and its beauty.

14. Parasnis, 20.

15. Ibid. Parasnis, 20-21; Tahmankar, 17-18.

16. Godse, 51.

17. Mahasweta Devi, 27.

18. Om Shankar Asar, 14.

19. Motilal Bhargava says she kept up her regular exercise and gymnasium practice and taught other women horse-riding, use of arms and wrestling. This is highly unlikely.

4. Years of Loss

1. John Kaye, *History of the Indian Mutiny of 1857-58 Vol I* (Connecticut: Greenwood Press, 1971), vol I., 53.

2. W.H. Sleeman to Maj. Malcolm, (undated), *Foreign Department, Political Branch*, 2 December 1853, Nos. 362-65.

3. Demi-official letter from Malcolm to Ellis, 29 October 1853 and Ellis's reply, 1 November 1853, *Foreign Department, Political Branch*, 2 December 1853, Nos. 362-65.

4. Malcolm to Ellis, Camp Amola, 2 November 1853, *Foreign Department, Political Branch*, 2 December 1853, Nos. 362-65.

5. R.R.W. Ellis to Maj. Malcolm, 22 November, 1853, *Parliamentary Papers, House of Commons, Vol.40, (1854-55)*, 57.

6. Ellis to Malcolm, 20 November 1853, *Parliamentary Papers, House of Commons, Vol. 40, (1854-55)*, 52.

7. From Ellis to Malcolm, Jhansi, 22 November 1853, *Foreign Department, Political Branch*, 31 March 1854, Nos. 153-183; Interview with Mahendra Lal Verma.

8. Maj. D.A. Malcolm to J.P. Grant, 1 December 1853, *Parliamentary Papers, House of Commons, Vol. 40, (1854-55)*, 52.

9. From J.W. Darlymple, Officiating Under-Secy to the Govt. of India to Maj. Malcolm, Fort William, 16 December 1853, *Parliamentary Papers, House of Commons, Vol. 40, (1854-55)*, 59.

10. Malcolm to the Secy, Camp Puna, 25 November 1853, *Foreign Department, Political Branch*, 31 March 1854, Nos. 153-83.

11. Ibid.

12. Kharita from Lakshmi Bai, forwarded by Ellis to Malcolm, Jhansi, *Foreign Department, Political Branch*, 31 March 1854, Nos.153-183. This letter does not have a date and Ellis' letter was mistakenly dated 4 November.

13. Vrindavan Lal Verma, 87.

14. Kharita from Her Highness, the Lukshmi Baee *Parliamentary Papers, House of Commons, Vol.40, (1854-55)*, 60.

15. Mahasweta Devi, 32-35.

16. Luchmee Bai's Kharita, *Khareeta from Her Highness, the Lukshmi Baee, Parliamentary Papers, House of Commons, Vol. 40, (1854-55)*, 60.

17. From Ellis to Malcolm, 24 December, 1853. *Parliamentary Papers, House of Commons, Vol. 40, (1854-55)*, 66.

18. Ibid.

19. Ibid., 65.

20. Translation of *Khureeta from Her Highness, the Lakshmi Bai,* 16 February, 1854, *Parliamentary Papers, House of Commons, Vol. 40, (1854-55)*, 74-75.

21. Verma, *Jhansi ki Rani*, 55-56.

22. Kaye, vol. I., 54-61.

23. Michael White, *Lachmi Bai Rani of Jhansi—The Jeanne D'
    Arc of India* (New York: J.F. Taylor & Company, 1901),
    11.
24. Malcolm to the Secy. to the Govt. of India, 25 November
    1853. *Parliamentary Papers, House of Commons, Vol. 40,
    (1854-55)*, 51.
25. Note by J.P. Grant, *Parliamentary Papers, House of
    Commons, Vol. 40, (1854-55)*, 67-69.
26. *Minute by the Most Noble the Governor General, dated
    17 February 1854, Foreign Department Political Branch,
    31 March 1854, Nos.153-83.*
27. Ibid.
28. *Minute by the Most Noble the Governor General of India.
    Parliamentary Papers. House of Commons, Vol. 40, (1854-
    55)*, 71-73.

5. Dethronement

1. Translation of a Gen. Proclamation issued by Maj. D.A.
   Malcolm, for distribution in the Jhansi Territories, 13
   March 1854, *Parliamentary Papers. House of Commons,
   Vol. 40 (1854-55)*, 79.
2. Mahasweta Devi, 57.
3. Interview with Dr Mahendra Lal Verma, Jhansi.
4. D.V. Tahmankar, 48-49.
5. Major D.A. Malcolm to Major Ellis, 15 March 1854,
   *Parliamentary Papers, House of Commons, Vol. 40, (1854-
   55)*, 79-80.
6. *Minute by the Most Noble the Governor General of India,
   25 March 1854, Parliamentary Papers, House of Commons,
   Vol. 40, (1854-55)*, 81.
7. From J.P. Grant, Secy. to the Govt. of India to W. Muir,
   Secy. to Govt., North Western Provinces, Fort William, 31
   March 1854, *Parliamentary Papers, House of Commons,
   Vol. 40, (1854-55)*, 82.
8. From Muir to Grant, 18 April 1854, *Foreign. Consultations*,
   5 May 1854. Nos. 127-129.
9. Sinha, 28.
10. From Hamilton to Beadon, 29 May 1855, *Foreign
    Department, Political Consultations*, 5 October 1855, No.1.

11. From Malcolm to Ellis, 11 April 1854. *Foreign Department, Political Branch*, 12 May 1854, Nos: 76-79.
12. From Ellis to Malcolm, 20 April 1854 and Malcolm to Ellis, 23 April 1854, Ibid.
13. John Lang, *Wanderings in India*, (London: 1859), 85.
14. To R. Hamilton from Malcolm, Gwalior, 25 April 1854, *Foreign Department, Political Branch*, 12 May 1854, Nos: 76-79 .
15. From Hamilton to J.P. Grant, 28 April 1854, Ibid.
16. To the most Hon'ble Marquis of Dalhousie from Lakshmi Bai, Jhansi, 22 April 1854, Ibid.
17. John Lang, 84-96.
18. Ibid.
19. Interview with Om Shankar Asar in Jhansi.
20. Chanderi saris are of very fine fabric that is a speciality of this region.
21. N.S. Prasad, *Jhansi Lakshmi Bai* (Bharata-Bharati Pustaka Sampada, Bangalore, 1975), 22.
22. Godse, 57-58.
23. John Lang to C. Allen, 8 June 1854, *The Memorial of the Maharanee of Jhansi*, 8 June 1854. From the Secy. to the Govt. of India, 21 June 1854. *Foreign Department, Political Branch*, 23 June 1854, Nos. 116-19.
24. Ibid.
25. Sinha, 28-29.
26. Sir Robert Hamilton, Agent to the Gov. Gen for central India to G.F. Edmonstone, Secretary to the Govt. of India, Indore residency, 23 August 1854, *Foreign Department, Political Branch*. F.C. 15 September, 1854, Nos. 33-34.
27. Hamilton to Beadon, 29 May 1855, *Foreign. Department, Political Consultation*, 5 October 1855, No.1.
28. Ibid.
29. Maj. W.C. Erskine, Agent Lieut. Governor and Commissioner of Saugor Division to W. Muir, Secy. to Govt. of NWP, Agra, Jubbulpore, 13 September 1855, *Foreign Department*, 1855, 28 December, Nos. 43-44.
30. Skene to Commissioner, Saugor and Nerbudda Territories, Camp Jhansi, 4 September 1855, *Foreign Department*, 28 December 1855, Nos. 43-44.

31. Hamilton to G.F. Edmonstone, 21 March 1857, *Foreign Department*, 3 July 1857, Nos. 23-25.
32. R.N. Hamilton to Sir J. Kaye, *Papers of William Coldstream*, MSS.EURO.D.706. I am grateful to P.J.O. Taylor for this reference.
33. Ibid.
34. S.N. Sinha, 34-35.
35. Godse, 55- 57.
36. G.M. Fraser ed., *Flashman in the Great Game*. The Rani of Jhansi or the *Widowed Queen* by Alexander Rogers is a play in which she is portrayed as the feisty and robust Rani who waits for her hour of revenge. (A. Constable & Co., Westminster, 1895).
37. Ibid., 66-67.

6. A Rebellion and a Massacre

1. Godse, 59-60.
2. For more details see, C. Hibbert, *The Great Mutiny—India 1857* (Penguin Books, New Delhi, 1980) and Saul David, *The Indian Mutiny* (Penguin Books, London, 2003).
3. For a more detailed discussion on the social composition of the soldiers, see Tapti Roy, *The Politics of a Popular Uprising—Bundelkhand in 1857* (Delhi: Oxford University Press, 1994), 33-37.
4. Gen. Orders by the Right Hon'ble the Gov. Gen. of India in Council, Fort William, 4 April 1844, *Foreign Secret Proceedings*, 4 May 1844, No. 123.
5. Suggestions in Regard to Sanitary Works Required for Improving Indian Stations, (Calcutta: 1864), 32.
6. S.A.A. Rizvi & M.L. Bhargava ed., *Freedom Struggle in Uttar Pradesh,* (Prayag Publications Bureau), 1939, Vol. III, 47.
7. Ibid., Rizvi, 29.
8. The 2nd Cavalry in Kanpur broke into mutiny on the evening of 5 June, Christopher Hibbert, 176.
9. Rizvi & Bhargava, 14-20.
10. Ibid., 26. This was according to Aman Singh, a sepoy of the 12th Native Infantry.
11. Rizvi & Bhargava, 49. Lalu Bakshi said this in his deposition when he was tried a year later. He was one of the Rani's

courtiers, who had been very active in the year following the rebellion before the British returned. When he was apprehended, he had to prove his innocence and since the Rani was already indicted, he had to prove his distance from her. The only way he could do so was to prove that he had been forced to join the Rani. Lakshmi Bai, he said, had asked him to recruit troops but he refused on the ground that he was no longer in her service and that she should first seek the permission of the British government.

12. Pir Zahur Ali, a soldier of the 14th Bengal Irregular Cavalry was the only person who said that the Jhansi Rani assisted the mutineers with provisions the same night. This does not ring true simply because they could not have required any assistance that evening.

13. Rizvi & Bhargava, 31.

14. Ibid., 19.

15. Ibid., 47.

16. Ibid., 7.

17. Ibid., 17.

18. Deposition of Sheikh Hingun Huqqabardar to Capt. F.D. Gordon, Deputy Commissioner of Jhansi, 6 March 1858. Rizvi & Bhargava, 31.

19. Verma, 136-140.

20. Rizvi & Bhargava, 43-44.

21. Ibid., 45.

22. Ibid., 32-33.

23. Ibid., 44.

24. Ibid., 33.

25. Ibid., 46.

26. Ibid., 34.

27. Ibid., 9.

28. Ibid., 21-22.

29. Ibid., 32.

30. Ibid., 35-39.

31. Ibid., 43-45.

32. Ibid., 47.

33. Verma, 177-78.

34. Ibid.

35. Ibid., 181-182.

36. Mahasweta Devi, 93.
37. Ibid., 94.
38. Godse, 63-64.
39. Roy, 105.
40. Sinha, 55.
41. Sinha, 55 and 57.
42. John Smyth, 12.
43. A. Fraser, *Boadicea's Chariot—The Warrior Queens* (London: Weidenfeld & Nicolson, 1988), 284.

7. Legendary Heroics

1. J.W. Pinkney, *Narrative of Events Attending the Outbreak of Disturbances and the Restoration of Authority in the District of Jhansi*, 513, para 37.
2. *Kaye's Mutiny Papers*, 287, Home Misc. Series, 725 (IOL).
3. Rizvi & Bhargava, 66.
4. Ibid.
5. Ibid., 66-67.
6. Ibid., 69-70.
7. S.N. Sen, *Eighteen Fifty Seven* (Delhi: 1957), 278.
8. Rizvi & Bhargava, 24-25.
9. V.L. Verma, 133.
10. Rizvi & Bhargava, 24-25.
11. J.W. Pinkney, 514, para 41.
12. Rizvi & Bhargava, 49-50.
13. Ibid., 58-59.
14. Ibid., 59-60.
15. Godse, 64.
16. Ibid.
17. Pinkney, 516-517.
18. Ibid., 522.
19. S.N. Sinha, 63-64, Pinkney, 522, Rizvi & Bhargava 51.
20. Substance of a Maratha news report from a spy of Gwalior, 1 October 1857, *Foreign. Department, Secret Consultations,* 18 December 1857, No. 840.
21. Lt. Col. H.M. Durand, off. Agent G.G. to Edmonstone, 15 October 1857, *Foreign. Department, Secret Consultations,* 18 December 1857, No. 838.

22. Rizvi & Bhargava, 70-71.
23. Ibid., 92-93.

8. The Gathering Storm

1. Lt. Col. H.M. Durand, officiating Agent Governor General for Central India to G.F. Edmonstone, Esq., Secy. to the Govt. of India, *Foreign Department, Secret Proceedings*, 18 December 1857, No. 453.
2. From Gordon to Erskine, 17 September 1857, *Foreign Secret Consultations*, 18 December 1857. No. 237.
3. News from Bundelkhand of 5 January 1858, *Foreign Department, Secret Consultations*, Nos. 114-15.
4. Translation of a Kharita from the Ranee of Jhansi to the Agent Governor General for C.I. dated 14 Jamadiolawal A.H. 1274 corresponding to January 1858, *Foreign Department, Secret Consultations*, 25 June 1858, No. 115.
5. Ibid., 25 June 1858, No. 115.
6. Rizvi & Bhargava, 221.
7. Ibid., 221-22.
8. From F.O.Mayne, Magistrate of Banda to C.B. Thornhill, Offg. Commr., 4th Division, Banda, 4 August 1858. *Foreign Department, Political Consultations*, 8 October 1858, No. 13.
9. Ibid.
10. Rizvi & Bhargava, 229.
11. For the interpretation of the use of religion, see Roy 50-53.
12. Rizvi & Bhargava, 225-227.
13. Ibid.
14. Ibid.
15. Kaye, 94.
16. Mahasweta Devi, 140-41.
17. T. Lowe, *Central India during the rebellion of 1857 and 1858* (London: Longman and Roberts, 1860), 166.
18. Ibid.
19. Ibid., 205-06.
20. Ibid.
21. Rizvi & Bhargava, 222.
22. Verma, 224.

23. Rizvi & Bhargava, 223.
24. Ibid., 224.
25. Ibid., 225.
26. Narrative of Events in the North-Western Provinces for the week ending the 14 February 1858, *Foreign Department, N.W.P. Narrative,* Sl.no. 77, vol. 82, 1858.
27. Rizvi & Bhargava, 227- 28.
28. Translation of a Proclamation issued by the Peshwa, Chirkhari, 26 February 1858, *Foreign Department, Secret Proceedings,* 28 May 1858, nos. 151-2.
29. Rizvi & Bhargava, 221.
30. Ibid., 224.
31. Ibid., 283.

9. Desperate Manoeuvres

1. Godse, 67-68.
2. Lowe, 207, Mahasweta Devi, 147.
3. R. Hamilton to G.F. Edmonstone, Secy. to the Govt. of India, Indore Residency, Camp Bheelonee, 12 March 1858, *Foreign Department, Secret Proceedings,* 30 April 1858, 137.
4. Abstract of Intelliegence, 11 February 1858, *Foreign Department, Secret Consultations,* 30 April 1858.
5. Lowe, 221.
6. From G.F. Edmonstone, Allahabad to C. Beadon, Calcutta, 16 March, *Foreign Department, Secret Proceedings,* 30 April 1858, No. 326.
7. Rizvi & Bhargava, 283-84.
8. Ibid., 286.
9. Verma, 190-91.
10. Rizvi & Bhargava, 290.
11. Ibid., 292.
12. Ibid., 292.
13. Ibid.
14. Ibid., 291.
15. Ibid., 293.
16. *Foreign Department, Secret Consultations,* 28 May 1858, Nos. 213-219.
17. Rizvi & Bhargava, 295.

18. Ibid., 295-296.
19. J.H. Sylvester, *Recollections of the Campaign in Malwa and Central India under Maj. Gen. Sir Hugh Rose*, (Bombay: Smith, Taylor & Co., 1860), 84.
20. Kaye, 106.
21. Rizvi & Bhargava, 299, Kaye, 107-8.

10. The Siege

1. Sylvester, 87.
2. Maj. Gen. Hugh Rose to Col. Green, Adjutant General of the army, Bombay, *Foreign Department, Political Proceedings*, 13 August 1858, No. 26.
3. This is Godse's version.
4. Godse, 66.
5. Verma, 234.
6. Godse, 66.
7. Sylvester, 87.
8. Rizvi & Bhargava, 299.
9. Letter from camp before Jhansi quoted in G.W. Forrest, *A History of the Indian Mutiny, Vol. III* (London: William Blackwood & Sons, 1859), 198.
10. Ibid.
11. From Hugh Rose, to Col. Green, Adjutant General of the army, Bombay, *Foreign Department, Political Proceedings,* 13 August 1858, No. 26.
12. Rizvi & Bhargava, 311.
13. Ibid.
14. Ibid., 322-23.
15. Ibid., 323-24.
16. Sen, 287.
17. Ibid., 287-88.
18. From Maj. Gen. Hugh Rose to Col. Green, Camp Jhansi, 13 April 1858, *Foreign Department, Political Proceedings,* 13 August 1858, No. 26.
19. Lebra-Chapman, 130 & 136.
20. Godse, 71.
21. Mahasweta Devi, 149.
22. Verma, 243-45.
23. Godse, 72-80.

24. Forrest, 217-18.
25. Rizvi & Bhargava, 325.

11. The Chase to the End

1. Sylvester, 88.
2. Thomas Lowe, 236 & 261.
3. Forrest, 218.
4. Ibid., 219.
5. Godse, 67-88.
6. Rizvi & Bhargava, 324.
7. Ibid., 334.
8. Mahasweta Devi, 181-82.
9. Smyth, 136.
10. Mahasweta Devi, 179.
11. Rizvi & Bhargava, 346-47.
12. Ibid., 351-52.

12. Queen Without a Kingdom

1. Rizvi & Bhargava, 345.
2. Narrative of Events for the week ending April 1858. From E.C. Bayley to G.F. Edmonstone, 12 May 1858. *Foreign Dept. N.W.P. Narratives*. Sl. No. 77, vol. 82, 1858.
3. *Foreign Secret Consultations*, 9 April 1858, Nos. 151-55, Rizvi & Bhargava, 352.
4. From Judge Cawnpore to W. Muir, Allahabad, 12 April 1858. *Foreign Department, Secret Proceedings*, 30 April 1858, No. 304.
5. *Foreign Secret Consultations*, 28 May 1858, No.128, Rizvi & Bhargava, 353-56.
6. *Foreign Political Proceedings*, 30 December 1859, Suppl. Cons. No. 651, 71-72, Rizvi & Bhargava, 356.
7. Rizvi & Bhargava, 357-358.
8. Ibid., 359-360.
9. Ibid., 360-361.
10. Ibid., 360-366.
11. Ibid.
12. Dated 1st Jumadoossanee, A.H. 1274, Sunday, *Trans. Of Tantia Topi's Orders*, 23, Home Misc., 727 A.
13. Ibid., 24-25.

14. Ibid., 28.
15. Ibid., 29-30.
16. Ibid., 25-26.
17. Ibid., 28.
18. Ibid., 42-44.
19. Godse, 78-79.
20. Verma, 298-99.
21. Rizvi & Bhargava, 369.
22. From Hamilton to Cecil Beadon, 5 April 1858. *Foreign Department, Secret. Proceedings*, 25 June 1858, No. 79.
23. Intelligence of 19 April 1858, *Foreign Department, Secret Proceedings*, 28 May 1858, Nos. 171-172.
24. Rizvi & Bhargava, 368-69.
25. Ibid., 318.
26. For a more detailed account of the battle, from Hugh Rose to Maj. Gen. W. Mansfield, Chief of Staff, Camp Gulauli, 24 May 1858, Forrest: *Selections from State Papers*, Vol. IV, 64-72, Rizvi & Bhargava, 313-21 and 370.
27. Rizvi & Bhargava, 371.
28. Ibid., 378-79.
29. Ibid., 404.
30. Ibid., 384-85.
31. Ibid., 387.
32. Ibid., 388.
33. Mahasweta Devi, 208.
34. Rizvi & Bhargava, 387-405.
35. Ibid., 381.
36. Ibid., 446.
37. Ibid., 412.
38. Ibid., 414.
39. Ibid., 416.
40. Ibid., 422-23.
41. Ibid., 425.
42. Ibid., 422.
43. Ibid., 435.
44. Report on the Affairs of Gwalior from the 24 May to the 20 June 1858, sent by S.C. Macpherson, Political Agent, dated Gwalior, 30 September 1858. *Foreign Political Consultations*, 31 December 1858, Nos. 4281-83, Rizvi & Bhargava, 463.

45. Godse, 109.
46. Rizvi & Bhargava, 436.
47. Mrs Henry Duberly, *Campaigning Experience in Rajpootana and Central India, during the Suppression of the Mutiny, 1857-58* (London: Smith, Elder and Co., 1859), 145.
48. N.S. Ramprasad, *Jhansi Lakshmi Bai* (Bangalore: Bharati Pustaka Sampada, 1975), 42-45.
49. Quoted in Antonia Fraser's *Boadicea's Chariot—The Warrior Queens* (London: Weidenfeld & Nicolson, 1988), 294.
50. Ibid., 295.
51. Parasnis, 223.
52. Ibid., 231-39.
53. Tahmankar, 163.
54. Ibid., 168. He quotes Ramchandra Vinayak, Deputy Vakeel of Indore.
55. Mahasweta Devi, 238.
56. Ibid., 242.
57. Fraser, 304.
58. From Col. Shakespeare to Cecil Beadon, Indore, 20 April 1860, *Foreign Department, F.C.,* 30 March 1860, Nos. 382-83.
59. To the Agent, Gov. Gen. For Central India from Foreign Depatment, Fort William, 12 September 1860. *Foreign Depatment,* Part A, September 1860, Nos. 111-13.
60. From J.B. Gubbins, Commr. 5th Div. to George Couper, Secy. to Govt. NWP, 20 December 1859, *Foreign Depatment, F.C.,* 10 February 1860, Nos. 115-26.

Epilogue

1. P.C. Joshi, compiled, *1857,* in *Folk Songs* (New Delhi: People's Publishing House, 1994), 47.
2. Lebra-Chapman, 66-67.
3. Alexander Rogers, *The Rani of Jhansi* or the *Widowed Queen* (Westminster: A. Constable & Company, 1895).
4. Tahmankar, 176.

Bibliography

PRIMARY SOURCES:
MANUSCRIPTS & PRINTED RECORDS

Manuscripts

A. *National Archives of India, New Delhi*

Foreign Department, Political Proceedings, 1830-1860 (selected volumes)
Foreign Department, Political Consultations, 1850-1859 (selected volumes)
Foreign Department, Secret Consultations, 1830-1860 (selected volumes)
Home Misc. Series (selected volumes)
Foreign Misc. Series (selected volumes)

B. *Uttar Pradesh Regional Archives, Allahabad*

Commissioner's Office, Allahabad, Jhansi Records, 1808-1857 (selected volumes)

C. *Uttar Pradesh State Archives, Lucknow*

Foreign Department, *North-Western Province Narratives*, 1858

D. *India Office Library and Records, London*

Home Miscellaneous Series, 727 A & Kaye's Mutiny Papers

Printed Records

Aitchison, C.U., *A Collection of Treaties, Engagements and Sanads Relating to India and Neighbouring Countries*, vol. v (Calcutta, 1892)

Atkinson, E.T., *Statistical Description and Historical Account of the North Western Province of India*, vol. I, Bundelkhand (Allahabad, 1874)

Brochman, Drake D.L., (compiled & edited), *District Gazetteer of the United Provinces of Agra and Oudh* (Allahabad, 1909); vol. xxiv, Jhansi; vol. xxi, Banda; vol. xxii, Hamirpur; vol. xxv, Jalaun

Census of the N.W.P of the Bengal Presidency taken on the 1st of January 1853 (Calcutta: 1853)

Cruz, A.D., *On the Political Relations Existing Between the British Government and Native States and Chiefs Subject to the Government of the North-Western Provinces as they Stood in 1840* (Calcutta, 1844)

Jenkinson, E.G., *Report on the Settlement of Jhansi* (Allahabad, 1871)

Montgomery, R., *Statistical report of the district of Cawnpoor (1848)*

Nevill, H.R., *Cawnpore: A Gazetteer Vol. XIX of District Gazetteers of the United Provinces of Agra and Oudh* (Allahabad, 1909)

Parliamentary Papers, House of Commons, vol.16 & 493, 1806; vol. 18 & 585, 1819; vol. 8, 1831-32; vol. 40 & 45, 1854-55;

Suggestions in Regard to Sanitary Works Required for Improving Indian Stations (Calcutta: 1864)

The Imperial Gazetteer of India vol. XIV (Oxford: Clarendon Press, 1908)

ON MUTINY

Pinkney J.W., *Narrative of Events Attending the Outbreak of Disturbances and the Restoration of Authority in the Division of Jhansi*

Parliamentary Papers, House of Commons, vol. 42 & 517 (1857-58)

Rizvi, S. A.A and Bhargava, M.L, ed., *Freedom Struggle in Uttar Pradesh*, vols. I-IV (Lucknow, 1959)

SECONDARY SOURCES: BOOKS AND ARTICLES

English

Ball, C., *The History of Indian Mutiny—Giving a Detailed Account of the Sepoy Insurrection in India, and a Concise History of the Great Military Events Which have Tended to Consolidate British Empire in Hindostan*, 2 vols (London and New York: London Print and Pub. Co., 1858-59)

David, S., *The Indian Mutiny* (London: Penguin, 2002)

Duberly, Henry Mrs, *Campaigning Experiences in Rajpootana and Central India, during the Suppression of the Mutiny, 1857-1858* (London: Smith, Elder and Co., 1859)

Devi, M., *The Queen of Jhansi, translated by S. and M. Sengupta*, (Calcutta: Seagull, 2000)

Fraser, A., *Boadicea's Chariot—The Warrior Queens* (London: Weidenfeld & Nicolson, 1988)

Fraser, G.M., ed & arranged, *Flashman in the Great Game— from Flashman Papers 1856-1858* (London: Barrie & Jenkins, 1975)

Forrest, G.W., *A History of the Indian Mutiny vol. III* (London: William Blackwood & Sons, 1859)

Frietag, S.B. ed., *Culture and Power in Benaras—Community, Performance and Environment, 1800-1980* (Delhi: Oxford University Press, 1989)

Gupta, P.C., *The Last Peshwa and the English Commissioners, 1818-1851* (Calcutta: S.C. Sarkar & Sons Ltd., 1944)

Hibbert, C., *The Great Mutiny—India 1857* (New Delhi: Penguin Books, 1980)

P.C. Joshi, compiled, *1857 in Folk Songs* (New Delhi: People's Publishing House, 1994)

Kaye, J.W., *A History of the Sepoy in India 1857-1858 vol I* (Connecticut: Greenwood Press, 1971) *vol. III* (London: W.H. Allen & Co., 1876)

Kincaid, C.A., *Lakshmibai, Rani of Jhansi and other essays* (anon, 1966)

Lang, J., *Wanderings in India: And Sketches of Life in Hindostan* (London: Routledge, Warne & Routledge, 1859)

Lebra-Chapman, J., *The Rani of Jhansi—A Study in Female Heroism in India* (Honolulu: University of Hawaii Press, 1986)

Lowe, T., *Central India during the Rebellion of 1857 and 1858* (London: Longman Green, Longman and Roberts, 1860)

Medhasananda Swami, *Varanasi—At the Crossroads* (Kolkata: The Ramakrishna Mission Institute of Culture, 2003)

Paul, E.J., *Rani of Jhansi—Lakshmi Bai* (New Delhi: Roli Books, 1999)

Ramaprasad, N.S. *Jhansi Lakshmi Bai* (Bangalore: Bharati Pustak Sampada, 1975)

Rogers, A., *The Rani of Jhansi* or the *Widowed Queen, A Play* (Westminster: A.Constable & Co., 1895)

Roy, T., *The Politics of a Popular Uprising—Bundelkhand in 1857* (Delhi: Oxford University Press, 1994)

Rushby K., *Children of Kali* (New Delhi: Penguin, 2002)

Sardesai, G.S., *History of the Marathas* (Agra: Sheolal Agarwal & Co., 1982)

Sen, S.N., *Eighteen Fifty-Seven* (Delhi: Publication Division, 1957)

Sinha, S.N., *Rani Lakshmi Bai of Jhansi* (Allahabad: Chugh Publications, 1980)

Sleeman, W.H., *Rambles and Recollections of an Indian Official* (reprint, Karachi: OUP, 1973)

Smyth, J. Brig., *The Rebellious Rani* (London: Frederick Muller, 1966)

Sylvester, J.H., *Recollections of the Campaign in Malwa and Central India under Maj. Gen. Sir Hugh Rose* (Bombay: Smith, Taylor & Co., 1860)

Tahmankar, D.V., *The Ranee of Jhansi* (London: Macgibbon & Kee, 1958)

Taylor, P.J.O., *Companion to the Indian Mutiny of 1857* (Delhi: Oxford University Press, 1996)

White, M., *Lachmi Bai, Rani of Jhansi-The Jeanne of D'Arc of India* (New York: J.F.Taylor & Company, 1901)

Hindi

Bhargava, M., *Jhansi ki Rani* (Aligarh: Bharat Prakashan Mandir, 1964)

Gokhle, R., *Jhansi ki Rani* (Varanasi: Rashtrabhasha Mudranalaya, 1957)

Hadirkar, S.B., *Rani Lakshmibai* (New Delhi: National Publishing House, 1968)

Khare, O.S. Asar, *Maharani Lakshmibai Aur Unki Jhansi—* serialised essays *in Dainik Jagaran* (Jhansi) pt. 1, 6 February 2000 to pt. 19, 14 August 2000

Nagar, A.L., *Ankhon Dekha Ghadar, Hindi translation of V.Godse's Majha Pravas* (Marathi) (Delhi: Rajpal & Sons, 1986)

Parasnis, D.B., *Jhansi ki Rani Lakshmi Bai—Marathi pustak ka anubad* (Prayag: Sahitya Bhavan Limited, 1938, Allahabad: Sahitya Bhavan Limited, 1964)

Verma, M., 1857 ki Kranti me Jhansi—essay in *Bundelkhand Diary* (20-26 June, 1999)

Verma, P., *San 57 ki Kranti (Itihas, Samiksha tatha Natak)* (Kalpi: Hindi Bhavan, 1951)

Verma, V.L., *Jhansi ki Rani Lakshmibai* (Delhi: Prabhat Prakashan, 2003)

Index